WRITING FOR MONEY

LORIANN HOFF OBERLIN

WRITER'S DIGEST BOOKS
Cincinnati, Ohio

To my husband Matt for his encouragement and love, and to my
children, Andy and Alex, who inspire me every day!

Loriann Hoff Oberlin welcomes interviews and speaking engagements. For
information, write to: P.O. Box 515, Monroeville, PA 15146-0515.

ACKNOWLEDGMENTS

Writing this book has truly been a pleasure for me. If it weren't for the cooperation of friends and colleagues, however, this could have become a very different kind of project! I'm grateful to a long list of important people, among them:

My parents, Elmer and Mary Jane Hoff, for instilling such a strong work ethic in me and providing the liberal arts education I continue to use each day of my career; and to my husband Matt and sons, Andy and Alex, for enduring my long stretches at the keyboard without complaint. You three are my biggest fans, and I'll never forget that!

Sharing their anecdotes, insights and expertise were friends and fellow writers: Lillian Africano, Shirley Agudo, Gordon Burgett, Frank and Patty Cappelli, Sheila Davis, Arlene Eisenberg, Connie Emerson, Patricia Gallagher, Vicki Lansky, Sandra Louden, Colleen McKenna, Doug McKinney, Bill McWreath, Holly Miller, Mary Beth Mueller, Pam Price, Fred Rogers, Hedda Sharapan, Helene Siegel, Tony Turo and Molly Wigand.

Literary agents Laura Cifelli, Alice Fried Martell and Pattie Steele-Perkins added helpful perspectives. Providing valuable assistance from the editorial point of view were Tom Clark, Chris McHugh, Nan Roloff Stine and Janice Wright. And, at least once in a career, someone special comes along—someone who takes a chance on you, presenting opportunities you never dreamed possible. That person in my career has been Jackie Barrett-Hirschhaut, and I'm grateful to work with her!

Of course, a manuscript begins with an idea and ends up as a book. My thanks to Bill Brohaugh who took a chance on me as an author; to Bob Beckstead for shepherding me and my manuscript through production; and especially to Jack Heffron, my editor at Writer's Digest Books, who not only made this book the best it could be, but who was a great guy to work with every step of the way!

ABOUT THE AUTHOR

Loriann Hoff Oberlin contributes to national magazines, greeting card companies, corporate and nonprofit clients. Her work appears in national magazines, including *Elegant Bride*, *USAir Magazine*, *The Saturday Evening Post*, *Woman's World* and *First for Women*. Formerly the publisher of a communications newsletter, she now shares her advice on finding freelance work and getting published in her writing workshops and public speaking engagements.

Here's how to study the market and approach editors.

SECTION THREE
Writing for the Public

professional etiquette and photographic skill can be
your passport to further feature articles. This chapter
leads the way.

What's not written is spoken. Learn the essentials of
writing broadcast copy, public service messages,
news and information.

SECTION FOUR
Commercial Work for Clients

Promoting products and services takes knowledge of
advertising outlets in addition to a special way with
words. Here's how to create client advertising.

Public relations is often an elusive practice, but with
the proper plan and skills, you can boost your client's
image with news releases, press kits, news
conferences and talk show appearances.

Business and technical writing pays big bucks if you
cater to corporate clients needing annual reports,
manuals, executive speeches and technical data.
Here's what you need to negotiate fees and set up
agreements with commercial clients.

SECTION FIVE

Long-Term Investments

INTRODUCTION

It was 1983. I had just graduated from Westminster College, a private liberal arts college north of Pittsburgh. While I had earned my degree in speech and broadcasting, what I really longed to do was write. As my husband reminded me years later, I must have said something to the effect of: "If only I could get paid to write. Wouldn't that be great!"

But having spent nearly four years enjoying the ease of a small Amish community, with one college bookstore and perhaps two newsstands in the entire town, I had a hefty load of decisions to make, not the least important of which was finding a job. Writing was a dream.

I never set out to become a freelance writer. Only by necessity did I land freelance work writing ad copy for a Pittsburgh department store. Like many young college graduates facing a competitive field and a recessionary job market, I also made my rounds in the temp circuit, typing and filing my way through advertising agencies, broadcasting stations and banks. I volunteered my writing skills for nonprofit public relations departments, wrote resumes for fellow job seekers, and penned an article for my alumni magazine. And when I finally did land my first full-time job, I kept the faith, determined to find ways I could weave my writing skills into my administrative tasks, recreating the position I was originally hired for.

Not long after, a friend from college made a simple observation. We had been commiserating about our job dissatisfaction when Doug said, "You know, Loriann, I've always admired how you've found ways to make money through your writing." In a time when many of our college friends had fought hard to use their degrees, I realized that I had been doing just that all along. And it felt great!

Looking back on those early writing days, I can clearly remember the advice I sought. I listened to anyone who worked in a communications field, asking copious questions about how they got started and how they did their jobs. I browsed the bookstore shelves for written guidance. It seems only fitting, now, that I offer this book to others, since Writer's Digest Books influenced my writing career from the start.

In the pages that follow, I'll offer you a myriad of freelance writing ideas—most of which I have used throughout my career to increase my skills and talents, and most certainly, to boost my bank account. The book is broken into five sections, for this is the way a typical writer's career progresses—from small projects with limited or no pay to larger ones requiring the commitment of many hours, months or even years. But writing careers can hardly be described as typical. So use this book to meet your individual circumstances, advancing to the chapters you are most interested in and following up with others when your confidence propels you to a new stage in your writing career. Each chapter contains information and contacts you may find useful starting out.

Some of the ideas may jump out at you, urging you to try them right away. Other ideas may linger, waiting for the right moment, years from now, when you seek another challenge, need a change of pace or simply have more time to tackle them. Regardless, all of the ideas you will encounter offer the potential for pleasure—and plenty of profit!

THE
FREELANCE LIFE

Chapter One

The Write Decision

No two writers are exactly alike. We come from both sexes, all races and out of every socioeconomic background imaginable. For some, the decision to write is forever delayed until that magical time in life when everything comes together in unison. Unfortunately, a good portion of this group never realizes its dreams or discovers its potential. Others never started with the intention of writing. Fate led them in that direction.

Some writers realize their passion for prose early on. Though I refined and focused my writing skills in college, I truly fell for words during my first year of high school. Yes, ninth grade and that presidential paper we were assigned really did its job on me! I remember it well. Some other kid had already selected John F. Kennedy, my favorite president, so I quickly grabbed the chance to write about Lyndon Johnson, figuring I could weave a good deal about the Kennedy administration into my paper.

I had so much fun researching this particular assignment that the effort it took to pull that paper together didn't seem like work at all. Fortunately, as a full-time freelancer, I feel the same way about most of the assignments I tackle today. But even with this recognition, it took a life passage for me to act upon what I had really wanted to do all along.

For me, motherhood made the difference. My first full-time job ended up being my last. It had served its purpose, given me much needed income and a look at the real world of business, but with no clear-cut future in sight, it was merely a job. Not a career. So when my son Andy came along, it was a perfect time for reflection.

I thought of that popular question we pose to children, and

instead, asked it of myself: "What do you want to be when you grow up?" I *was* grown up. I *knew* what I wanted to be. I just had to make the decision to do something about it.

In my case, I didn't have the financial luxury of not working outside the home, but I was able to return to my old position on a part-time basis, knowing it would be much more difficult to find a job as a member of the unemployed. I asked my local printer if he knew anybody who needed writing or desktop publishing services. I sent out resumes, scoured the want ads and registered with the placement services of Public Relations Society of America (PRSA) and International Association of Business Communicators (IABC). In one of these organization's newsletters, I discovered a few leads.

Four months after my part-time return, my boss cut my hours. Fortunately enough, I had landed a nonprofit public relations client of my own the very same month. The arrangement fit perfectly into my schedule. I could continue to work two days at my old job, one day for my new client and still have a few hours in the week to pursue additional opportunities and spend time with my infant son. And, the public relations experience I had developed all those years on my first job could now be put to use earning pure profit for me, not an employer. I urge all beginning writers to take careful account of where they are, just as I did. Many times, you'll find that the experience you've garnered along the way can launch you into a new career.

MOONLIGHTING

Freelance writing is a natural extension of a professional communicator's talents. Any job that requires you to write every day, develop an eye for accuracy, meet deadlines and attend to clients' needs has the foundation for freelance work. If you're employed in corporate communications, public relations, advertising, broadcasting, teaching or consulting, most employers will not view your after-hours writing as a conflict of interest, unless you are engaged in commercial freelancing, taking time away from your daily job-related responsibilities or directly competing for clients.

In my case, if I had returned to my job as a full-fledged employee, there would have been a definite conflict of interest. I couldn't, in good faith, start up my own moonlighting venture without it being in competition with my nine-to-five job. But because my boss was not engaged in public relations work any longer and insisted that I work as an independent contractor, that issue was put to rest. Legally, I was self-employed, responsible for paying my own quarterly taxes, social security and retirement.

Of course, whether you actively promote your outside efforts is another matter. My advice is to keep a low profile, promoting your services only to those who can hire you, and maybe to a few close friends and associates who could recommend you. You don't want to raise questions that haven't even been thought of yet, and by alerting your boss or company to your moonlighting, you *will* raise those questions in the minds of others.

OTHER REASONS FOR WRITING

While motherhood and the need for extra income motivated my efforts, other writers are struck by a myriad of circumstances: giving up a career and transferring to another locale; unemployment; disabilities; marriage and homemaking; personal, career or creative satisfaction; educational status and the need to meet school expenses; or retirement. All of these life passages spur such a decision. Still others dream of seeing their name in print. Occasionally, that dream turns into the lofty goal of making a mark, contributing to the betterment of the world you'll someday leave behind. When you think of how popular genealogy is today, it's hard not to remember Alex Haley and how he touched so many with his best-selling novel *Roots*, how John F. Kennedy inspired a generation of Americans with *Profiles in Courage*, or how Al Gore has made an impact with his bestseller *Earth in the Balance*.

CAUTION: QUICK DREAMS

Just as life passages motivate you, life's realities may humble you. If you have to keep working to pay the bills and merely survive each month, the choice has been made for you. You'll have to combine your nine-to-five work with your freelancing goals. Even those of us with gainfully employed spouses need to make every hour of the workday count.

Very few writers rely on their writing career as their major source of income. Scott Turow wrote much of *Presumed Innocent* while commuting to his law office in Chicago. It took him eight years to complete the book. Writing advertising copy by day, Danielle Steel wrote her first novels late at night. Today, she reportedly earns $25 million a year. And Dr. Kevin Leman, who has given parents a real handle on raising families, churns out his pop psychology, self-help books, and for much of his publishing career, maintained a private practice in Tucson, Arizona.

Most of the writers I meet or read about advise beginners to be wary of risking their day jobs for dreams of quick success through writing. I followed the road to full-time freelancing slowly, gradually. One year after reducing my hours, my boss lost an important client, and thus, some business. Guess whose hours got cut again? Now I was down to one day a week. While many friends and colleagues urged me to quit altogether, I resisted. For me, the work routine was down pat. I knew the tasks, and the people I was accustomed to seeing provided a much needed social outlet. And even one day's income met some of my bills.

In the long run, I was able to look at each setback and my ultimate departure from this position as blessings in disguise. These experiences forced me to search out new ways of meeting my financial needs, and I've been a lot better off over the years. Perhaps the best lesson the whole experience taught me was that if I could run a business for someone else, I could do the same for myself. And I did.

CUTTING LOOSE

No one can tell you when the time is right to begin treating your writing as a business in itself. Sometimes circumstances will force your hand. You may be caught in corporate downsizing, or you may decide you want no part in either the mommy or the daddy track—you simply want to create your own track. Alternatively, you will just have that sixth sense inside telling you that now is the time. If you complete an inventory of your skills, identify your most salable talents and research the markets thoroughly, you'll be doing all that you can to insure a profitable start. Your journey may be slow and steady or sudden and swift. My advice is to begin gradually, not just because I did, but because financially it's the safest way to start.

If opportunities don't turn up immediately, you may need to broaden your search for freelance work. If so, contact your local United Way and ask if there are any member agencies who cannot afford full-time public relations personnel. Meet with the executive directors of these nonprofit organizations and try to sell them on using a freelancer, even on a trial basis.

Scour the classified ads for communications jobs and try to convince the company that they could use you as a consultant instead of a full-time or part-time employee. Look to government agencies, businesses and associations, and use the same tactic. Or, approach your employer and try to transform that relationship into your first paying client. Those who are already pleased with your work will frequently be the first to sign on, knowing you are dependable.

Invariably, the day will come in your writing life when you receive more acceptances than rejections. Your self-addressed, stamped envelopes will be returned with checks, and people will begin to comment favorably on your work. Once you've freelanced for several years and steady income flows from a variety of sources, you can think seriously about putting your writing career on the full-time track. But a steady stream of sales can also lure you into a false sense of security about your success and your income potential.

Never get too comfortable, for as the self-employed in any industry will tell you, you never know what the next month will bring. That editor who has been feeding you constant work could be out of a job next month, and the new editor could favor friends she has worked with in the past. You might have to start all over selling yourself. On the client side, mergers and acquisitions do away with departments and managers. Changing market conditions determine budgets for outside consultants and the work that can be sent to specialists. In today's economy, no job is completely secure, and that goes double for any freelance efforts. Starting on your own takes a great leap of faith, but so does staying in business for the long haul.

Establish yourself in whichever area(s) you have the best shot in. Write a few articles on speculation, and maybe you'll land a published piece. Voilà—you have your first clipping! Clippings lead to confidence and the ability to sell on queries alone. Assigned articles, if accepted, pad your bank account, and if rejected, will most likely earn you a kill fee for your efforts.

As your career progresses, you'll begin replacing those "bread and butter" assignments with larger, long-range projects that have higher income potential. Yes, the day *will* come when you will turn down an assignment.

In commercial work, the same progression takes place. One client well served and satisfied will lead to portfolio pieces others will inquire about. Happy clients talk. Word of mouth and a good track record of meeting deadlines and producing quality material will establish you in the community and industry. In time (sometimes months or years), don't be surprised if jobs come directly to you. You'll no longer have to seek them out.

Soon, the work you easily fit into a Saturday afternoon or evenings at home will require the commitment of days strung together. Securing written contracts and putting several clients on retainer will signal that it's time to become your own boss and set up your business as your main vocation. But proceed with caution. Be sure to calculate what it will cost to provide your own health insurance, tax and social security payments, insurance, legal fees, overhead, office rent, even secretarial support— all those things your employer takes care of, and the things you rarely have to think about.

JUST SAY NO

If you're like many writers, including yours truly, you'll begin by accepting every assignment that comes your way. That's perfectly understandable, and wise. Not only are you looking out for your finances, but you're also building a valuable portfolio and testing your skills. But after a while, you'll need to turn down an occasional writing job (and if you don't, you'll kick yourself). No one can make this decision for you, but nowhere is it written that you must write everything that's offered to you.

Some of my best breaks were passed along to me by other freelancers who had progressed to a higher plateau in their careers. They either didn't have the time, didn't need the money, or were well versed in the art of saying "no" and meaning it. Perhaps they had other, better-paying commitments. Let's face it, some writing jobs pay lousy, but we take them to get the credit, the clipping and the connections. Or, we take them simply to buy groceries without depleting the cash machine. Overextending your time, on the other hand, isn't worth the risk to more important assignments where you might gain additional assignments further in your career, a chance at more money or the prestige of a particular publication.

Ask yourself what you really want. Set clear priorities among markets and projects. Write these down periodically. I do mine at the start of every new year. Remind yourself of them. Writers often wonder if by turning down assignments, they'll be passed over in the future and lose the contacts they worked so hard to make. I've had this concern myself, but I've been pleasantly surprised to find that most clients and editors call again. These people don't just want a writer. They want a good writer, and I suppose I've proved my worth to them over the years. You will too. The thought you put into saying "no" will help determine whether you should specialize in one form of writing or remain a generalist.

There are times when I shake my head at myself. I've often felt like a jack of all trades and a master of none. I'm also not very good at saying "no." Until this book came along. Faced with a deadline, twenty chapters and resource information to collect, I learned that two-letter word quite quickly, and even enjoyed using it on occasion. But only after five years of public relations consulting, teaching, newsletter publishing, greeting card writing, newspaper stringing, magazine freelancing, travel writing, fiction attempts and focusing on book proposals could I streamline my writing life.

For me, having many irons in the fire has been both helpful and exhilarating. I have thrived on the diversity, and while I am cutting back, I cannot imagine the day when I don't have my hands in several different areas. Some writers see it differently, believing that if they channel their creative energies into only one area (maybe two), they will become better known as an authority. These professionals also feel they can make just as much money, or more, through specialization. That's the positive side.

The downside is that in a tight economy, your income is tied to only one or two sources. If you specialize in advertising, for instance, that's often the first budget cut in a recession. If you focus on travel writing, beware that consumers might curtail their travel plans, thus resorts and hotels may advertise less. Travel editors see their stories cut from issue to issue. Therefore, they assign fewer articles and need fewer writers.

THE DAILY GRIND

As you make the decision to write, understand the true life of a freelance writer. No two writers are alike, and no two business days are exactly the same. Each has its triumphs and challenges.

For instance, in any given day, I might field a half-dozen phone calls from a client, make follow-up calls regarding freelance leads or queries I haven't heard back on and begin research on an article that's due next month. I'll also proofread a manuscript for another magazine, organize my materials for my weekend writing workshop, begin developing a new batch of greeting card captions, jot down ideas for a future proposal and continue work on this nonfiction book.

Of course, I still need to carve out enough time to read the morning newspaper, peruse a magazine or two, and continue turning pages in the latest novel or nonfiction book I'm reading. It's essential to make time for reading, for if you want to write well, you must read widely.

Each day, I'm reading the work of others, cultivating new assignments, developing important contacts, learning about the industry, and seeing my work in print. After about four years of full-time freelancing, I filled the majority of my work days with writing, but it wasn't always that way. In the beginning, marketing yourself, querying editors, and assembling packages of your published pieces requires at least half of your time, if not 75 percent of it. Writers just starting out are surprised to learn how little time they will spend writing in those initial stages of their careers. Often this is the most sobering reality, because writing is what they have been called to do. It's what they love and long to do when they sit down to work. But before writing comes selling.

Next comes research. If you haven't visited your library in a long time and made friends with the librarian, this is the time to do so. Also, you know that post office you visit to pick up registered mail or buy an occasional roll of stamps? Get ready to treat it as your second home.

Working for yourself means that fun and frustration go hand in hand. The novelty of trying out new equipment and home-office toys will be tempered by your swearing at your software when it doesn't work the way you want it to. You'll test old talents and discover new ones you never even knew you had.

You'll meet influential people that some might give up a limb for, but you'll also be willing to sacrifice your own soul if only to have the support of another writer who could understand how rotten your day has been. What is supposed to be work may somedays seem like a constant job search, no matter what area of writing you choose to concentrate in.

If you're developing client leads for commercial work, get ready to knock on a lot of doors, also, if not physically and in person, then by direct mail and telephone contact. Freelancing is not for the faint of heart. If you think you are outgoing and gregarious as you read this chapter, just wait until a year from now. You will be more outgoing after learning the fine art of give and take, gentle persuasion and overall compromise. For all of these reasons, freelance work requires a certain amount of bravery mixed with a healthy dose of tenacity. And I haven't even mentioned patience.

One of the perils of this business is the slow pace at which it moves. You mail off a manuscript, wait your obligatory eight to ten weeks and pounce on your postal carrier every day. Still no word. What should you do?

You send off a polite reminder and still no answer. Has it arrived safely? Did an editorial assistant spill coffee on it? Was it so bizarre an idea that it's permanently tacked up above the water cooler for everyone to gawk at?

You pick up the phone, only to find out that Editor X has left the magazine, but Editor Y *may* have received it. You send another set of materials along just in case, this time to Editor Y's attention. By now, nearly four months have lapsed, and you are no further along than when you originated the idea.

I've had editors lose two and three sets of materials, request long-distance faxes and then tell me that they liked the idea but had assigned it to another writer just last week!

I've had clients sign off on work to be done and wait months to pay my invoices, and I've negotiated new hours, fees and projects only to wait weeks for a contract to be typed or a check to be cut.

Patience and persistence are both prerequisites in the freelancer's job description, and I'll admit that my lack of the first quality and my mastery of the second have done me in on occasion. On any given day, it's a tough call when to cross the line between the gentle art of persuasion and being a persistent pain in the neck. In the end, we're all human — writers, editors, clients and colleagues. We can only do the best we can with each assignment, and hope that others will fully understand our good intentions, our work ethic, and yes, our need to make a living, too.

Take your job seriously and be disciplined about everything you undertake. Live and work one day or one week at a time, maintaining an organized course, but allowing for sudden starts and stops along the way. Know that in all creative fields, the highs will be incredible peaks of pleasure, sprinkled with some glamour at times. Egos will soar. But the lows can plummet you into despair. There will be days when your self-esteem will be hanging by a thread. Keep it all in perspective.

BEATING THE BLUES

For this reason, I learned early on to develop what I call an encouragement file. I keep this file in a special drawer. I don't think anyone else even knows it's there. Looking through this file, I have saved a photocopy of my first "big" check, letters from former students telling me how much my course helped them, even my KDKA-TV internship evaluation where I received an A+ recommendation during college.

The Christmas card I received from an account exec I traveled with is in there, forever reminding me of the "Super Mom" title I got at the end of that press trip. I tuck away cards and notes from editors, along with other encouragement from clients, newsletter subscribers and friends around the country who have spotted my articles. Devotional readings and some of my minister's sermons inspire me and help me turn mistakes into triumphs. My first article for *USAir Magazine* brings back memories of setting an important goal and achieving it. There's even a hastily scrawled note to myself that was the origin of the book you're now reading.

Your own collection of kind words, achievements and sources of strength can offer you encouragement on days you need them the most. Sometimes just knowing that your efforts have touched another person gives meaning to an otherwise empty day. Believe in yourself and in the work you produce. It makes a difference. But no one else will remind you of this, if you don't take the time, now and then, to remind yourself.

Other ways of beating the blues include getting out of your home office, enjoying the company of other writers and learning from their experiences. For me, that's been one of the greatest aspects of press trips. Traveling with writers from across the country gives me tips on photography, names of agents, an "in" at another publication, and always, the sense that my colleagues struggle with the same issues I do. I've learned their ways of collecting from slow payers, their strategies for breaking into the book business or their methods of promoting their writing careers. I've often appreciated bouncing ideas, matters of etiquette or industry questions off another living, breathing writer who was sitting down with me over a drink.

You can increase your likelihood of these professional exchanges by joining writers groups or starting one of your own. By attending writers conferences, you can also meet editors and agents who can boost your career. That's how I met a national magazine editor and an agent, and I didn't even need to leave my hometown to do it.

Finally, I firmly believe that hanging around winners pays off. Surrounding myself with successful people somehow convinces me that I can achieve my dreams, too, whereas spending time with nonachievers seems to hold me back. I also try to avoid naysayers since I hate to be told what I can and can't do. If told I can't do something, my response has always been: Watch me!

Pessimism prevails too frequently. I don't need it, and I don't know any other writer who does. Surround yourself with people who will give you a pat on the back and a healthy dose of hope now and then. Watch the winners in your circle of friends and associates. Study them, learn from them, and reap inspiration from them. You won't just *feel* like a winner. You'll be one!

Chapter Two

Home-Office Hurdles

An essential element in boosting your creative energy, increasing your productivity and convincing others to take your writing seriously is your work environment. If you write as a hobby, you can curl up on the living room sofa and be perfectly happy, but if you undertake your writing as a business endeavor, carving out a suitable work space needs to be given top priority. If you rent space, many of these techniques for furnishing and equipping your office will also work for you.

As writers, we are lucky that our craft melds so wonderfully with whatever we call home. Whether we reside in a studio efficiency or a sprawling estate, we can tackle our work each day without leaving our own four walls. Still, it's surprising how many writers view their work space or lack of one as an obstacle to their writing efforts.

Know that the work space you carve out today will probably not be the one you rely upon in two, three, four or even ten years. Just as your writing career will grow and take sharp turns you never expected, so will the physical demands change as they relate to the work you produce. The greeting card writer can start out with a batch of index cards, a set of stationery, a few notebooks and a typewriter. The book author, on the other hand, will require shelves of research material, filing cabinets, a word processor or computer, a laser printer, a writing surface, a comfortable chair, a telephone and most likely an answering machine.

When I began freelancing in earnest, my husband and I owned a small garden apartment—two bedrooms, with a walk-in closet, a utility room and a large living, dining and kitchen area featuring a built-in table. Well, my infant son occupied one room and the washer and dryer sat across the hall with our cat's litter box. Not good choices there!

We stashed so much stuff in our walk-in closet that it should have been declared a disaster zone. Our bedroom housed our Macintosh in a quiet corner, but with quarters so tight, there was no room left to write, no place to spread things out and no convenient access to the telephone. That left the kitchen table, where our son Andy sat in his baby bathtub some evenings and where our cat played whiffle ball in the middle of the night. And on occasion we ate there too.

You can imagine my frustration at setting up and tearing down each time I needed to work. It sometimes took me longer to assemble my workstation than it did to get the actual job done. My stationery was stored in the bedroom, and my paper clips and staples were tucked away in another closet (parents will understand these child-proofing measures!). My reference books sat in the living room, and the telephone hung on the kitchen wall.

I held out hope, knowing that the imperfect would become perfect as soon as we built our home. But in the meantime, I had to make money for that dream to ever be realized. So I endured, and so will you, if you face a similar lack of choices.

TRANSFORMING ANY SPACE

The first step in establishing a home office is to survey your surroundings, finding out what spaces aren't being used to their full potential. The ideal situation is a room you never seem to use. This ideal room just happens to have a telephone jack; several strategically placed electrical outlets; plenty of bookshelves; natural, fluorescent and incandescent lighting and so much space that you'll be sure to get lost in it. Of course, it has a door!

If you don't have this ideal room, you're not alone. Most writers don't. So, look at every square foot of space — underneath the stairs and at the top of them, in corners of the kitchen, in sections of the garage or in vacant but dreary spaces, such as laundry or utility rooms.

In their book *Working From Home* (Jeremy P. Tarcher) Paul and Sarah Edwards show a diagram of a freestanding "office in a box" manufactured by Nordisk. This folding and expandable unit sells for approximately $600.

Home Offices & Workspaces (Sunset Books) shows you how to transform almost any home space into a workspace. I found this book helpful when my husband and I finished off our basement, creating my home office. We used every available inch of space by adding shelves above the water meter and closing off electrical boxes, HVAC unit and water heater with doors. We used the space under the stairs for file cabinets, storage and a closet. Our electrician added recessed lights, plenty of electrical boxes and the capacity for future phone lines.

Getting the Work Done

Some of the work was too tough to tackle alone. Major renovations require the advice and skill of experts. Decide what you can do on your own, and what jobs will prove frustrating and impossible. Strike a happy medium as we did, hiring out some of the jobs and doing what you can yourself. Get bids, seek advice from home improvement books and video tapes, and ask friends and family to give you a hand. Approach the entire remodeling project in a series of stages.

After all, if you're working out of a corner of a kitchen while you add on to your home or undertake a major remodeling effort, you might be losing that all-important tax break from the Internal Revenue Service (IRS). The sooner you can complete the project, the more efficient your writing services will become and the more money you will save since your home office could save a bundle in taxes (see chapter three).

OFFICE FURNITURE

You'll soon realize that writing surfaces differ depending upon the tasks to be performed on them. With the amount of time you'll spend in your office, make sure everything is ergonomically correct.

For instance, if you intend to write at your desk, you'll want this piece of furniture to be generally twenty-nine or thirty inches off the ground. However, if you will be typing or computing, the height changes to twenty-six or twenty-seven inches. And while older office furniture may be the right height, don't forget to measure the width. Today's computer monitors and keyboards require more room than yesterday's typewriters.

If you prefer an L-shaped arrangement, you'll want an adjustable chair. When I type, I raise the chair. The wrong chair height can lead to carpal tunnel syndrome, an aggravating condition for many writers whose hands remain tilted at an angle over long periods of time. An improper chair will also cause back and circulatory problems, muscle strain, varicose veins and swelling in the legs.

If you expect to host clients in your office, or if you just want to chat with your children from time to time, you'll need some places for people to sit. In my basement office, I built a small seat right into the wall unit across from my desk. This way, I don't need to take up any additional space with more chairs, and I'll have one less expense.

Other decisions you must make include what filing system you will use. I prefer to have a set of hanging files immediately accessible, so I ordered my office furniture from a company whose pieces can be configured various ways. I also have a separate cabinet that locks for business stationery, toner cartridges and film — things I don't want young children to get into.

EQUIPMENT YOU CAN'T LIVE WITHOUT

To develop the right contacts with editors or communicate with commercial clients, you'll need a telephone. However, with the competition for your purchasing power these days, there are a myriad of models to choose from.

Writers I know who work from home appreciate having a telephone that features a speaker phone option, auto-redial and call waiting (which is actually a service, but I'll throw it in here). If you have pets or children, a mute button comes in very handy for those instances when you want to hear the other person, yet have concerns about background noises.

An answering machine is vital. While some people are put off by voice mail and answering devices, many more have come to rely upon them. Editors are busy people. So are most clients you'll be dealing with. If they choose to call you, whatever they have to say is important — important enough for you to spend thirty dollars or more on some system you're happy with. I like the kind you can use to screen calls while working or the models you can access when you're away from the office. I also prefer to give my callers as much time as they need to complete what they have to say (probably because I'm guilty of leaving such long messages!).

Another piece of equipment, probably the least expensive on the list, is a calculator. Whether you use it to add your expenses, invoice your clients or deal with printers on costly quotes, have a calculator handy so that your math is accurate.

Computer Considerations

Writers wrote in the days before electricity was ever discovered, but transport any of us from the computer generation into that era and you'd witness a revolution. Most of us are so accustomed to our PCs or Macs that we could never go back to a manual typewriter.

This is not to say that you cannot become a writer if you don't already own a computer or word processor. You can. There are many writers of greeting cards, fillers, features, and even fiction who write just this way. But more often than not, they get frustrated retyping their work. In the case of best-selling novelists, they might prefer their old manual typewriters, but chances are good their secretaries have much more modern equipment. Computers generally cost more money. No one will argue that. However, their value far outweighs their cost—professionally and financially.

If you had to retype an entire page and proof it all over again because of one error, wouldn't you be tempted to overlook that mistake? "Oh, it's not so bad after all" . . . "Maybe the editor won't even catch it" . . . or, "A little bit of correction fluid won't hurt." If you can hear yourself uttering these kinds of excuses, face the facts. A computer will increase the professional look of your material. It will save you time. With time comes efficiency, and with efficiency comes increased profits. Don't be afraid to spend a little money if it means adding to your success.

Yes, computers may cost more, but today they are just about standard in every office. More and more editors request diskettes so staffers won't have to retype the material. And if you even think of extending your services to newsletters, know now that desktop publishing is the accepted way of producing such material. If you don't have this kind of equipment, you will surely be competing against other freelancers who do.

Printing Technology

Purchasing decisions are not so clear-cut when it comes to types of printers. Publication listings in *Writer's Market* (Writer's Digest Books) will often indicate which editors accept dot-matrix hard copy and which ones want letter-quality submissions. That doesn't necessarily mean that these publishers with higher quality requirements are off-limits to you. For one or two years, I wrote for markets that didn't require letter-quality work. My dot-matrix printer was one of the high-density models, and that was all I could afford in those initial stages of my career. On the few occasions I needed better output, I either begged a few laser copies off my husband (who had a printer at work), or I took my diskette to a service bureau and paid for the copies from their machines. This route was certainly cheaper than owning my own. But the day came when I couldn't justify sending editors anything less than laser copies. So I researched several vendors, found one that I liked, and broke down and bought it. Today, I'd be lost without my laser printer.

When you reach that stage in your writing career, a major purchase like a laser printer makes a lot more sense. You'll be able to depreciate the expense over several years, and your editors will thank you for the increased legibility and their decreased eye strain.

Before you invest in such an important piece of equipment, try to predict the future. If public relations, newsletter publishing or self-publishing may be a part of your career, think seriously about purchasing a laser printer that is PostScript compatible. Suffice it to say that this is a writing book, not a computing one so I won't go into the details of PostScript. The bottom line is that you cannot print PostScript files or applications if your hardware is not compatible. And many graphics fall into this category. It's an important factor when selecting a laser printer.

Finally, be sure that your laser printer has enough memory, or you may have trouble printing more complicated documents. Four megabytes should be sufficient. And take into account the replacement supplies you'll need to operate any printer you consider. The tab for toner and developer cartridges as well as drum replacements can add up. Ask how long these supplies usually last and be sure to keep at least one cartridge of toner on hand at all times.

EQUIPMENT YOU CAN ADD LATER

Other equipment you will find useful includes a photocopier, fax machine, postal meter, paper cutter, tape recorder, modem and portable computer. But owning all of these items would add tremendous cost to your writing business. Depending on where you live, you may be able to survive fine without these capital expenditures.

I live near two office superstores. What one store doesn't have, the other most certainly does. Each has a self-serve photocopy department, and each will send or receive faxes for me. At this writing, I pay three cents per photocopy and one dollar a page for local fax transmissions. For long-distance service, I've found that my favorite superstore buys large blocks of telephone time that makes long-distances faxes just slightly higher in price. Besides, it's very rare that I need to fax to an out-of-town editor, and when I do, I'm usually reimbursed for the expense. Because these services are so convenient, and I actually look forward to getting out of my office at least once a day, I won't be investing in these big-ticket items anytime soon. If your work requires a lot of long-distance deliveries or personal messenger services, a fax machine can often save on fuel consumption.

Also, if you do a lot of commercial work for clients, a fax machine helps to certify in people's minds that you are indeed professional. In fact, it's advisable to have a separate business phone and a dedicated fax line as clients prefer to work with freelancers who appear successful, not strapped for cash.

If you don't have office superstores near you, perhaps your local printer has a self-serve copier or would be willing to make copies for a slight charge. Many large grocery stores also offer this convenience. If neither is an option, ask a local company if you can work out an arrangement for occasional use of the copy machine.

Now, let's look at the other equipment. Each of my superstores has a paper cutter, and that's the last thing I need curious little hands coming across in my home office. I check my post office box every other day, so making trips there eliminates the need for my own meter.

I do own two small tape recorders—a microcassette version and a regular cassette recorder that, with a handy little device I bought, plugs right into the telephone. This device makes phone interviews a snap.

A modem enables you to send files electronically, from one computer to another and cuts down on the paper trail. Last, there's the temptation to buy a portable computer. Many writers I travel with own one, but they are writers who do great volumes of work or spend more time on the road than they do in their offices. Many are also authors who need to keep plugging away at large projects.

If you decide to make this investment, be sure your laptop is compatible with the system you use each day. Make sure it has enough memory, that the keyboard seems comfortable to you, and that you have a way of backing up your data. Laptops take a lot more abuse than desktop computers so don't just settle on the lowest price available. Shoot for quality, and always invest in a carrying case to protect it while travelling.

STOCKING SUPPLIES

If you're starting from scratch, there are a few essential office supplies you'll need to purchase or order ahead of time. Not all will pertain to your type of writing business, but they include: a calendar or datebook, blank cassette tapes, reference books (especially a good dictionary, thesaurus and small spelling/divider book to grab quickly), bookends, computer diskettes and storage boxes, correction fluid, large mailing envelopes or manuscript boxes, file folders, glue or rubber cement, index cards, mailing labels, marking pens, notebooks (especially a portable kind), padded envelopes, paper, paper clips, pens and pencils, pencil sharpener, postage stamps, three-ring binders, a ruler and T-square, scissors, stapler, staples and staple remover, sticky notes, tape (transparent and packaging varieties), typewriter ribbons or toner cartridges, and a typing stand.

In addition, if you truly want to look professional, invest in stationery, matching envelopes and business cards. Visit your local print shop and work with your printer to create a pleasing design. Having my own desktop publishing system, I save money by designing my own camera-ready artwork. Whatever course you choose, make sure it's professional, and that you've carried your design theme through on all printed matter.

Editors have seen all the cutesy images writers come up with — the quill pens, computer screens and more. Many advise against labeling yourself "Jane Doe, Freelance Writer." If you offer writing and public relations, then say so, using a descriptive, but professional phrase — something like "Writing Services & Public Relations Counsel" underneath your name.

Anytime you update your stationery, ask your printer to make notepads, cutting the old paper down to size and adhering it together. You can use this, and other handy scraps, to jot down telephone notes, write first drafts or entertain your youngsters when they, too, want to play office. All writers have plenty of paper left over. Several trees contributed to this book, even before the printing press. At least by conserving the back sides of paper and reusing shipping materials, I feel like I'm contributing in some small way to saving the environment.

Greeting card writers and those who send a lot of packages ought to invest in a personalized stamp that contains your name and address, as well as telephone number. This cuts down on unnecessary paper through mailing labels. I also have a stamp that says "Requested Material," which I use (with a red stamp pad) to call attention to packages landing on my editors' desks. Of course, I only use it when the material was truly requested, not sent on speculation.

Finally, if your services extend to photography, you will want to own a 35mm camera and plenty of film. Allow for growth as your skills improve. This way you can add lenses, filters and other equipment later on. If you do a fair amount of newspaper work, it might be wise to invest in a second camera to carry with you for black-and-white photos. Some photojournalists I know own one single lens reflex (SLR) and a less expensive, automatic camera for this reason.

You can purchase most of your supplies at office superstores, supply outlets, drug stores, grocery shops or through direct-mail catalogs. Beware of telephone scams trying to sell you products you don't need. These scams prey on all offices, convincing people that they need things they truly do not. In one office where I worked, a temporary employee gave the go-ahead for a whole case of toner. We owned neither a copier nor a laser printer. These salespeople can be sly, so be forewarned!

SAVING MONEY

Now that you're establishing yourself as a small business (even if you remain a sole proprietor), ask whether suppliers offer business discounts. Apply for these wherever you can. The savings can add up in everything from film to photocopies.

Check the classified sections for deals on used equipment, furniture, estate pieces, auctions, second-hand stores, warehouse clubs, garage or moving sales. You'll often be able to pick up gently used items and save a lot of money. Proceed with caution, however, when purchasing anything electronic or delicate (such as camera equipment).

Building your own furniture or ordering unfinished pieces also saves money. Never pay full price for furniture in a retail showroom. Ask for a better price and inquire about floor models that might be available. The same goes for accessories, lighting fixtures and carpeting. Floor models and remnants might suit you fine.

If you live on the East Coast, take advantage of the time differences by placing your West Coast calls after 5 P.M. E.S.T. In fact, you could try calling some offices in New York between 5 and 5:30 P.M. as many editors stay after hours. And when mailing or expressing packages that need to get there fast, check second day service on the slip. If the area you're sending to isn't too far away, your package might even arrive one day sooner, saving you money.

IT'S YOUR OFFICE

Whatever your home office turns out to be, make sure it's efficient. There's nothing worse than trying to be creative in surroundings that aren't comfortable for you. Remove anything that will hinder your capacity to concentrate. If you're working in the kitchen, and the dishes in the sink bother you, you've got a problem. Either move your office or take two minutes to clear the clutter.

Your home office doesn't need to compete for coverage in *Architectural Digest*. It just needs to work for you. And the tools of your trade don't need to be fancy or high tech, either. Aim for the most professional look with whatever you can afford.

Chapter Three

The Business of Writing

F reelance writing might seem glamorous so far — deciding which assignments you'll take on and which you'll turn away, discussing your craft with other writers, editors and agents, and trading in the daily commute to equip your home office. However, without planning properly and developing some business acumen, your dream of a freelance career could become a nightmare.

In a nine-to-five job, workers most likely have resources including a receptionist, secretary, accounting department, marketing and public relations specialists, planners, a personnel manager and maybe even an in-house print shop. Not any more! Put another way, when you're self-employed, you take on all of these jobs, and you take out the garbage too!

DEVELOPING A BUSINESS ATTITUDE

Gene Perret gives great advice for becoming the writer you aspire to be in *Shift Your Writing Career Into High Gear* (Writer's Digest Books). Perret reports that people get promoted in their careers not because others think they can do more, but because they already have demonstrated that they can. Only you can decide what kind of writer you want to become. And only you can make it happen.

Your first step in this direction should be the process of writing itself. Write every day. I'm not telling you something that you haven't read in other books or magazine articles, but the concept is so crucial to your career that it bears repeating.

Choose the time of day that's best for you. It might be first thing in the morning when you feel freshest. It could be in the afternoon after you've tackled the morning mail, returned phone calls and run an errand or two. It could be in the evening after a day's work, or it could be after the kids are in bed and the rest of the world is quiet. It doesn't matter when it is, just so long as you stick to your goal of writing something everyday.

You say you have no time. You say it's impossible to write every day what with your family responsibilities, full-time job and other commitments. Well, I have another book for you. *The 30-Minute Writer* by Connie Emerson (Writer's Digest Books). Here you'll learn how to break writing assignments into manageable segments. Time will no longer be an obstacle. When Connie first told me about the concept of this book, I became excited. As both a working mother and an overextended writer, I needed some guidance. I needed this book. If you're like me, you may need it too.

The next hurdle I usually hear is writer's block, but truthfully, writer's block is the antithesis of creativity, and for my tastes, drastically overstated. Sure, there are days I must sit down to begin writing, and I'd much rather be doing something else. But I've got bills to pay. Writing has always been a way of meeting my financial needs. Whether it's been paying off a loan, saving for a house, setting aside savings or rewarding myself with a major purchase or home improvement, there has always been something tangible I could conjure up to help me overcome that hurdle.

I go to my office in the morning, and treat my work as I would any other job at a newspaper, magazine or public relations department. I start writing. What I come up with might not be the best I can do, but it's a start. Sometimes, I go over yesterday's work, polishing and rewriting it. I think a lot of writers do this to sharpen their creative spirits. Once they begin the process, they learn quickly to revise, move on and get their writing done.

If bills don't break the block for you, stop to recharge your batteries. You should write every day, but nowhere does it say you must write eighteen hours a day. When you need a change of pace, take a walk, read a book, see a movie or get involved with a hobby unrelated to writing. You'll soon feel ready to get back to work.

COMBINING KIDS AND CAREERS

You've heard my feelings about nay-sayers—people who tell others what can and can't be done. When I was pregnant with my children, I listened to plenty of people predict my future for me, most of them telling me how difficult it would be to combine kids with a career. I'm here to tell you that it can and definitely should be done. It's a wonderful lifestyle, at least for me. But for a writer to develop a business attitude, she needs to write. And that rule about writing every day still applies.

If you want to take your writing seriously (and have others do the same), you'll need to strike a child-care arrangement that works for you and your family. My preference is for off-site care, but that might not be the best solution for everyone. I say that based on my own experiences and from talking with other writing, working moms. If a child knows one of his parents is around, he'll want to interact, not with the caregiver but with his mom or dad. It's natural. It's flattering. But it doesn't help you get the work done.

Part-time child care and preschool have tremendously boosted my productivity. It helped not only me, but benefitted Andy tremendously. I urge other writers to recognize the need for occasional child care and search for solutions that will be productive, not disruptive. But I do understand how difficult it can be. My second son Alex was born three months premature, and after getting him healthy, the last thing I wanted to do was risk illness in organized day care. So I made the most of nap times and enlisted the support of my husband to baby-sit evenings and weekends. Perhaps you can find the help you need from neighbors, nearby relatives, teenage babysitters or mother's day out programs. Whatever your situation, put a priority on finding child care that's there when you need it.

DEVELOPING A WINNING ATTITUDE

By now, I hope you have learned that you are only as productive as you want to be, and you have developed support systems that help you achieve that end. If you still need a push, read Napoleon Hill's *Think and Grow Rich* (Fawcett), available in calendar form, as well. So what about other smart business decisions?

Doing business with the right people promotes your image. In the case of a client of mine, we established a promotional relationship with the Pittsburgh Penguins hockey team, the back-to-back Stanley Cup champions. In addition, our celebrity spokesperson was a children's recording artist gaining national acclaim. Both of these affiliations helped to get our message out.

But they also helped us align with other companies and individuals purely on the basis of association — people who had the power to underwrite additional projects and work with us to create community awareness that we couldn't have achieved as easily on our own. Remember, hanging around winners pays off!

FOLLOW-UP IS CRUCIAL

As my husband and I returned from vacation many years ago, the urge to turn my travels into a published piece moved me to type a manuscript and send it off to a start-up publication. This was my first attempt at freelancing in the magazine market.

Wanting to follow accepted protocol, and yet a little bit naive about the business, I never really followed up as I should have. Surely, if the editor had wanted the manuscript, she would have called, so there was no need for a long-distance phone call to New York. Right?

A year later, feeling I'd given up too fast, I thought about reworking the piece and resubmitting it. To prepare, I ordered some back issues of the magazine and perused them one afternoon. An article in one of the issues seemed familiar, so familiar that I suddenly realized it was mine! And I hadn't even had the thrill of rushing to the newsstand to buy out all the copies.

While editors should not run material they haven't paid for, I'll accept a good part of the blame for what happened. I made all the typical first-time mistakes — submitting on speculation, not following proper manuscript form, and not listing my name, address and telephone number on top of the first page. Obviously, my manuscript got separated from my cover letter.

After a quick call to New York, I did get a check. But, I learned my lesson about the need for follow-up pretty fast that day, and it was a lesson I'll never forget. Making things happen takes more than a leap of faith. It, too, is a smart business decision.

In this case, it required the ability to be confident about my work and its potential for that magazine. It required the ability to pick up the phone and convince an editor, or at least entice her to find my material (buried on her desk) and give me an answer. Writers should make the most of all communication — calls and correspondence (since this demonstrates the writing ability that you'll ultimately be judged upon).

Having broken the bad habit of hesitation, I'll admit that all of my well-meaning, and I hope, well-timed phone calls haven't always met with receptive responses over the years. With some people you can connect; with others, it will never work. One thing's for sure: Follow-up is crucial to the success of any freelance writer.

Never let queries or work sit in limbo longer than six months without prodding the process along through written correspondence, at first, followed by a short phone call. Maybe there's a good reason for lag time. Right after I had an article accepted in the *Pittsburgh Post-Gazette*, an eight-month delivery strike broke out, and everything was put on hold. Pushing, in this case, would not have helped the strike negotiations.

Certainly, if you have no other market in mind for your manuscript or query, then patience might pay off. If your editor has a good excuse for needing more time, give it to him. But if ideas sit for well over a year, I would press a little harder.

MANUSCRIPT MECHANICS

After reading about the mishap with my first sale, you can surmise that following proper manuscript form makes a lot of sense. Your name, address and telephone number are generally placed in the upper left corner. Directly across from these, in the upper right corner, you should indicate the rights you are selling. Underneath, estimate the manuscript's length. On the third line, I sometimes place my social security number, just to round out each side, but this isn't required by all editors.

Skip a few spaces and center your title, with your byline underneath. Drop another two or three lines and begin your manuscript, remembering to double-space. On all subsequent pages, type one or two words identifying the manuscript and your last name, separated by a slash mark. Then, put the page number. When you come to the end of your story, indicate the conclusion by using "−30−" or "−###−" as these are standard symbols, recognized throughout the writing industry.

Use nonerasable paper (at least twenty-pound stock) and leave ample room in the margins for your editor's notations. I place a vertical staple in the upper left corner, but only for short articles. Never try to staple long manuscripts. These should be secured with a rubber band and submitted in manuscript boxes. Always enclose a self-addressed, stamped envelope (known as the SASE).

If you need to know how to prepare and present other types of writing projects, consult *The Writer's Digest Guide to Manuscript Formats* by Dian Dincin Buchman and Seli Groves (Writer's Digest Books).

PUT EVERYTHING IN WRITING

I'm often amazed that many misunderstandings result because no one required a written record. It may be difficult for you to insist upon a signed agreement all the time, but when you do, both parties have a clear understanding of what the writing job entails, any special requirements and the deadline it demands.

I can remember a travel article I once wrote, following the format of a feature with a sidebar filled with handy, "how to get there" information. It landed on the magazine's cover. When the new editor called me for another story, I asked if the sidebar would still be a part of the manuscript package. She said no, but to put that information in the body copy. So that's how I wrote the piece. That conversation guided me.

Unfortunately, when I turned in the article, she felt it wasn't focused enough. She wanted to get rid of the miscellaneous details I had made sure to include. A rewrite resulted.

Two things could have helped this situation. A written description of the assignment from the editor's perspective, and lacking that, my faxing an outline detailing my understanding of the work to be done.

In another instance, I queried an editor of a regional magazine and was told to send in the article. The editor even gave me a deadline, price and publication date. I began the writing, took an overnight trip to complete the research, and was putting the finishing touches on the piece when I called this editor again. To my dismay, she had forgotten the details of our conversation.

This editor had asked another writer to do a similar article for the same issue. Now, she wanted to combine the two contributions. I also learned her definition of an assignment—an article idea originating with the editor and handed out to the appropriate writer. Because I had come up with the idea, I queried, and I called to follow up, my editor didn't consider this an "assignment." To her, it was merely an article on spec. I finally learned my lesson of sealing everything in print.

Written agreements don't just protect details of work to be

done. They play a vital role where money is concerned, especially in commercial work. Businesses merge. New managers take over where old ones left off. Some clients may go through short-term cash flow problems. A signed agreement gives you something to protect your claim and something to refer to when you call on account of late payment.

By signed agreement, I'm referring to a document as simple as a letter. If a business deal requires a more formal contract, seek an attorney to look it over. But you can draft a letter, and if you ever need to go to small claims court, this ought to help your case. Add a line that says something to the effect that "I hereby agree to the terms of this letter and agree to be legally bound by it." Provide a place for the recipient's signature and date, and ask that the letter be returned to you.

If you are on retainer, a written letter should also establish a maximum of hours worked, a price for overtime extended to your clients and a review period that is mutually agreeable. This protects you from working at the same rate for years on end, and it relieves you of guessing when it would be appropriate to broach the subject of renegotiation. You'll feel a lot more comfortable and be able to discuss money matters from a position of confidence and strength.

KEEPING CAREFUL RECORDS

Written records of your work serve another important purpose. Keep a log of submissions, along with photocopies of cover letters, manuscripts, queries and other correspondence, as this delineates your work as business-related (more on that in a moment). A three-ring binder or filing system suits most writer's needs.

You should employ a similar method for recording income, invoices, expenses, car mileage and computer usage. Recording bank deposits with enough notation is also important if you're ever audited.

Smaller publications will frequently send only a check without a perforated stub. Photocopy all of these checks and attach them to the invoices you used for billing. Note that the invoice was paid and be sure to record the income in your ledger.

You don't need to have a degree in accounting to come up with a system you are happy with. I created record-keeping forms with a few columns and a series of blank lines. I keep a calendar by my computer to log hours I've worked on it, and each time I use my car for client appointments, travel research or business errands, I record the mileage I've driven.

An added bonus of keeping sufficient documentation comes when you are vying for new business or negotiating for higher fees. If you've carefully logged your hours and projects, you'll have a head start at compiling an accomplishments sheet for your client or prospective buyer to review.

TAX CONSIDERATIONS

The expenses I described above are tax deductible because I am self-employed, I make a profit every year, and I have no outside office. But this book is not a tax guide. Each year, tax laws change. Your circumstances and the current regulations will determine what tax advantages you can reap from your freelancing efforts, but it's safe to say there are many. My advice is to keep copious records and receipts—whether you believe you will be entitled to a tax deduction or not. In fact, I believe all self-employed people should carry a small receipt book with them (or at least a pad of paper) to request receipts if they're not automatically given.

To obtain many of these tax deductions, your writing must clearly be recognized as a business endeavor rather than a hobby. To prove this point, the IRS requires that you earn a profit in three of the past five years. To take the home-office deduction, you must use your work space solely for business purposes. That regulation disqualifies a spare bedroom, a den or a corner of the kitchen.

Obtain the services of a certified public accountant who can help you at tax time. You will find an accountant's services especially helpful when it comes to filing your quarterly, estimated federal, state and local taxes and when filing any forms for outside help you might hire (such as 1099s). As with any complex matter, read up on the subject. Personal finance magazines, newspaper articles, tax guides and books about self-employment will help you. Kiplinger Books has a particularly good annual tax reference.

EASING THE CASH CRUNCH

Regardless of the methods you employ or the records you keep, most small businesses must learn to survive with limited (or no) cash flow. Setting aside six to twelve months of living expenses to tide you over is your first step in easing the cash crunch. Following up on written agreements ranks second. If an editor agreed to pay on acceptance of the completed manuscript, hold her to it. If your client signed off to pay in thirty days, place a call on day thirty-two or thirty-six, if you haven't received payment by then.

Of course, you improve your chances of collecting promptly if you write for those publications that pay on acceptance, not on publication. *Writer's Market* lists each publication's policies, but be sure to confirm this in your written agreement. I know writers who swear they'll never write for payment on publication, but I'm not one of them. There are some pretty prestigious magazines who operate this way, and while I try to negotiate a better arrangement, getting paid sometime is better than not getting paid at all. But for me to justify the long wait, the credit has to be worth it.

In commercial work, invoicing your clients promptly will enhance early collection. Some writers wait until the end of the month. Others invoice upon completion of each project or portion thereof. Never carry your clients' expenses as this is a surefire way of getting yourself into debt. Help your clients set up their own accounts with printers, photo suppliers and mailing houses, and have all bills for these services go directly to the client. In the case of nonprofit organizations, this works to their advantage because their tax-exempt status saves them money.

The day will come, however, when your best efforts at organization and debt collection fail to produce a check. If you are given a long list of reasons why you must wait, at least ask for a percentage of the payment. Major creditors demand such, and so should you. Keep after the issue. Make your name known and your presence felt.

Several years ago, I accepted an assignment from a national parenting publication. A few weeks later, a different editor took over and killed the project. I was offered a kill fee, but weeks and months passed. No check appeared, and the new editor wasn't returning my phone calls. I finally called the accounting department and pressed the issue. I did receive my kill fee. To me, $250 was worth the extra effort; $25 might not have been.

INCREASING CASH FLOW

As in all businesses, money seems to validate writers. It often motivates us, and it certainly makes others sit up and take notice of what we do. If cash isn't coming your way, there are a number of strategies to make certain that it does.

While writing on speculation is usually frowned upon by professionals, it's also accepted as the norm when breaking into free-lance writing. You can't get assignments based on queries if you have no clips. You can't get clips if you never publish. So writing on speculation is often a first step and last resort.

That's OK. Just be sure to limit the number of articles you write this way. In the initial stages of my career, I wrote three articles on spec for a motor club magazine after the editor said she wanted to see them. Well, she never used them, and never gave me a reason. She lost my trust, but I lost out on three sales. Don't let this happen to you.

Another way of increasing your income potential is to know what the market will bear. Ask other freelance writers what they charge for similar assignments, but take into account their years of experience and the locale they live in. *Writer's Market* gives you a guide, but you'll need to do some of your own research wherever you live and work.

Also, review your rate structure from time to time. We writers forget that corporate workers receive cost-of-living increases, end-of-year bonuses and the like. Some of us are lucky just to receive a holiday greeting at the end of the year! Resist the temptation to sell yourself short. After all, you must include in your fees your costs for health care, overhead, vacation time, retirement and taxes. If you've established a firm track-record of consistently meeting client needs, demand what you are worth!

Pay particular attention to the rights you sign away, never selling all rights to a magazine. Avoid work-for-hire agreements, which mean that you relinquish all rights to the work you were hired to complete. However, when you are starting out with greeting card companies, you will probably have to sell all rights. Be familiar with the differences in rights (again, *Writer's Market* can guide you) and think to the future. If you maintain the option for future sales, make sure you exercise this option. Too many writers put time and effort into one sale and file it away for posterity. Periodically, try to place these reprints with other markets.

Finally, write with extension value in mind. With a different slant, you can sell a newsworthy topic or personality profile many times to a variety of markets. I did this when I learned from my research that Fred Rogers, whose show is produced in Pittsburgh, would be celebrating twenty-five years on public television in 1993. Fortunately, I learned of this nine months ahead of schedule. All told, I was able to produce a question-and-answer interview for *Hemispheres* (United Airline's inflight), an article on Pittsburgh for *The Saturday Evening Post*, a profile of *Mr. Rogers' Neighborhood*, a reading article, a travel piece on a Mr. Rogers' theme park and a child-care story for parenting newspapers across the country. In addition, I received a finder's fee for an idea I presented to *USA Weekend*, and I made contact with *People* magazine.

ETIQUETTE AND ETHICS

Having said that, I must add some basic rules to follow when trying to maximize your sales potential. In the above example, I had developed a good working relationship with Family Communications, Fred Rogers' production company in Pittsburgh. They trusted that I would place stories only in reputable publications, and they also knew that I kept in touch with and ran my ideas past their public relations staff.

If someone grants you an interview for one publication, it does not mean you have license to market that interview somewhere else. In my case, I collected quotes and research over many months, faxing questions back and forth, following up by telephone and sitting down in person with Mr. Rogers himself.

Don't misrepresent your credentials. Never tell someone you are on assignment for a publication when you are not and watch that others don't either. I once got help from a convention and visitor's bureau for a trip I was arranging to California. The office intern asked what magazines I wrote for and where I'd be placing the story. I told him I was still pitching stories and confirming assignments, but gave him a list of my past credits. Months later, I read in the bureau's newsletter that I was "on assignment" for these publications. I was not pleased with the way he had misrepresented me.

Another etiquette issue surfaces when people you interview ask to see your article before you turn it in. Allowing sources to preview your story would be allowing a form of censorship. The public expects reporters to work uncensored and free of such constraints. We journalists shouldn't have to fear that our sources will change their recollections, words or ideas to a more acceptable point of view. Also, by giving this kind of advantage to one source, you would give that person unfair insight into the information your other sources gave you. Clearly identify yourself as a writer or journalist researching a story for publication. Take great care in quoting your sources, and if need be, repeat what you've written down to insure accuracy.

Making such ethical choices can be tough. During my research of Fred Rogers and the Neighborhood, I was in the running to write an in-depth feature for a local publication. The editor knew I had interviewed him for *Hemispheres* and asked to see a copy of the article, months before it would appear in print. She said she wanted to see my style, but I would not send it.

In a letter accompanying other clips, I wrote something to the effect that "if I were in my editor's shoes, I think I'd want to see the piece I contracted with a writer before anyone else." Sure, I could have written "not intended for publication" across the top, but by allowing her to read a completed assignment for another magazine, I would be handing over my research, my angle and the questions my editor at *Hemispheres* and I had carefully selected.

EXPECT REJECTION

No matter how well you have honed your business and writing skills and mastered the lessons of professional etiquette, rejection rears its ugly head. Expect it. And don't run from it.

Editors reject manuscripts and queries for a multitude of reasons, most of which we'll never understand. Rare is the editor who scrawls a personal note in the margin of the form letter to explain why your idea didn't make it. Perhaps the suggestion was already assigned to another writer or maybe the section you were interested in is staff written. Maybe it's already been completed and remains in overset for a future issue. Perhaps your query wasn't targeted enough or maybe it was too focused for the magazine's readers.

Advertising or lack of it plays another important role in rejection. Most publishers (read: editors) must meet their advertisers' needs, for in publishing, advertising often pays for the magazine. If there isn't advertising to support an editorial idea or if the idea doesn't meet a need for an existing advertiser, your idea could be golden, but it's not publishable.

Finally, maybe there's real merit in the rejections you have received. Maybe your idea needs to be more clearly defined, your writing skill honed and improved. Maybe a rewrite is in order, especially if you haven't looked at the material in several months.

After accepting the reasons for rejection and not personalizing the blow, give up the grief. I got very down on myself because a favorite magazine of mine, one I had researched thoroughly, could find no home for my ideas. My husband said, "If you never write for that magazine again, what difference will it make? Will your career be over?" When I really thought about it, I understood his point. It *hadn't* made a difference. That year turned out to be a good one. Those rejections *didn't* hold back my career. I urge you to ask yourself the same questions. Move on. Reroute those queries to other markets. You'll never know what sale awaits you if you don't.

PROMOTING YOUR WRITING CAREER

I'm sure by now that you've caught on to my freelancing approach. I'd describe it as proactive, in the least, slightly assertive at best. But in this competitive industry, a discussion of self-promotion is paramount to the success of your writing efforts.

It's sad to say that the number of consumer and specialty publications has shrunk over the years. Some magazines have slashed their pay scales for freelance writing, and others have eliminated the need for outside editorial work altogether. With these facts in mind, know that if you don't promote your writing, other writers will promote theirs.

The beginning writer won't require news releases, press kits, publicity photos, give-away gadgets and publicists. We'll save this discussion for chapter twenty, realizing that these investments pay off when you promote books. In addition, other resources such as *The Writer's Guide to Self-Promotion and Publicity* by

Elane Feldman (Writer's Digest Books) are devoted to explaining publicity and promotion in much greater detail.

For now, focus your efforts on writing clear and concise correspondence, establishing a good reputation among clients and editors and building an impressive selection of published clippings.

Often your letters will make your first impression. List your credits and areas of expertise in the final paragraph of your query letter. In essence, answer that editor's question: "Why should I assign this story to you?" Once you've developed quite a biography, with articles, books, commercial projects and teaching assignments, you might want to develop a separate sheet of writing accomplishments to include with your pitch letters. Of course, invest in good letterhead and proofread everything that leaves your office. Business cards will add that extra touch of professionalism.

Building your clippings might require an additional ounce of effort. Just as you would clip, date and cite the source of articles you retrieve for your own use, be sure to do the same for others. Trim your articles neatly, taking great care to tear, not mutilate the samples you've collected. Using rubber cement, do the best paste-up job you can manage, remembering to include the masthead of the magazine you wrote for. If you don't have the masthead, just type the name and date of the publication on top. Use correction fluid to disguise any specks or lines that don't belong.

Take your paste-up to your local printer or self-serve copy center and learn the art of photocopying, with lightening, darkening, reduction and photo enhancing commands. This skill in itself will carry you far, for newspaper clips yellow over time, and articles torn out of magazines fray around the edges, creasing where you don't want them to. Photocopy each clip you publish, and build a file with several sets ready to grab, seal into a large envelope and mail.

In fact, I attribute my willingness to write letters and send clippings to the sale of this book. Several years into my writing career, I wrote to Bill Brohaugh, the editorial director of Writer's Digest Books, and offered to be interviewed as a freelance writer in one of their books. While no opportunity existed, I was pleasantly surprised when Bill invited me to submit book ideas. If I hadn't taken the initiative to promote myself, I might never have written the book you're now reading.

When undertaking commercial work, photocopies and clippings are just as necessary, even though you'll be showing off originals in your portfolio. You can spend a lot of money on savvy portfolios, but I prefer to use a handsome three-ring notebook, with individual plastic protectors for my work. As long as your notebook doesn't shout "school supply," I think it will do just fine.

I purchased my portfolio at a specialty office supply store. It's burgundy with gold trim on the edges, and it looks much more expensive than it was. But each time I've met with prospective clients, it's done its job. I try never to leave it behind. Instead, I offer the client a photocopied set of selected clippings, usually those that closely pertain to the work we're discussing.

Use these clippings to send to others who inquire about your services. If you think someone you know would enjoy reading your article, send them a copy, along with a polite note. A little self-promotion never hurts as long as it's appropriate. Never pass up the opportunity to see your name in print. When asked for an interview, give one. This is how you establish yourself as an industry expert. Offer to teach a class. It will create further name recognition.

Speaking before civic, church or student groups lends even more prestige. Ask your local librarian if a talk hosted by a resident writer would be welcomed. If offers don't come to you, seek them out, volunteering to speak gratis if you can afford to do so.

As you put together a steady string of public speaking engagements, be sure to confirm details well in advance and immediately prior to your engagements, especially when any travel or overnight accommodations are involved. You should also write an introduction for your host. Being introduced at a local college as "Larry Oberlin Hoff" confirmed the need for me to insist upon accuracy. The absent-minded instructor who did the dishonor—a speech professor, no less—left the bio I had handed him in his office. I started my presentation one down, and felt at a disadvantage for it.

Even if you aren't a published book author, you can still speak at colleges and bookstores that sponsor special events. One of my favorite bookstores publishes a bimonthly newsletter featuring craft demonstrations, storytelling, informational lectures and even fashion shows. Seek out these types of opportunities and make the most of them.

Tell everyone you know that you're a writer. Sure, you'll run into those few who may patronize you with an "isn't that nice" or "oh, really dear." It's true that anyone can call himself a writer, but once the clippings and the checks start coming in, you can hold your head high (and watch people's reactions!). Just remember, word of mouth starts with yours.

In every article you submit, take two extra minutes to craft your own bio at the end of the manuscript. Many magazines like to identify their contributors and their accomplishments. If you write two or three sentences, you won't leave anything to chance.

Write op-ed pieces for your newspaper or send a note to your local features editor, explaining your area of expertise and adding that you will have an upcoming article published. If you've interviewed a major newsmaker or celebrity, the same tactics apply. When people compliment you on the great article you wrote, suggest that they write a letter to the editor of that publication. Such good wishes will further your foothold there.

You might ask your writer's group if they need speakers, and don't forget the networking opportunities at writer's conferences. Even if you aren't a featured speaker, you can participate in group discussions, ask insightful questions and cite examples from your own work, if called upon. But don't forget to dress for first impressions. When I attended my first conference, I was amazed at how many participants showed up in blue jeans and tennis shoes.

To promote to clients, develop a brochure, selling others on the services you offer. Ask satisfied customers to contribute quotes, if you feel this might help. Make sure the sales piece you produce is professional, that it accentuates all that you do and does not advertise any lack of expertise.

With all this talk of soliciting new clients, let's not forget the importance of maintaining your client base (including editor relationships). Each Christmas, I make sure I send greetings to those I've worked with throughout the past year. In fact, I usually go one step beyond with the editors I've repeatedly worked with. I send them a tin of homemade rum balls, made with island rum brought back from one of my numerous travel assignments.

After one of my editors accidentally gave out her birthdate, I scrambled for a piece of paper to write it down. Now each year, I usually send a card and a small gift. I do this because she's been so helpful to me throughout my career. If we hadn't hit it off so well based on our work together, my guess is that we would be good friends anyhow. Over the years, I've tried to remember to say congratulations on a promotion, goodbye and good luck, and always, thank you. Other freelancers I know do the same, approaching greetings and gift-giving in a professional, yet friendly manner.

Some might think all this smacks of buttering up, but I don't believe so. I send such gifts to say thanks, and I think the editors I work with appreciate the gesture (and rumor has it they like the rum too!).

Never underestimate the value of good exposure to your writing career, and don't write off the kind of writing you do as unworthy of people's attention. Getting others to recognize you, your finished products and your hard work increases sales and brings more projects, and profits, your way.

Chapter Four

Journalistic Foundations

No matter what kind of freelance career you choose, your ability to write clearly and concisely is essential. In fact, mastering this skill is not only imperative to the success of any communication effort, but it's also your ticket to landing more assignments and earning additional income.

Nowhere did I learn this better than during my three months as an intern in the public affairs department of a TV station. I was able to hone this important skill, and some of my work appeared on the air. Hours of writing ten-second public service announcements paid off. Years after that experience, I can see how it has helped me achieve success in various forms of my writing.

Let's face it: You can say only so much in ten seconds. Every word *must* count. In my case, people relied on these spots to let them know the who, what, when, where, why and how of the events or nonprofit services I wrote about. That's a lot to cram into a few words, but if you practice long enough, as I did, it will become inherent in your writing style.

As you read through this chapter, the concepts may seem vaguely familiar, reminding you of high school English class or Journalism 101 in college. You probably have seen these principles before, but after studying them again here, I hope you'll see them in a different light—as keys to higher profit and professional potential.

THE FIVE Ws AND THE H

As I've described, these are the foundations of all journalistic writing: who, what, when, where, why and how. These questions are essential for your reader (or listener) to have a clear grasp of the information you are presenting. Leave out one of these, and you'll cause a certain amount of chaos.

Imagine the listener tuning in to a radio station. Music creates the ambiance in the background while he is cooking dinner, washing the car or sitting down at work. The disc jockey reads a PSA for a benefit concert to be held over the weekend, only the spot never mentions when it will begin.

The listener, familiar with the organization or town, might just show up at the time these events normally occur. What if he's wrong, and shows up an hour after the performance has begun? His wife yells at him for not getting the information straight. They've both just blown a Saturday evening, wasted money on a babysitter, and now they're angry with one another.

OK, so my example might be a little far-fetched. The point is that there is much information, written or broadcast, competing for your time. Forget an essential fact, and the communication effort fails. Your job as a writer is to make life easier on your readers and listeners, not harder. So remember the five Ws and the H, and you and your audiences will be better served.

In my writing classes and workshops, I often add a sixth W for the benefit of my students. I encourage them to ask *who cares?*, for if no one besides the author does, you've got a real problem with your writing from the start. It's a reminder to make sure that there is actually an audience for your subject matter. If you answer "no one" to the question, rework your topic until you can come up with a positive response.

INTERVIEWS—THE SEARCH FOR ANSWERS

Now that you recognize the importance of the five Ws and the H, how do you get the answers? Enter the interview—the technique writers use to satisfy our curiosity and provide us new information.

Interviews bring real people and substance to our writing. Since many writers are generalists, relying on a broad base of liberal arts knowledge, we rely on the insights, perceptions, thoughts, reactions and feelings of others to guide us through the unfamiliar territory of a new story or topic. Others, particularly authorities in the subjects we're exploring, relate experience and offer explanations far better than we can on our own. Good writing thrives on diversity. Readers enjoy the opinions of others, and they can relate to personal involvement in our stories much easier than straight summation of the facts.

For all of these reasons, interviewing becomes another essential skill. Writers conduct interviews in three ways, according to Michael Schumacher, author of *The Writer's Complete Guide to Conducting Interviews* (Writer's Digest Books). These methods include in-person, telephone or through-the-mail interviews. As a freelancer, I've conducted all three types, with the most common being over-the-phone interviews. These normally offer convenience when a personal visit is impractical. Telephone interviews also save time and money. If you're getting paid only fifty dollars to write a story, then travelling across town eats into your productive time. Unless you're doing in-depth profiles, question-and-answer pieces or extensive research, a phone interview should suffice.

Finding the Right Source

As part of my clipping and filing procedures each month, I keep an eye open to experts, both local and national, who might have something to offer if I have queries outstanding or if my client could use the information. I file the clipping (with the person's name, title and affiliation) accordingly. I use a similar approach when watching television, making note of featured guests on talk shows and news reports. In fact, I always try to keep some blank videotapes next to the VCR so that I can quickly pop one in and record a news program I can use for research.

Newsmakers and authors make valuable resources for articles, columns, news releases, newsletters and book chapters. These sources surface at the strangest times—in the doctor's office as you peruse magazines or at the bookstore while you're combing the shelves for an entirely different project. Carry paper and pen with you at all times. When you spot appropriate information or a beneficial source, you'll be prepared to write it down.

Researching Your Subject

Before you make that phone call or personal visit, draw up a list of questions. To do this well, you'll need as much information as possible. Go to the library and flip through the *Reader's Guide to Periodical Literature*. Interlibrary loan is often handy when your local library doesn't subscribe to a particular publication you need. *The New York Public Library Desk Reference* can also help as you track down statistics and seek to understand information that's new to you. If your subject is local, ask community leaders, the person's secretary or the person herself for background material. Most people are more than willing to oblige.

For in-depth assignments, read everything that's been written on your subject (or at least as much as you can get your hands on). The research rule of thumb suggests that more is always preferable to less. Proper research saves time, and I'll reiterate: Time is money. Don't spend the precious moments you have with your interviewee seeking answers to questions you could have obtained elsewhere. People you interview will be pressed for time. State who you're writing for or whether you're using the interview for a spec submission; most people have a reputation to uphold and want to know the publication they'll appear in.

Conducting the Interview

If you do your homework ahead of time and arrive or phone when you're supposed to, you're off to a good start. It's usually helpful to chat briefly just to break the ice and establish a rapport with the other person. If you wish to use a tape recorder, do ask permission first (but don't rely on technology alone as it has been known to fail).

When I gained access to Fred Rogers for an in-depth interview, I took along my brand-new tape recorder, which Mr. Rogers quickly dubbed "fancy." It was fancy, all right. So fancy, I forgot that the voice-activate switch was on, and only snippets of my interview actually recorded. Fortunately, I took careful notes. Rogers' slow-paced speech and willingness to repeat something helped me immensely. But learn from my mistake: Make sure your equipment is working and know how to operate it.

Begin your list of questions early in the interview. With celebrities or highly recognized individuals, it's easy to get carried away in conversation. Fred Rogers made me feel so comfortable and so good about myself that I could have spent the entire afternoon listening to and learning from this fascinating man. But we writers must resist the temptation to chat beyond those first few minutes.

Get to the heart of the subject at hand, but save the probing questions for the middle of the interview. By this time you will have developed a certain level of trust, and you'll receive better responses. If you wait until the end, your time may be cut short, and you'll never get to the critical questions at hand.

When interviewing, ask questions that are open-ended and attitudinal as opposed to those that solicit a yes-or-no response. Probing questions often begin with "how" or "why." If your subject stops short of giving you all the information you need, ask her to expand upon the last answer or cite specific examples. And when you must cover controversial or sensitive subject matter, phrase your questions carefully. Lead by saying, "Your critics charge . . ." or "It's been said. . . ." Watch the pros (such as Barbara Walters) on television and see how they develop a rapport and navigate through difficult questions.

Finally, when your interview is over, double-check the accuracy of spellings and quotations you're unsure of. Transcribe any taped material and fill in your notes as soon as possible. When writing your finished story and inserting your quotations, try to put your subject in the best light possible, unless including an error in language or sentence structure serves a purpose in your story, as with quoting young children or the uneducated. I usually fix a minor mistake in grammar or syntax because I know that we're all a little more casual in our speech than we are in our writing.

THE INVERTED PYRAMID

Now that you have answers to your questions and mounds of research, it's time to assemble your information. Journalism graduates will surely remember the drawing that by now is a classic. It's the upside-down triangle, otherwise known as the inverted pyramid. Instructors test their geometric skills to demonstrate an important writing concept. The drawing depicts the fullness that's embodied at the top of whatever you write. In other words, all the important information finds its home in the beginning of your story.

I'm referring to the material we covered earlier — the who, what, when, where, why and how. These questions deserve answers in your lead sentence, where your reader will develop an interest in your story or decide to pass it over for some other item. A lead sentence or paragraph creates a mood. It says to your reader, "You're going to smile while you read this story," "Get the box of tissues ready," or "When you put this down, you're going to be compelled to act." Whatever the result, your lead grabs your reader, hooks him into paying attention and sets the foundation for what follows.

There is another reason for the inverted pyramid. Not only does it remind you to stack the important information at the top, but it also guides you as you complete the rest of your work. Envision the pyramid as a funnel. As you tell your story, you'll be dealing with less and less important material. When your editor goes to copyfit the article into the newspaper, she may have to cut a few lines at the bottom. But, if you've done your job well, the information that's sacrificed won't matter to your reader, for you have remembered to include all the important concepts higher up in your piece. If you write to please your readers, you'll be pleasing your editor, who will be more apt to pass further assignments your way in the future.

TAKE ONE: ACTION!

Does your writing skip or simply stroll along the way? Do your words evoke images so that the reader can see and believe instead of read and merely trust? Active and visual writing are two elements that sell a winning manuscript.

If your writing moves along aimlessly, bogged down with too many words, why not lighten the load? For example, if I offer a brochure to market my services, I might say:

> Service is provided to clients through writing in the form of public relations work such as newsletter design, desktop publishing and media relations.

But consider this alternative:

> I provide writing and public relations services including newsletter design, desktop publishing and media relations.

Which sentence would convince you to hire me? The second example gets to the point a lot faster, uses fewer words and communicates more directly.

That's the power of the active voice. It's crisp. It's clear. It communicates, using far fewer words. By contrast, the first sentence reads as if no one wants to do the work. No one wants to take responsibility. It's a prime example of the passive voice and the problems associated with it. Ever wonder why so much academic, bureaucratic and legal documentation shouts with the passive voice? Because it's the easy way out. No one has to put a name on it. No one has to take responsibility. Changing your sentences from the passive to the active voice might not make every sentence dance, but it will pack a lot more punch into what you say.

TAKE TWO: CUT!

Just like it happens on a movie set, the cut follows the call for action. In writing, much of what we write cries out for such treatment. If your writing runs on with too many words, eliminating passive construction is your initial first-aid measure. Next comes cutting the clutter.

In the classic writing book *The Elements of Style* (Macmillan Publishing) Professor William Strunk says:

> Vigorous writing is concise. A sentence should contain no unnecessary words, a paragraph no unnecessary sentences, for the same reason that a drawing should have no unnecessary lines and a machine no unnecessary parts. This requires not that the writer make all his sentences short, or that he avoid all detail and treat his subjects only in outline, but that every word tell.

When you sit down with your first draft, ask yourself, again: Does every word count? In many cases, you'll find words to weed out.

Clichés are frequent word wasters, yet we're all guilty of using them, at one time or another. See, I tricked you. I just used a cliché (at one time or another), and for a split second I didn't even notice it, and you may not have either. I just wrote it. It sounded right. But that's the problem. We're so accustomed to hearing clichés that they indeed sound as if they belong.

Next time you edit your work, question your comfort level with your favorite clichés: as a last resort; by the same token; by any stretch of the imagination; don't rock the boat; get the ball rolling; it's fallen on deaf ears; just in the nick of time; or, swept under the rug.

You get the idea. And don't put these culprits in quotation

marks either, for that only calls attention to poor word choice. Cut them. Throw them away, and try something new—something fresh.

If you need additional help weeding unnecessary words, purchase a copy of *The Elements of Style* (also available on videocassette). Careful writers take the time to review this material periodically, and believe me, it pays off no matter how accomplished you are.

Write Tight by William Brohaugh (Writer's Digest Books) also tells us how to express our thoughts with grace and power, using not only the right word, but the right number of words. This book will surely help you develop the skill of clear and concise writing.

Of course, as we weed words, we must avoid robbing our writing of the right rhythm or maintaining the richness of a time-honored work. Take the Bible passage that's read at so many Christian weddings—I Corinthians 13:2-3. In the *Revised Standard Version* of the Bible, it reads:

> If I speak in the tongues of men and of angels, but have not love, I am a noisy gong or a clanging cymbal. And if I have prophetic powers, and understand all mysteries and all knowledge, and if I have all faith, so as to remove mountains, but have not love, I am nothing.

Then, look at *The Living Bible* version:

> If I had the gift of being able to speak in other languages without learning them, and could speak in every language there is in all of heaven and earth, but didn't love others, I would only be making noise. If I had the gift of prophecy and knew all about what is going to happen in the future, knew everything about *everything*, but didn't love others, what good would it do? Even if I had the gift of faith so that I could speak to a mountain and make it move, I would still be worth nothing at all without love.

Which passage is richer? Which calls out to a person more than the other? Finally, which is more concise? Admittedly, *The Living Bible* is a paraphrased version, and one I've found useful on many occasions. But as a writer, I would choose to maintain the integrity of the older version rather than sacrifice the beauty for a newer, trendier way with words.

It's also important to remember that while we must edit language for clarity, we shouldn't sacrifice colorful language. In some instances, colloquial flavor, regional dialect and historical context might be called for and should not be tampered with.

ELIMINATING SEXIST LANGUAGE

We've already discussed how clichés are built into our vocabulary. So is sexist language. It's ingrained in our culture, and while the women's movement brought it to our attention in the early 1970s, it still appears in our writing and speech. Unless there is a rich, time-honored passage (such as in I Corinthians 13), a lot of the references we read can be updated for the present.

Years ago, United Technologies ran an advertisement in the *Wall Street Journal* titled "Let's Get Rid of 'The Girl.' " I loved it then, and I still do, for it sums up the need for eliminating sexist language. I read it in almost every workshop and class I teach. I'll share it with you, as well:

> Wouldn't 1979 be
> a great year
> to take one giant
> step forward
> for womankind
> and get rid of
> "the girl"?
>
> Your attorney says,
> "If I'm not here
> just leave it with
> the girl."
>
> The purchasing agent
> says, "Drop off your
> bid with the girl."
>
> A manager says,
> "My girl will get
> back to your girl."
> *What* girl?

Do they mean
Miss Rose?
Do they mean
Ms. Torres?
Do they mean
Mrs. McCullough?
Do they mean
Joy Jackson?

"The girl"
is certainly
a woman when she's
out of her teens.
Like you,
she has a name.
Use it.

©United Technologies Corporation, 1979

This may be cute, but the point is that if you use sexist language (or any offensive writing or speech), it shows you're out of step with the times. It signals a lack of professionalism and puts your editor on guard for future slip-ups.

In class, I ask my students to complete a sexist language quiz. In one column, I list words or phrases such as businessman, fireman, salesman, stewardess, watchman, and of course, girl in the office. I leave a blank space next to each word and ask them to come up with as many non-offensive alternatives as they can, without using the suffix "—person." It usually takes the class a while to complete the exercise, but the end result is always the same. Men, and women, walk away with a heightened sensitivity and a broader vocabulary.

Replacing hackneyed expressions with more socially conscious choices is challenging. It's easier to just switch between "he" and "she" but many writers (and readers) find this technique distracting, not to mention wordy. Instead, rewrite your sentences in the plural, replace "he" with the second person "you," or substitute the plural "we/us/our" or "they/them/their" for "he/him/his," as in "Writers must avoid sexist language whenever they can" instead of "A writer must avoid sexist language whenever he or she can."

If sexist language continues to haunt your style, create your own quiz, as I did, listing the offending words in one column, and alternatives in another. Your self-study project will become a thesaurus for future assignments, and this will make your writing stronger.

BEGINNING TO END

In my explanation of the inverted pyramid, I discussed the basics of lead sentences and paragraphs. Not only does the important information go here, but that information creates a mood and a feel for what's to come. In my own writing, I only pose a question to my reader if the situation truly warrants it, and if I use this approach, I never allow the reader to turn off by answering "no" to whatever I've posed in my lead.

In addition, I avoid beginning my leads with quotations from others—not because other sources aren't valuable; they are. In fact, it's tempting to let the people I've interviewed have the first say. But I believe their input is best contributed after I've built a case for their credentials, after I've established the story to the point where the reader begs for more information from an identifiable source.

Quotes ideally belong in the body of your story. Remember to identify those you've interviewed early on. Don't wait until the end of a long sentence that stretches into a paragraph. Instead, identify your source midway through the sentence, continuing with the quote after you've established your expert's credentials in the reader's mind. Don't be afraid to use the word "said" to attribute your phrases, and don't use quotations when the information cited is fairly general. Use quotes to set off something that stuns the reader or reveals significant remarks. Paraphrase anything of lesser importance.

Quotations are also quite appropriate for conclusions when you want your sources to have the final say. Many quotes have long-lasting impact. So do firsthand anecdotes or a basic restatement of your theme. No matter what type of conclusion you use, your ending needs to wind down your story and provide a sense of closure.

SUMMING IT ALL UP

By now, you've learned the techniques of establishing a good lead, writing like a journalist, eliminating unnecessary and offensive language from your manuscripts, and bringing all your hard work to a satisfying conclusion. How do you know you've covered all the important points? Careful review should answer that for you. Ask yourself these questions:

- Does my lead identify the kind of story I'm writing and what I expect the reader to feel along the way?
- Is my message clear?
- Do I hide behind the passive voice, or do my verbs shout action?
- Do my sentences limp along or lunge forward, propelling the reader to a new level of understanding?
- Are my sentences diverse enough? Or, do they cry out in sing-song "subject, verb . . . subject, verb"?
- Have I weeded all unnecessary words? Clichés?
- Have I eliminated any sexist, racist or otherwise offensive language?
- Do my words evoke images? Can my reader "see" what I'm writing about?
- Are my quotations or dialogue stilted? Do they sound natural when read aloud? Have I used quotation marks to identify ideas that any fool could have said, or have I used them when I truly felt there was something significant to say?
- Have I created good transitions between paragraphs?
- Does my conclusion wind down the story and provide a sense of closure?

If you've answered all of these questions, you've done all you can to practice the basics of journalistic style, writing clearly and concisely. Your next step is an obvious one, albeit somewhat dreaded. Now you must put your work before an audience, or an editor. In the chapters ahead, you'll learn to do just that.

FAST-CASH PROSPECTS

Chapter Five

Fillers, Hints, Humor and More

Getting published quickly will boost your self-confidence as a writer and increase your cash flow. It means that someone has liked your work. Someone has placed a value on it. Someone was so moved that she wrote you a check. Indeed a $15 sale means as much to the beginning writer as $1500 does to the contributing editor of an upscale magazine. And as I've often told my students, $15 works for me, and for you, at the grocery store or in the bank.

Fillers and short pieces make these quick sales possible. In the time you could spend composing, typing, revising and printing a query letter, you could have gathered the same amount of information, drafted a manuscript, sent it out and sold it. Once you sell it, you suddenly have clippings. You've become a published writer, and you'll move quickly onto another successful assignment.

You can write several fillers in the amount of time it takes other writers to produce the first draft of a feature. With several short manuscripts landing on different desks, you also increase your chances of acceptance.

But time and stacking the odds aren't the only reasons writing fillers is effective. By consistently proving your skills and producing publishable material, you are opening editorial doors with each short piece you write. You become a writer with a name, face and voice. Chances are good they'll remember you when you pitch a longer piece in the months or years to come. Also, when you reach a standstill in your writing day, you can recharge your creative battery by quickly switching gears and writing something fun—something fast.

WHO BUYS FILLERS?

Much of what we read today is service-oriented journalism. It's material that makes the reader healthier, wealthier, wiser, more attractive, better liked and better adjusted. Small pieces are no different in their focus, and they provide the apprenticeship you'll need for tackling longer length works later on.

Take a look at the magazines you read, or browse the newsstand. You'll see a lot of small sections devoted to service-oriented information. Busy readers eat these up, for they are items quickly read, grasped and put to use.

Check to see if the filler pages give bylines. That's a sign that a variety of writers are contributing to the section. Check the masthead to be sure these aren't staff writers. It's an important distinction. In *American Baby*, a regular freelance contributor has traditionally been responsible for the Crib Notes column. Obviously, it would be a waste of your time, not to mention the editor's time, to send submissions to this column. However, a cursory look through *Writer's Market* shows that *Expecting* takes submissions of fifty to one hundred words for the Happenings column; *Woman's Day* welcomes contributions for the Neighbors and the Tips to Share columns; and *The Saturday Evening Post* publishes anecdotes and short humor of approximately three hundred words in its PostScripts section.

MEETING EACH MARKET'S NEEDS

When writing fillers, your ability to write clearly and concisely is put to the test. Many magazines give word counts to guide the writer of short pieces. Others do not, but you can come up with your own guide by counting the words yourself.

What one magazine editor considers short, another newsletter editor may consider long, but usually, short pieces are defined as anywhere from forty to three hundred words. Regardless, you must make each word count. Practice. If your first draft runs long, put it down for a few hours. A fresh look often allows the writer to pinpoint a word here or a phrase there that can be cut without sacrificing any meaning. Soon you'll tighten the whole piece.

FINDING IDEAS FOR FILLERS

Before I sat down to write this chapter, two articles from my morning newspaper jumped out at me. They weren't major world events. They weren't even on page one. They were buried inside but valuable just the same. The one small article talked about coffee awakening people's mental power, while the boxed item beside it discussed the new mail codes that help automate mail delivery.

An astute writer would see these as the foundation of great fillers and use such news reports as research. Think of the possibilities for the coffee tip. Office workers and executives rush to the coffee cart every morning. Homemakers sip their favorite brew while caring for the kids, watching the morning news or chatting with their neighbors. College students rely on caffeine to pull an all-nighter. Similarly, we all rely on the U.S. mail to make it through. Every business counts on it. Kids feel special when they tear open a birthday card or holiday greeting. And I don't need to tell you how many writers look for letters and checks in those deliveries every day as our source of income.

These are just three easy market possibilities — starting points writers can use to customize the information they come across and write fillers for their audiences. You could take one news report and gather more ideas. With additional research and a new twist each time, you can boost your income through several sales. And both of the ideas I cited came from paying attention to the newspaper, which most writers read everyday.

Converting large ideas into the succinct is another source for filler ideas. When I interviewed Fred Rogers, I had a longer feature to write, but using that research, I wrote a filler featuring the only life-size Mr. Rogers' Neighborhood of Make-Believe in the country, and sold this to a travel magazine.

HOT HINTS

Another great method of creating fillers stems from using that which has proved useful to you. I've done this quite frequently with *Communications Briefings*, a newsletter that bills itself as a monthly idea source for decision-makers.

I'm sure you've come across publications that welcome hints about saving money, helping the environment, keeping house, tending to the garden or caring for the kids. If you've come up with a new way to solve an old problem, send it in. What's the worst that can happen? The editor doesn't run it. But if it's brilliant, you'll be a couple of bucks richer.

Connie Emerson, who has written fillers for years, suggests a good technique for testing your hint's originality. Check them out with friends, she writes in *The 30-Minute Writer*. "Chances are, if they've heard or read similar ones, they'll tell you," Connie says. She also encourages writers to market product-related hints to manufacturers. Just find out first whether the company pays for such contributions before you share your nifty idea.

RECIPE WRITING

If you're a writer who loves to cook, stir up some sales by sharing your culinary talents. There are a lot more opportunities in this market than you might think.

The obvious target is the food magazine market, but often recipe sales to these publications are linked to the full-length articles they buy. Women's magazines feature recipes every month. But don't limit your search for sales. Extend it to include parenting publications whose readers always look for lunch box surprises and nutritious snacks; singles and senior citizen magazines run single-serving recipes and tips on easy-to-prepare foods; the college crowd needs to master the fine art of cooking with a crock pot and hot plate; religious magazines offer tips to readers who need to adapt recipes to feed large congregations gathered for a fellowship dinner.

Watch for contests. Pitch the idea of a recipe card to a greeting card company. These are popular, particularly during the holiday season. Also, local chefs, restaurants, caterers, nonprofit organizations or even celebrities might need help compiling a recipe book for their own promotional purposes. Point out that by hiring a professional writer, the book will sell more copies, yielding higher profits for everyone involved. With new dietary findings released all the time, and with people travelling all over the globe, the demand for relevant recipes and foreign cuisine is increasing.

Doris McFerran Townsend wrote a handy book for those who want to pursue a career in recipe and cookbook writing called *The Way to Write and Publish a Cookbook* (St. Martin's Press). It's worth reading, especially for the chapter on how to make money on your community cookbook. Even if you undertake such a project, without pay, the experience you gain will be valuable. Just be sure to get proper credit for the work you do. Then, you can apply what you've learned to your own cookbook pitched to a major publisher.

If you have commercial clients, consider including recipes in the client's publications. But be sure the recipes are accurate. A nonprofit organization where I once worked included in the newsletter recipes their volunteers used at a cookie sale. An angry reader pointed out a glaring error. The recipe had listed two "tbsp." of baking powder among the ingredients instead of two "tsp." The irate caller stated that if a cook tried this recipe, as printed, it would have caused a minor explosion in the oven.

I don't know whether this is true, but be warned and kitchen-test your recipes before they hit the print shop. In her book, Townsend shows a sample of a test sheet she uses to double-check recipes for accuracy. This test sheet lists various items that affect the recipe, including weather, pan preparation, times and temperatures and then leaves room for a complete listing of ingredients, your comments and conclusions.

In finding ideas for your recipe sales, remember that service-orientation applies here as well. Why not take an old favorite and make it easier for today's busy two-career couples? Or make it healthier for the millions who must watch their cholesterol and fat content? Make it meatless for the vegetarians among us? Or, make it more palatable for moms and dads to feed to their kids?

I'm sure that when headlines broke regarding the unhealthy nature of some Chinese dishes, a lot of writers (and editors) cringed. But if astute writers listened closely to those health reports, they could have discovered great follow-up potential writing about how to make Chinese cuisine, as we know it, more authentic and a lot healthier by adding greater portions of rice and vegetables.

Cooks often wonder when their recipes deserve a wider audience. My recommendation is to serve your secret dish to family and friends in your own home or whenever you're called upon to contribute a dish to a neighborhood gathering, church dinner or office picnic. When your guests continue to rave about your culinary creation, it's time to send it in.

Finally, don't forget about approaching those manufacturers just as you did when trying to sell your hints. Food, cookware and appliance companies all feature recipes with their products, and those recipes in your Sunday circular may not have originated in some corporate test kitchen. They may have been served to some writer's family first.

"Whatever I'm testing for my books is what I feed my family for dinner, which doesn't always sit well with my children," says Helene Siegel, author of *The Ethnic Kitchen* (HarperCollins) series. "After writing several ethnic cookbooks and serving things like tongue stew and chilaquiles night after night, my 12-year-old son requested that my next book be something American, so we could have hot dogs and hamburgers like normal people do!" If you're fortunate enough to have adventurous eaters to sample your kitchen creations, take them up on their offer, or try telling them that they're expanding their culinary horizons. It's worth a try!

To increase your profits writing recipes, sprinkle your sales with low-fat, low-cholesterol and low-calorie ingredients. These days, people are more prone to break old habits and try new health-conscious recipes. Stick to ingredients that are readily available across the country. In fact, there's a trend toward using more fresh ingredients and fewer canned items in recipes. Expensive and hard-to-find ingredients frustrate cooks feeding families on a budget.

If you're skilled in photography, send along a photo of your food. You may have to learn some techniques from an experienced food stylist, but a tempting photo may clinch the sale for you.

You'll also improve your chances of getting your recipe collections published if you use an occasional recipe from famous chefs or cookbook authors. Isn't this stealing, you ask? Actually, no it isn't. A fact cannot be copyrighted, and in this case, it means the recipe's ingredients and the order in which they're listed and used. For other elements of a recipe or cookbook (i.e., captions, explanations, comments and methods) copyright does apply. Obtain permission if you're reprinting for profit and carefully cite the source.

WRITING TECHNIQUES FOR FILLERS AND RECIPES
Whenever you write fillers, particularly recipes, remember that every word must count. Cut right to the action, followed by the results. Use imperative verbs such as "keep," "make," "place,"

"sprinkle" and "use" to convey the action required. Writing with a commanding voice isn't always required for fillers, but since every word counts, this technique helps get your idea across as succinctly as possible. For example:

Dust your light bulbs to cut down on the electricity used.

Or, use an infinitive in the beginning of your phrases to grab the reader's attention. In this case:

To extend the life of your frozen concentrate, add a little extra water to the mix.

Also, define your problem early on if there's any doubt as to who might care about your tip. To get others to sit up and take notice, you might write:

Rudolph won't be so cute when you catch him munching on your landscape designs. Purchase a deer fence and put it over your bushes this winter.

In the above example, notice how I used the conditional word "when." The same applies to the word "if." Conditional words help readers grasp your message and mentally make it their own. Finally, write instructional fillers, and certainly recipes, with a sequence in mind. Specific stages help the reader grasp the action along the way.

In recipe writing, Siegel says titles have an obligation to tell the truth as you sell the recipe. "Try to include the flavors that really sound good or provocative together, without stretching too far," she says. "For instance, if there's only ¼ teaspoon of ginger, I'd leave that out of the title. Also, avoid superlatives or overly cute titles as the results can be disappointing. What if the world's best brownie only tastes so-so? Is the author to be trusted?"

Because the demand for cookbooks has increased over the years, so have the requirements. Cookbooks can no longer tempt their readers with mere mouth-watering recipes. Authors must pay attention to their prose — their descriptions, their cultural information, and their tips for shopping and for stocking a well-equipped kitchen. As you make your writing descriptive and entertaining, also assume that the typical reader of your book has no prior knowledge of cooking. By writing step-by-step instructions, you won't offend your experienced cooks, but by leaving out necessary tips, you will offend the beginners. Never use vague measurements such as "a pinch of." Be as specific as possible.

Finally, be sure to list first all ingredients your reader will need, in the order they are used. There's nothing more frustrating than getting halfway through a recipe only to find you don't have one essential ingredient. Since word-of-mouth is your best publicity, the last thing you want to do is anger the cook.

COMEDY WRITING

Local and national comics constantly search for fresh, original humor to keep their gigs alive. Since they don't have a lot of time to write their own material, they often turn to the freelance joke writer. Public speakers need these services just as much. Most metropolitan areas have at least one comedy club where the entertainers may also need such a boost of creativity. And, radio personalities also rely upon freelance material to help their morning shows wake us up.

Watch the Comedy Channel and other cable television specials devoted to this form of entertainment. Punch around your radio dial to find out who is funny. Read the radio/TV column in your newspaper to see which radio disc jockeys are winning the rating wars.

From your research you'll ascertain what comics are joking about. It's often a matter of putting a new spin on an old idea. Use pop culture as a guide. The baby-boom generation can be a good barometer of trends. Thumb through publications that are geared to them. *People* magazine might be good for this. *USA Today, USA Weekend, Parade* and TV newscasts and magazine-type shows also focus on trends.

In addition, each time there is a presidential election, newspapers and magazines across the country feature news on what's in and what's out. For instance, when Bill Clinton defeated George Bush, the game of horseshoes fell by the wayside, and Americans started enjoying the saxophone. Cats were in, dogs were out. And fast food fascinated those who used to enjoy a good old Texas barbecue. All of this trivia is grist for the humor mill.

Poking fun at human nature or the irony of situations is another frequent comedic ploy as are exaggeration and satire. A parody of a popular movie plot, political event or well-known incident may also work in your comedic routines.

During your market research, observe the comics, studying their monologues and making note of each individual's word choice, sense of timing and attitude. Try to capture the style of the comic you want to write for. Are the jokes subtle or direct? Do they require a lot of set up beforehand?

When you've gotten a real feel for the humor market, you can gauge your own potential and match it to the many types of comedy that exist. If you're more on the serious side, there's no sense trying to write something funny. It's not you. It will backfire. The same goes for anything off-color. Stick to what you feel comfortable with and what you can master.

Crafting Comedy

When writing comedy, you can add a third "C" to the mix of clear and concise style. That "C" stands for clever. Try your jokes out to make sure they really work. Remember that the longer you take to set up the joke, the more your audience will expect. You'll probably find this out in testing your material. If it takes more than five sentences, trim it.

Make sure to vary your jokes. If they are all the same, the routine will not work as well. Also, as mentioned, it's important to write within the style of the comedian you're working for. Your best guide will be observing the comic. If you can't do this in person, ask for videotapes to study. And if you're still having trouble writing your gags, get a copy of *Comedy Writing Step by Step: How to Write and Sell Your Sense of Humor* by Gene Perret (Samuel French), which discusses the skills you'll need, the second income and career you can create and the jokes and sketches that will lead you there. Perret's *Comedy Writing Workbook* (Sterling Publishing) is also loaded with concrete examples, many of which you may recognize from old TV shows and sitcoms. His workouts will surely put you through your paces.

Testing Your Wits (and Theirs!)

When do you know if your jokes are funny enough? Well, as in many other forms of writing, there is no absolute. You must trust your instincts to know that you've done your best.

Refrain from sharing uncompleted gags with others. Do yourself and these others a favor by finishing your work, and once your enthusiasm has been transferred to print, share all you want. The worst-case scenario is that you have the makings of a great comedic line or sketch and you share your preliminary thoughts with another friend who promptly puts down you and your idea. Now what do you do? You're shattered. Your confidence is shaken, and you may not want to continue. When a work is completed, it can stand taller and stronger on its own merits, facing constructive criticism without being destroyed.

How do you know when to draw on good taste before you offend someone? "Humor is a powerful and beautiful force, but it can cause pain if misused," says Gene Perret in *Step by Step*. "You simply have to be objective and learn that if a joke runs the risk of offending someone, you drop the joke rather than take the chance."

As with all forms of writing, you'll need to be open to the rewrite. If you're not satisfied with your comedy, let it sit and try working on it later. But, if your routine has a tight deadline, you'll have to come to some quick decisions about its worth. Don't worry it to death.

Marketing Your Humor

If you want to start out in comedy, some will tell you that you must move to Los Angeles or New York. But other industry sources agree that humor is everywhere, and there's no place like home to start out, working banquets and local clubs while you hone your skills. Frequent the places where comedy is performed. Visit your local comedy club and get to know different club owners. Ask them if they'll post notices that you are available.

Advertise your services in professional publications such as *Standup*, the newsletter of the Professional Comedian's Association (in New York City), which also publishes an annual directory. *Comedy USA* provides an in-depth industry guide that is updated annually between February and March. It's essentially the yellow pages for the comedy industry, listing comedians, agents, managers, publicists, comedy clubs, comedy club bookers, talent coordinators for TV shows that feature standup comics, comedy writers, cruise bookers, competitions and festivals.

Finally, market your work by taking a chance on your favorite comedian, sending him a batch of your jokes along with a release form. Famous comedians have been known to buy material this way, but don't rely on this as your primary marketing method.

In comedy writing, you'll often be paid by the joke or by the monologue. It's not uncommon for buyers to purchase a few of the jokes and pass on the rest. If that happens to you, increase your sales potential by contributing the rejected jokes to a gag sheet, frequently used by radio personalities. While the pay rate is minimal, you will be recouping something for the effort you put into your work. For a listing of gag sheets, check out the market section of *Radio & Records*.

PUZZLES AND BRAIN TEASERS

Another way to make people smile is to challenge them. Let them match their wits with your clever words. When you're tired of standard writing projects, but still want a creative challenge, puzzles and brain teasers offer profit potential.

Study the magazines devoted to puzzles and games. General-interest magazines also devote space to such entertainment. Focus on those that feature entire pages of crosswords, word searches, word scrambles and quizzes.

In your research, you'll notice that many magazines center their puzzles on a central theme. A publication devoted to cruising, for instance, might feature nautical terminology. Once you have your theme in mind, resource books will help you as you brainstorm for a list of words pertaining to your subject. Frequently, you can skip reading the entire book and find exactly what you need by gleaning the index. Compile a list of literally hundreds of words. You'll want much more than you'll actually need.

Remember to match your pattern of squares to the number traditionally run in the magazine. An editor will throw up his hands and throw out your submission if it blatantly exceeds the set of squares fitting the format.

While puzzles, searches and scrambles are addicting, so too are quizzes. Here, however, the quality of your quiz will be judged more harshly. You'll need to tempt readers and offer a reason for them to complete it. If you sprinkle your quiz with a touch of humor, an element of intrigue or a hint of excitement, you'll be better off than creating a bland, straightforward quiz.

REFERENCE WRITING

While most encyclopedia companies use experts in the fields of medicine, history or other specialties, some occasionally look to authors and freelance writers who specialize in a particular area. If you look at the list of contributors to these major volumes, you'll see many sources cited.

So how do you get started in this field? Your best bet is to visit a library with an extensive reference section, get to know the encyclopedia companies and their styles. Study the contributors' credentials. If after a little research, you feel you can compete with academicians who keep up on developments in the field and ponder the scholarly journals, then write a brief letter of introduction to the editor in chief at the encyclopedia firm you have in mind.

In your letter, sell yourself with your expertise. Send published clippings, book promotions and releases, and perhaps a resume. Your best bet at breaking into reference writing is to be a connoisseur of current events. Know which sections of the encyclopedia will need to be updated. For instance, if you were a reference writer with knowledge of the Soviet Union, you could have gotten work when communism collapsed. Just be careful that you don't offer your expertise to more than one firm or a conflict of interest could easily arise.

If you aren't a scholar yourself, perhaps you know one. It's true that some firms are reluctant to use writers who aren't academically credentialed. But that doesn't have to stop you. You can align yourself with an academic who has the expertise you lack. Terry Hori, managing editor at *Encyclopedia Britannica*, says, "Some of the most successful articles I've received have been from husband-and-wife teams. A collaborative effort is something we certainly look for."

Hori also points out that encyclopedia yearbooks offer additional opportunities for writers who can combine a flare for magazine article writing with a reference approach. In fact, writing for yearbooks can sometimes pay better than the work in standard reference volumes.

When you write for encyclopedia firms, remember that you are writing for an audience of nonspecialists, not for your colleagues. You must limit your esoteric remarks. You must explain fully the significance of events and ideas. Never assume that your reader will be as familiar with the subject as you are. Stick to basic principles and developments. Avoid highly technical details.

Many encyclopedias are written for English-reading persons throughout the world. Therefore, limit parochialism. Instead, write to achieve a universal understanding. Objectivity is also a prerequisite in all that you produce. In quoting authorities, always note the person's credentials upon first reference, explaining her relevance to the subject at hand. Finally, since encyclopedias remain in homes, offices and libraries for years, you must try not to date your material. Avoid statistics that are sure to change. Eliminate phrases such as "recently," "at present," "fifteen years ago," or "just last year."

HOW TO GET STARTED

Just as students don't graduate and advance immediately to the executive suite, writers must start small and pay their dues. Writing fillers, hints, humor and recipes provides excellent starting points for freelancers. If you have expertise, reference writing provides the same.

• Peruse newsstands, send for newsletters and scan the listings in writing directories, searching for publications that accept fillers, recipes, jokes or puzzles.

• Send an SASE to these publications, requesting writer's guidelines.

• Remain alert to the latest trends and the current events making headlines. These are the foundation for fillers, salable recipes and humorous gags.

• If you've developed an expertise in one subject area, send a resume with published samples to the editors at encyclopedia publishers.

• Test what you write, but only when your work is complete. Share your hints and humor with friends. Serve that favorite recipe to anyone who will try it. Remember, all writers start by writing and succeed by putting their work before an audience. Select your audience today, and start writing.

Chapter Six

Greeting Cards

In 1993, the Greeting Card Association estimated that 7.4 billion cards were purchased. Greeting cards generate approximately $5.6 billion in U.S. retail sales with an industry growth rate of approximately 2 percent. Creating snappy sayings and sentimental expressions is your ticket to sharing in the wealth!

Writing greeting cards (and captions for other self-expression products) is ideal for the writer with only bits and pieces of time. Captions can be conceived just about anywhere—as you shepherd your children to school in the morning, commiserate with your co-workers over lunch, or sit and watch TV by night. Ideas may soon come to you out of the blue. By channeling these sudden sparks of inspiration into real words and salable phrases, you can carve out a nice little living, and have a lot of fun doing it.

Sandra Louden, a greeting card writer who is working on a book on the subject, began writing captions to earn extra money while staying home with two young children. She made her first sale after three months of perseverance and today has sold hundreds of sentiments.

"When I first began, I had only two hours a week to spend on caption writing," Louden says. "It's not the amount of time that's important; it's how you use the time you do have."

STUDYING THE MARKET

The greeting card industry continues to change and evolve. Those cards you have stashed away in shoeboxes underneath your bed might bring back fond memories and smiles, but they won't reflect the needs of today's card companies. Visit card counters and gift shops to discover what types of cards consumers are currently purchasing.

I used to think "you've seen one greeting card, you've seen them all." Then I took a class in greeting card writing. What's selling today is not the same love-and-flowers concept that people embraced in the past. Today's messages are much more finely tuned. Years ago, there were "thinking of you" cards, but today, you're much more likely to see "thinking of you because your pet died" or "I'm so sorry you have a terminal illness."

Get to know the different card companies, their range of verses, lines of cards and other product outlets. Don't limit your search to one shop in your neighborhood. Send away to mail-order companies specializing in cards, posters, mugs, T-shirts, notepads and beverage napkins. Notice who publishes the serious versus the silly, or the risqué rather than the religious.

Broaden your geographic horizons as well. Some paper-goods companies are better known in different parts of the country. Whenever you travel for business or pleasure, be sure to pop into several stores, even at the airport. You'll be surprised at the diversity of products you'll find. Look at every visit to a store as an opportunity to learn something new about this ever-changing industry.

INDUSTRY EXPECTATIONS

If you know very little about the greeting card industry, here is an important fact: Ninety percent of all greeting cards are purchased by women. Molly Wigand, author of *How to Write & Sell Greeting Cards, Bumper Stickers, T-Shirts and Other Fun Stuff* (Writer's Digest Books), has coined a great tip for male writers in this business. "Except when otherwise noted," she says, "you are a woman!"

Indeed the ability to think like a woman, empathize with others and tap into the feelings of love, friendship, sadness, sorrow, joy and elation are all prerequisites for a career in greeting card writing. Editors will also expect you to spot trends as much as the writer of fillers, hints and humor.

Differentiating between the needs of direct-mail companies and retail-oriented firms is also essential. Nan Roloff Stine, creative writing supervisor at Current Inc., reports that writers often confuse the two. She says that with direct mail (companies that sell their cards and gift items through catalogs, rather than at the point of purchase), people buy a batch of cards to keep on hand, not knowing who they'll send them to months, even years, down the road.

The buyer in a retail shop, however, usually browses through the rack with a particular recipient in mind. This means that mail-order companies have a more limited range of sentiments. Whereas travel cards, engagement wishes or specific birthday greetings ("Happy Birthday to the Boss," for instance) might be very appropriate in a store setting, these captions don't generate much volume in catalog sales. Instead, aim your all-purpose greetings like thank you, friendship, sympathy, general birthday and holiday wishes to the direct-mail companies, and be sure that the verses you send will apply to the masses. Editors buy cards that can be sent by one person or several people at a time.

Spotting demographic trends is essential to writing effective cards. In the 1990s, we witness the graying of America, according to the Greeting Card Association. Seniors represent a new and growing consumer group. Their findings also indicate a need for cards that reward and encourage healthy living, such as cards for kicking the smoking habit. The spread and fear of the AIDS virus has also brought romance, monogamy and marriage back in style. Greeting card companies need cards to reflect these lifestyle changes as well.

Writers can learn the specific needs of a company by conducting their independent research, scanning the listings in *Writer's Market*, and sending away for "needs lists." These lists are frequently tied to the deadlines editors face. Greeting card writing is not a hit-or-miss endeavor. It's much better to write your verses around the specific needs of an editor than to write simply what comes to you. Keep a list of the ideas you generate, but submit only what is needed.

Know the style of greeting cards companies produce. Contemporary prose cards tell it like it is, using gentle but realistic language. These are often conversational in tone. Traditional cards, on the other hand, feature rhymed or metered verse. These are the sentimental favorites. In fact, the sales of these conventional cards allow greeting card companies to take a shot, now and then, at new and different lines.

Studio cards are humorous greetings that reflect everyday life with their short and snappy sayings. Finally, alternative cards use both humor and contemporary prose to reflect current life, frequently dealing with single parenting, job loss, terminal illness, the environment, addiction and more. Understanding the differences between these types of cards will help you converse with your editors, understand their needs lists, and ultimately, lead to bigger and better sales.

COMMON MISTAKES

Not studying the markets is the most common error freelancers commit. Beginning writers tend also to stick with the similar and safe, much to their detriment. They'll spot a successful caption and send in one just like it. They feel their new creation will sell. But in many cases, it won't, especially to the smaller companies that do not feature as many captions in their lines. Stretch yourself, giving the editor a reason to buy the verse. Bring a fresh approach to an old idea. Most important, know what your editor needs, and be flexible.

Newcomers may believe that if one editor has rejected their work, all will surely do the same. Veteran caption writers will tell you that's nonsense. In my own rejections, I've had editors indicate that they already had something similar in the works. But even if your editor doesn't scrawl that note in the corner, never give up on your caption. "Never call anything a rejection," says Molly Wigand. "Just send it off somewhere else." Again. And again. If it comes back half a dozen times with a rejection, give it more thought. Heed any advice that's been passed along. Frequently, by changing just a word or two, you can increase your chances of a quicker sale. Never underestimate the power of the rewrite, if that's what it takes.

A final error freelancers commit occurs when they send off their treasured verses and cease to sell any others. It will often take weeks for an editor to reply to a single batch. Some will return a set of rejected captions, yet hold on to others for months, routing them to colleagues for their feedback. Keep the creative energy alive. Send off another batch to another company. But don't simultaneously submit the same captions. It's a surefire way to alienate two editors who may end up each wanting to purchase the same verse.

CREATING CAPTIONS

Come up with ideas for the kinds of cards you enjoy buying, sending and receiving. By doing so, you'll be most familiar with the range of possibilities in store.

All captions begin in the idea stage. I often give my students a word association exercise — three occasions or reasons for sending cards such as new baby, juvenile birthday and woman-to-woman friendship. Under each category, they must list as many words as they can associate with the category. They write down all possibilities and eliminate none. There are no dumb ideas in the brainstorming process.

Your list will be different, but under new baby, it could include: joy, hugs and kisses, gift from God, bottles, rattles, stuffed animals, cuddling, lack of sleep, smelly diapers. You can see the range of possible captions — everything from the warm and fuzzy to the religious and serious, and even the humorous.

If you try word association and you're still stumped for ideas, put a new spin on an old problem. Pretend you're writing a parenting card or a woman-to-woman friendship caption. Fact: Children have always been a challenge to entertain since the beginning of time. But in the 1960s, there were no video rentals, computer games and cable music channels. So the problem may be the same, but the solution completely different. Greeting cards reflect the culture in which we live and how we deal with such challenges.

Look at a subject from a totally opposite perspective. After all, some savvy creators took a dinosaur, a threatening creature in children's eyes, and transformed him into a purple, singing and dancing sensation. Do the same with other ideas. Just remember that regardless of your technique, you must convey a greeting. No greeting, no sale.

Draw on your own circumstances, gaining the sensitivity you need to create powerful messages. Take yourself back to the innocent child bursting with the thought of Christmas. Try to remember what it was like when someone close passed away. Life's sorrows increase our capacity for compassion. When my second son remained in the hospital for two months after his premature arrival, the experience taught me to see birth, daily coping, and even the prospect of death in a whole new light.

When your idea is formed, you must next construct me-to-you messages. These greetings can be full of playful humor, but they should never contain a slam of any sort. Political, ethnic or sensitive subject matters are taboo. We all know of at least one person who disguises her digs as "I'm only teasing." Write to build up, not tear down. Test your humor. If the reader laughs, you're probably not hurting any feelings.

Me-to-you messages are an important concept to successful greetings. If you get stuck on this point, write down the message you're trying to convey — without the right words, rhyme or meter. Writing it down, keeping it in front of you helps you focus on the message.

Divide captions for the proper comedic effect, enough to deliver a laugh or a groan without giving away the punchline. Using a list of threes comes in handy in the division process. For example, I created this caption for pet owners:

> Pets serve many purposes. They keep Mom company when she needs it. They fetch the newspaper for Dad, and . . . . they finish the kids' meals when you're not looking. Have fun with your new pet!

See the element of three and the way it works? As a writer, you can take an example from real life and stretch it to fit the format. In this case, I remember feeding an occasional hand-out to my dog underneath the family dinner table. My mother wasn't too fond of dogs to begin with, and I know our dog had no journalistic cravings. But you get the idea.

Listing threes isn't the only way to communicate a message. If you like to draw comparisons, use that approach. If you're tuned into clichés and pop culture, rework a phrase society has grown accustomed to. If you're skilled at riddles and rhymes, you might try using these techniques.

Rhyme and meter can enhance a me-to-you message, or get in the way. If you can make your verse more beautiful, more interesting or more moving by using these techniques, do so, but never let rhyme and meter get in the way. Don't force the meter. Allow the accent to fall on the syllable it would naturally fall on in everyday speech.

With religious captions, some companies require their verses to reflect a Bible verse. If that's the case, always be sure to cite the chapter and verse and which Bible translation you are using.

No matter what technique you use to create your captions, test their salability on others. If your sentiment achieves the desired effect, then by all means, send it!

SUBMITTING VERSES

Most cards have both an outside and an inside verse; some have just one. When typing your messages, you must follow proper submission style.

Develop a code, using your initials or those of the company you're sending to. If I send to Current, I may use CUR, or GIB when writing to Gibson Greetings. Assign a separate number for each verse, leave a space and indicate the type of card in parenthesis. Let's take my pet example that I used previously:

LHO-001 (New Pet)
(GRAPHIC: Mother, father, sister and brother enjoying the family dog)

O: Pets serve many purposes. They keep Mom company when she needs it. They fetch the newspaper for Dad, and . . . .

I: . . . they finish the kids' meals when you're not looking. Have fun with your new pet!

Not all cards require a graphic indication. Maybe this one doesn't even need one, but I've shown you where to describe a potential illustration, just in case.

Type your captions on plain white $3'' \times 5''$ cards using the example above. Submit six to twenty cards in a batch, accompanied by an SASE. A cover letter isn't necessary, unless you want to introduce yourself. Just keep it brief.

Make sure you proofread your cards and correspondence. Everything should be typed neatly. For those writers who live off their laser output, do not despair. You can purchase index cards and the compatible software for laser printers. These cards are much more expensive, but if you line everything up properly and print a test on plain white paper, you'll save money and waste fewer cards on your mistakes.

REASONS CAPTIONS FAIL

When you see your SASE return in the mail, and you feel its thickness, you'll want to frown. But don't give up. There are plenty of reasons captions fail, most of which you can't control. Perhaps your caption wasn't universal enough. Your topic might just be too obscure, and the editorial staff believes there wouldn't be enough of a market to demand such a card. Editors share captions with their colleagues. What one editor loves, another may veto.

It could also be that your caption just isn't sendable. Maybe it's too blunt. Maybe it's too touchy a sentiment. Maybe in time, the card would sell, but then again, maybe not. There was indeed a day when divorce cards would have been considered taboo, but today no one would question their worth.

Maybe your captions aren't funny, or they're corny. If your editor reads it and says "I've heard this before," chances are good it's just too familiar to the public. Despite all your hard work, perhaps someone beat you to the editor's desk with a great idea.

Finally, captions can fail because of poor format, because the writer was adamant in her claim that "my friend loved them," or because she inundated the editor all in one batch. If you follow proper style, proceed in a professional manner and submit a limited number of captions (no more than twenty in one mailing), your work will either succeed or fail on its own. And that's all you can do.

Writers who do not understand the greeting card industry frequently fail because they ask for royalties or outrageous fees. Most captions are sold on a work-for-hire basis, with you signing over all rights to the material.

In addition, beginners shoot for the stars at the start of their careers. As of this writing, there are three top greeting card companies—American Greetings, Gibson Greetings and Hallmark Cards, Inc. Each employs a large staff of writers, and each prefers to work with established freelancers recognized in the industry. Yes, it would be wonderful to have your friends enter their neighborhood Hallmark shops and pull your captions off the rack, but it might be more likely to win the lottery. Start small, work hard, perfect your craft, and then, move on to bigger sales.

SOMETHING TO STRIVE FOR

Sandra Louden wrote a verse for Current Inc. that won the Louie Award in 1991. Her card depicts a mom looking in on her two children at the end of the day. The caption reads:

O: If only I could think of them as sleeping . . .

I: . . . instead of recharging.

The Louie Awards are the greeting card writer's equivalent to a musician's Grammy or an actor's Oscar. Sandra's card won in the Best Humorous Friendship Caption Category (for a card costing under two dollars). Only greeting card publishers may submit entries for Louie Awards, and these entries will be judged on imagination, emotional impact, artistry, the harmony struck between the card's visual elements and verse, sendability and the overall product quality and price.

If you do your job well, and your card racks up the sales, who knows what honors may be in store! Such recognition will surely boost your career and convince future editors to take a chance on you.

SELLING MORE SENTIMENTS

To further your reputation and earn more money with greeting cards, keep your name and accomplishments in front of the editors you work with. Find editors you can build relationships with and who are willing to review a volume of work (in increments, of course).

Keep abreast of their needs by phoning occasionally. I've had editors tell me that they don't mind such calls if they're brief and infrequent (I would not advise calling more than every other month). Send for a needs list if you want to be more respectful of their time.

Join the Greeting Card Creative Network based in Washington, D.C. that produces a talent directory linking the efforts of writers, editors, artists and photographers. It's terrific publicity and a boost to further sales.

Hook up with an equally ambitious artist friend who may be able to offer illustrations. If you can offer complete writing/illustration packages and your own line of products, you may even be able to strike a deal to earn royalties in the years ahead or you may choose to self-publish your work.

Finally, broaden your sales base with ideas for posters, bumper stickers, mugs, T-shirts, notepads, sticky notes, beverage napkins, plaques and more. A whole array of giftware and paper goods depends upon creative writers like you! While some editors may convert a card caption into a successful self-expression product slogan, feel free to suggest any possibilities you have in mind.

HOW TO GET STARTED

$ People send cards to share their innermost feelings, to brighten another's day or to mark an occasion or an important life passage. Your caption could be the vehicle to the greater understanding that takes place between two people. If that's not beautiful enough, the business aspects will surely persuade you. Greeting card writing requires very little overhead and few supplies. And, it doesn't require great blocks of time.

• Learn to spot trends and keep abreast of the times, but don't seek to revolutionize the greeting card industry.

• Select six to ten companies, to start with. Attach a sticky note to your SASE, requesting a current needs list and writer's guidelines. Address your outer envelope to the editorial department (or a particular line at a larger company).

• Keep a journal of ideas, recycling rejected ones right away. If your ideas are repeatedly rejected, check them for limitations— situations that apply to only a few people and not to the masses.

• Be sure you've conveyed a greeting written in the form of a me-to-you message. Create a card for one person, but written so that thousands can identify with it.

• Add your name to the talent directory published by the Greeting Card Creative Network in Washington, D.C. Editors use this when they need to find experienced writers in a hurry.

• Consider the sales potential of self-expression products as a way of making more money with your captions.

Chapter Seven

Resume Writing

I t's a sobering thought that there will always be people out of work, and it's a given that professionals will seek to climb the corporate ladder. If you have a flare for self-promotion and a good vocabulary of adjectives and verbs, try the lucrative field of resume writing.

Any freelancer can add resumes to his or her repertoire. Marketing your skills as a resume writer becomes even easier if you live and work near employment agencies, large corporations and companies, colleges, universities, vocational institutions and law schools. Students make good clients. Executives make even better ones.

SELLING YOUR SERVICES

What does resume writing have in common with encyclopedia sales? Both resumes and encyclopedias are valuable resources. Both cost money. But in both cases, people often feel they can do without them, relying upon their own resources.

Part of your job as a writer is to sell your potential clients on the importance of a professionally written and prepared resume. I can't think of a better person to write a resume than the freelance writer, who is forced to self-promote and sell services every day.

Convince job candidates that with an impressive resume they may get an interview they couldn't secure on their own. Still another selling point: The cost of a resume is small compared to the lifetime of higher earnings it may garner for the professional candidate. While you, as writer, cannot guarantee any of these outcomes, you can use each as a convincing reason candidates should employ your services. Just remember (and remind people) that your job is to produce the most professional-looking document possible. Beyond that, your clients must sell themselves.

In competition with you are school placement offices, which frequently assist students in developing resumes free of charge. However, the bulk of the writing usually falls on the student. In the corporate world, outplacement firms are often contracted to assist laid-off workers. Be aware of your competition and be able to state why job seekers should use you instead. Sell them on the fact that you are a professional writer, not merely a typist.

Promote your resume writing services by posting flyers at libraries, placement offices, student unions or gathering spots. Place classified ads in school newspapers, daily papers, community advertisers, or executive magazines and industry publications. If you have access to a computer bulletin board, try sending a message through this route. Incorporate such words as "fast," "professionally written" and "satisfaction guaranteed." If you can accommodate rush jobs, state this as well.

It's up to you how specific you want to make your publicity or advertising. In some cases, you may want to advertise a price, but if you feel you'd be giving easy information to your competitors or that people would disqualify you too soon, just entice them to call you. Then when you answer the phone, you can turn on the sales pitch. On your flyer, list your telephone number and the hours you can receive calls from job seekers.

GETTING TO KNOW YOUR CLIENT

Years ago, I moved within close proximity to a community college. Many of the people I wrote resumes for never needed one before. I created a questionnaire. As people called in response to my flyers, I would reach for one of these blank forms and begin filling in the information I needed as we spoke over the phone.

In that initial conversation, I would obtain the name, address, phone number, and the date of the appointment we scheduled to begin work. I'd ask the person to bring to that meeting dates, specifics, copies of previous resumes and other pertinent information. Before ending the call, I would reiterate the expectations, just so we were clear. I'd spend a specific amount of time interviewing the client. Then I'd write a resume for his review, sending it through the mail or meeting a second time to get approval. I would deliver two copies, which the candidate could take to his printer, and I would finish the job by a certain date.

I preferred to meet my clients at the community college, usually grabbing a cup of coffee in the cafeteria and filling out the rest of the form. If your market includes professionals and executives, meet your clients in their offices (if they're being outplaced) or in your own office to keep things confidential. Then again, if you work out of your home and don't relish visits by strangers, a coffee shop will do.

I found that I had to limit the time I spent with my clients. Otherwise, we'd get carried away in conversation, and the time ate into my profits. The fees you charge will often dictate this. If you charge a client hundreds of dollars for a resume, you might be expected to spend a little extra time. But most of us write resumes for far less. I felt that forty-five minutes to an hour allowed enough time to cover the essentials, and if I felt the client was getting off track (or giving me a tale of woes), I'd politely glance at my watch and remind him of the time allotted. Most people will not want to pay extra for chat time.

During the interview, look for signs of achievement whether they be dollar figures produced, funds raised or percentages of sales and productivity that were increased. Ask about responsibilities or projects the candidate initiated and completed. Employers like to see signs of self-motivation and accomplishment. Good writers are usually able to listen attentively, ask thought-provoking questions and pull just the right information out of their clients. For instance, if your client self-financed his education, use this in the resume. Don't forget military background, educational credentials, outside interests and special honors or achievements. You'll need to showcase your clients' talents and tap into their hidden skills. This is vital when you're writing a resume for a career changer or a homemaker reentering the workforce after raising a family.

Look for ways you can translate everyday tasks we take for granted into bigger skills that, if undertaken in the workplace, would achieve great recognition. Examples include organizational and budgetary skills, the ability to handle several tasks simultaneously and effective time management. Volunteer or church-related work comes in handy when your client has taken a leadership role with large groups of people. Including such community work is fine as long as you don't overdo it. If you do, the employer may wonder if this candidate has time to devote to a full-time job.

Today's resumes limit a lot of personal information that used to be standard in years past. There is no need to list marital status, spouse or age. Some employers prefer you do not include this information so that charges of discrimination cannot be leveled against them.

WRITING RESUMES

When you finish interviewing your client, you're ready to write. In the beginning it may take one to two hours to write the resume and receive approval, but with practice, you'll be able to churn out more resumes in less time, thus increasing your income.

Be sure to produce an error-free document. Having another person proofread helps ensure accuracy. Nothing will destroy your reputation faster than a slip-shod job.

Resumes require a clear and tight writing style and an effective use of action verbs and adjectives. Avoid passive voice. If you recall from chapter four, the reason the passive voice pervades much of today's writing is that no one wants to take responsibility. Some one *must* take responsibility when searching for a job. That someone is your client. As the writer, you can accomplish this through the words and style you choose.

There are plenty of good resume writing books on the market with lists of good action verbs and samples of attractive and effective formats. Ten Speed Press offers some excellent resources including *The Overnight Resume* by Donald Asher, *The Resume Catalog: 200 Damn Good Examples* by Yana Parker, and *What Color Is Your Parachute?* by Richard Nelson Bolles. If in doubt as to the format you should use, stick with a conservative approach over anything that calls too much attention to itself.

Resumes should be concise, but if the material warrants two pages, by all means use it. I'd think long and hard before I went to three pages, however, unless your client is a high-powered executive. Most formats work backwards, listing employment history and educational background from the most current position held. Pay particular attention to gaps in employment and try to explain these. I once wrote a resume for a blue-collar client who had numerous gaps in his career but many small jobs to his credit. It was a challenge indeed, but I succeeded in grouping categories of jobs under appropriate headings to lessen the effect of the gaps.

Resume writing requires that you shed as much positive light onto bad situations as possible. In cases where your client was dismissed, try using phrases such as "will explain personally" or "prefer to keep confidential until interview."

Two rules govern resume writing and they may seem completely conflicting. Number one: Do not hold back. If ever a person is to shine, a resume is the place to do it. Number two: Don't lie. It's sure to backfire as headhunters, personnel officers and others check facts and credentials. You can highlight responsibilities so that others will recognize your client's talents more readily by using the right verbs. But never, under any circumstances, should you invent fiction on their behalf. The result could destroy your reputation along with theirs.

GENERATING ADDITIONAL INCOME

Before setting up shop as a resume writer, you'll have to investigate what the market will bear. A young college student will not be able to pay the fees a corporate executive could afford. Check classified advertising, ask employment agencies what they charge and call your local copy shop for prices they charge for typing alone. Remember that you'll be writing *and* producing finished copy so build both into your price. Charge extra for rush jobs or same-day service.

Word of mouth will be your best advertising vehicle, and after it has taken effect, consider increasing your fees. Your services will be in demand. By creating resumes with your own desktop publishing equipment, you'll be able to offer laser copies. This is a selling advantage, but also an expense that you need to include in your fees. You can certainly enter the resume writing market without a laser printer and page layout software programs, but these assets will help you increase your output, writing image and sales potential.

Finally, offer to write customized cover letters to go with your client's resumes. To sharpen your letter-writing skills, read *200 Letters for Job Hunters* by William S. Frank (Ten Speed Press). In some cases, one good draft is all that's required. A smart job seeker will take the bulk of the letter, adapt each position's circumstances and use the material you create many times over.

Always include the "ask" in your cover letters, whereby your client asks for the informational interview, the job or the next step in the job-selection process. For tips on how to write effective letters, turn to chapter four, which focuses on solid writing.

HOW TO GET STARTED

$ By writing resumes, you'll earn quick cash with a small investment of time, while helping someone seek better opportunities in life. You'll sharpen your interviewing, writing and selling skills. You'll improve your own resume by writing them for others. And you'll keep the cash flowing while working on longer range, harder-to-pay-off projects.

• Research your market. Flip through the yellow pages and note the listings under "employment contractors," "printers" and "resume services." Ask for informational interviews with some of these professionals, finding out what the market will bear and who your best prospects are. You may land a lead or two.

• Put flyers in libraries, colleges, student union buildings and placement offices. Advertise your services in school newspapers, executive magazines, community magazines and industry publications.

• Charge more for two-page resumes. Offer to produce cover letters at an additional charge.

Chapter Eight

Proofreading, Editing and Indexing

Anywhere you see words in print, there has been a proof-reader, steadfastly checking and double-checking spelling and punctuation. Anywhere there is a publication, you can be sure there has been an editor. And, for most nonfiction books you've read, an indexer has helped you get through the material without your even realizing it.

All of these tasks enhance the value of the published piece. But for you, all of these jobs can be completed by the industrious writer who wants to build better industry contacts, learn more about the publishing business and earn extra money.

PROOFREADING

Without a proofreader, we would be bogged down, or downright stopped, as we read through the daily newspaper, unwound with a good novel or pondered an important financial statement. Thus, there are plenty of takers if you've perfected the blue-pencil routine and practiced your standard proofreading marks.

Not only will you find work in major publishing houses, but you'll also find opportunities at print shops, typesetting firms, magazine and newspaper offices, in-house corporate printing departments and university presses. If you have specialized knowledge, say of medical terminology or scientific jargon, start your search for work with companies and publishers specializing in such highly targeted material.

No matter where you work, you'll need that steady sense of proper spelling, grammatical accuracy, and an aura of nit-pickiness about you to succeed. Typographical errors slip into text so easily, from the author composing at the keyboard to the typesetter keying a flawless manuscript into the system, so you can see why a potential employer would want to thoroughly review your skills.

While most firms or publishing houses follow one of the standard stylebooks (like the AP or *Chicago Manual of Style*), many others have developed an additional house style with which all matter representing the organization must ascribe. If your employer has no such stylebook, perhaps it's time to create one. Stylebooks, if only a few typed pages, help proofreaders, writers and editors remember their preferences from issue to issue or from book to book, thereby giving everything a uniform appearance. A good memory is a skill for the proofreader, whose job it is to remember page after page the fine points of house style.

Another known rule of thumb: Never proof your own work. We all tend to marry what we write, and when we read it, we see what we think is there rather than what actually is. While one person may be assigned the proofing tasks, it's always helpful for another person — writer, editor or publisher — to cast a second or third careful eye. Proofreading from a hard copy or printout is also much easier on the eye than proofing from a computer screen.

Professional proofreaders use standard markings known throughout the industry. *The Writer's Digest Guide to Manuscript Formats* by Buchman and Groves can help you learn these proofreading marks.

Finding work in proofreading begins as any search for freelance or nine-to-five work. A letter of introduction serves best when you can cite examples of prior publication experience and mention knowledge of specific subjects. Make sure your resume highlights this background as well. Employers require you to take a test — in person or through the mail — to prove your aptitude. They'll often give you a proofreading test or sample article to correct.

Besides the obvious markets of small to large publishing houses, university presses, publications and printing establishments, professional placement services may require proofreading of clients' resumes and letters. *Literary Market Place* (available in most libraries) includes listings of publishers and editorial services open to proofreaders.

Look to the classified ads in the newspaper, professional journals or in *Publishers Weekly*. In addition, the Editorial Freelancers

Association in New York City serves as a clearinghouse for all types of editorial personnel and offers meetings, educational opportunities, publications and a job phone line with paid membership.

Proofreading usually pays by the hour, but perhaps you can strike an understanding for a retainer with a regular client. Ask other freelancers what they charge or inquire with your local printer to guide you.

EDITING

Most anyone who needs a proofreader can also use an editor, and frequently, the same person wears both hats in smaller operations. While proofreaders concern themselves with the finer points of the printed product, editors concentrate on the acquisition, development and content of the written work. Content editing begins as soon as a project is developed. Copyediting concerns itself with the line editing of facts, figures, punctuation and such. Depending on your skills and interests, you may want to specialize in one of these editing areas.

The freelance editor works closely with publishers and other freelance writers, helping writers present what they mean to say more clearly. An editor's work begins in the idea stage, and through the ability to recognize marketable concepts and to organize several issues in advance, the editor brings all these pieces together to form the project's content. Editorial work requires knowledge of grammar, spelling and punctuation, in addition to a basic understanding of graphic arts, photography and what looks appropriate on a page. Often editors are called on to commission artwork.

The job also requires a strict deadline orientation, the ability to handle several issues simultaneously, interpersonal skills, and of course, writing proficiency. In publications that sell advertising, editors must work well with the sales staff, apprising them of each issue's theme, cover story and major articles. The sales team benefits by knowing which advertisers to target for particular issues while the editor learns about existing advertisers, their needs and how future editors can meet them.

"It helps to be a perfectionist because after all, your job as editor is to strive for the best quality possible—error free," says Shirley Agudo, who once worked in corporate communications before becoming an editor at *Pittsburgh's Child*. "Truthfully, I don't think you can train someone to be an editor without the inherent skills of spelling, graphics, grammar and a good imagination. You either have such talent or you don't."

To find editorial opportunities, the freelancer looks to the same outlets that the prospective proofreader does, but with the emphasis on small concerns since larger ones employ full-time personnel. Classified ads can help, but in many cases, editorial positions are filled without extensive searches. When Agudo left her job and moved overseas with her family, word of mouth travelled well. Publishers, printers and businesses are good places to start your search. If you want to broaden your geographic sights, the Editorial Freelancers Association might be able to help you locate appropriate publications. *Writer's Market* and *Literary Market Place* also include listings of potential employers.

On the Job as Editor

All of the skills mentioned as prerequisites for the editor's job play an important role in your day-to-day duties. You may also find it valuable to plan your editorial schedule or calendar several months, perhaps even a year, in advance. In many cases, your advertising sales staff and publisher will consult with you in doing this.

In the beginning, it's helpful if you stick to using a regular stable of writers. Some may have standard columns they contribute. Others may write full-length cover stories or be known for their lively and fascinating fillers. As you settle into your role as editor, you can take chances on new or even less experienced writers.

Since shepherding assignments will take up a good bit of your time, you may find it necessary to set artificial deadlines. There's nothing worse than being on deadline, ready for press, and waiting on this month's cover story. No one needs to know the method to your madness.

Editorial Perks

Freelance editing pays per hour, per day, per issue or per month. You'll have to judge each situation individually, but the income is usually steady, and any freelance writer can tell you how reassuring that is. To increase your cash flow, however, you should negotiate fees for additional work. For instance, if you write articles rather than farm them out to other writers, make sure you will be compensated beyond your editorial salary. Job descriptions need to be clear about which standard items in the publication the editor writes as part of her job, and which are additional duties.

No matter what type of publication you edit, the experience will certainly help you punch up your own work, forcing you to recognize your weaknesses and be more cognizant of your strengths. You'll learn a lot about the publication process, and most likely, develop a greater empathy for the editors you submit to when wearing your writer's hat.

MANUSCRIPT EVALUATION

Several writers I know use the skills they've developed writing articles to help novice writers get their start. Reading and evaluating the market potential of novels and nonfiction projects also helps them pocket additional income.

Before you set up your own critiquing service, be prepared to answer that ever-present question that runs through the mind of every consumer with money in hand: Why should I use you?

Your answer must include a level of achievement in your own right, such as a string of published novels, a signed contract or two, or extraordinary contacts in the publishing industry. You'll also need to highlight your broad reading background, your knowledge of publishing trends and the critical eye you've developed for spotting errors.

If you can successfully package all of these skills, promote them to fellow writers through classified ads in writer's magazines, writer's newsletters, conferences and flyers posted at libraries. There are always beginning writers who need and flock to the support of published pros.

Be sure your written information states exactly what you will do for the fee you charge. Maybe for fifty dollars, you'll review a synopsis and three sample chapters, or maybe a synopsis only. Many writers charge by the number of pages, in increments of twenty-five to fifty dollars.

Specify how you'd like the work to appear. On one project I edited, I assumed the writer would give me a double-spaced manuscript. I assumed wrong. Those handwritten corrections proved tiresome to read.

Your written promotional material should not guarantee a sale or a polished manuscript in return. These are two elements novice writers hang their hopes on, so anticipate this ahead of time. You can only promise to evaluate the manuscript, point out its strengths and weaknesses, suggest solutions to the problem areas you've pinpointed and give the final pat on the back or kick in the pants to get the writing project completed.

When I helped a child psychologist by reviewing the first few chapters of a book he'd been laboring over for quite some time, I truly liked the material. I like to read pop psychology books, and had become familiar with the works of leading authors, and I thought this man had what it took to become one of them. I enjoyed reviewing the material and offering guidance. But, I couldn't offer the quick-fix I think he was originally seeking. If I had, I would have been ghostwriting and that would have demanded much more work, not to mention much higher fees. (See chapter twenty for information on collaborative writing.)

In addition, had I offered the quick-fix myself, the text would have reflected my style rather than his. I recommended that he take the same rapport he had developed with patients, TV and live audiences and translate these into the book where his style would surface. I typed my comments in letter form and offered as much encouragement as I could. In the end, evaluation comes down to honesty, inspiration and a bit of guidance. That's all you can offer as there simply are no guarantees in publishing.

INDEXING

A book without an index is like a library without a card (or computer) catalog. Imagine how disorganized a project would be. Indeed, it's frustrating to walk to the bookshelf, grab the right reference, and never know where to find what you're looking for. A book's index solves all that.

Many authors rely upon the services of an experienced indexer to compile all the information in proper form. Individual authors, book and periodical publishers, universities, small presses and government printing offices are potential markets for the industrious indexer. In fact, in many book contracts, the cost of indexing is usually charged against the author's royalties.

If you can save this expense, it means more money to you.

For additional job leads, get listed in *Literary Market Place*. If you're new at this task, test your skills first on your own projects or on a friend's book. Library experience and prior editorial work offer you great advantages in selling your services to others.

The techniques of indexing vary, depending on how you like to work. Indexes are made up of individual entries. These consist of a heading, possible modifications or categories, and the page numbers they can be found on.

Most indexers scan the book's page proofs and mark entries and page numbers onto index cards. Use one entry per card. To double-check your accuracy, proofread these cards against the page proofs. Once you alphabetize the cards, you analyze the entries for duplication, consolidating these when you can. You cross-reference various listings for easier access, and you conclude by typing the finished index.

Other indexers use the ABC approach. On whole sheets of paper, they list entries under the corresponding letter and alphabetize their entries later. Try both methods and decide which is best for you.

HOW TO GET STARTED

Proofreading, editing and indexing offer opportunities to learn more about the publishing industry, build better contacts, improve your writing skills and earn extra money. Evaluating manuscripts allows you to share your knowledge with less experienced writers.

• Look for opportunities at publishing companies, print shops, periodicals and university presses. Small publishers and businesses are more likely to need freelance editors while individual authors may appreciate an indexer's services.

• Consult your local yellow pages when developing your list. Writing directories include potential employers. Consider placing classified advertising in some of these.

• Familiarize yourself with standard proofreading marks and common indexing techniques. Aim for consistency.

• Advertise your manuscript evaluation services by word of mouth and classified ads.

Chapter Nine

Teaching

While you're setting your sights on publishing in major magazines or writing the great American novel, sharing your knowledge with others boosts your self-confidence and your bank account, and reaps hidden rewards as well.

As an instructor, you'll be perceived as an expert. Beginners will come to you eagerly seeking instruction, advice and encouragement. Editors will respect you for your willingness to help others, and business people will be more open to using the services you provide. But you'll also receive regular paychecks. This is the best benefit.

There's no limit to teaching opportunities. Whatever kind of course you can create and research, you can propose to business and trade schools, companies, corporations, public schools, continuing education programs, professionally run seminars across the country, even college and universities. If you don't fit the gray-haired professorial profile, don't despair. For all of these noncredit teaching outlets, you'll only need to know more than your students, enough to field questions and speak from personal experience. To gain an edge over your students and better research your course material, sign up for instructional workshops at writers conferences (and someday you may find yourself teaching one of these workshops).

Colleges and universities will rely heavily on your advanced degrees and publishing credits in determining whether they will hire you to teach in their credit courses. While any teaching requires good organizational and interpersonal skills, these are paramount in the academic classroom. You'll need to spend greater blocks of time researching and preparing your lectures, counselling students in their work and grading their assignments.

Business and trade schools usually require an emphasis on writing letters, memos, reports and other forms of business correspondence. In fact, businesses themselves may want to bring you in to address a particular deficiency that's widespread among employees, such as memo writing. These workshops are generally held on the employer's premises.

Public schools may need journalism teachers and adult sponsors of the high school yearbook or newspaper. In these roles, you'll be guiding students who contemplate careers in writing and journalism. You'll also need to have a college degree and several education credits under your belt including some student teaching experience.

The most popular form of teaching is, by far, the adult continuing education programs that have sprung up all over the country at community colleges and universities. These are frequently held in the evenings and on weekends because the majority of the students are adults employed in other careers or students who are enrolled in degree programs. No course credits are earned, but occasionally certificates can be awarded.

Many freelancers who create popular workshops and classes in these evening divisions branch out into independent seminars where they have greater control and earn much higher incomes.

Throughout this chapter, we'll focus primarily on continuing education and professional seminars. Regardless, your challenge is to create an intriguing course description that will excite students into registering for your class, participating in it and learning from it.

WINNING THEM OVER

Your course description will be your primary publicity vehicle so take your time writing it, including an objective, a general description and a curriculum outline. Most continuing education programs run workshops spanning a few hours to several sessions or classes held weekly for two to twelve weeks. In the latter case, you may be required to submit a weekly outline of the topics you'll cover. In the beginning, limit your course length to three to four hours for a one-day session as people think long and hard before committing an entire day to something new. If your course will meet weekly, stick to six or eight weeks rather than ten or twelve.

Tempt your students with a course description they simply can't resist. You want them to feel that they absolutely *must* sign up for your course or they'll miss something important. To convince others of your course's perceived value, use words such as "how-to . . . you . . . new . . . and proven." Combine these suggestive words with action verbs — "discover . . . earn . . . make . . . or succeed."

When I developed my freelance writing course, I deliberately kept the focus on money because no matter what my students' backgrounds, they all sought additional income. Not only did this tactic help attract students to my classes, but it meant the difference between a course that was offered and one that could have been denied.

In Pennsylvania, state budget cutbacks have affected the types of continuing education courses colleges can offer. If you develop a course outline that meets "occupational" as opposed to "avocational/recreational" criteria, the college has a better chance of receiving state funding.

Writing, public relations, desktop publishing, newsletter production and public speaking classes all have the potential of helping people in new or existing careers. If you were the director deciding which classes to cut and had to choose between one of these and, say, "Basket Weaving for Beginners," which would you cut from the roster?

Write your descriptions with careers and advancement in mind. Don't make lofty promises that students will get rich or change their lives (even though they very well could). Advertise the class so that potential participants bring a lot of hope and promise with them that first night. Be honest about class content. If there is a lot of hands-on work involved, tell them. If there are prerequisite courses, state these in your description. Sometimes, you can tempt potential students by saying "Find out the six essential steps to successful article sales." Of course, don't list these six points in your promotional copy. Unveil them in your lectures.

Finally, as you submit your proposal and course description, you'll need to think about course materials. In some programs, you can establish a separate fee students pay to buy these materials from you. Think carefully about what you'd like to give to your students. Most participants love handouts. Ask if the college covers the cost of photocopying your originals. A materials fee should be presented along with your description so that it can be included in the course catalog.

I've included issues of *Writer's Digest* that featured ways writers could make money freelancing. I added information on correspondence schools, newsletter samples, how-to booklets and special discounts pertaining to books and magazines my students might be interested in. These materials gave the students starting points for further information.

In many continuing education programs, courses must attract a minimum number of students or else the class is cancelled. To ensure I get enough students, I often develop my own flyers, posting them at libraries or around the community college itself. These flyers are simple, but professional. They frequently do not include the price, and I omit that on purpose. I don't want to give anyone a reason to dismiss what I have to offer without careful consideration. I want them to think about it and inquire.

I've often sent notices to the newsletter my writers group publishes, to the college's student newspaper and yearbook offices and to the school's writers club. Often, I ask editors of suburban papers to list my workshop or course under the calendar of upcoming events. Perhaps your cable channel runs such community announcements free of charge. All of these efforts increase enrollment, and that's what counts. You can't receive a paycheck if your course gets cancelled.

DETERMINING YOUR APPROACH

I'll never forget my first night as an instructor. My class was called "Public Relations Made Simple." I had organized my materials, picked a savvy suit out of my closet and arrived to set up my room ahead of time. I took roll and started lecturing without a hitch. Everything was running smoothly. Until I handed out my first writing exercise.

"What's this?" a lady three rows back asked.

"Oh, it's just a little exercise to help you determine your writing skills," I told her. Sensing her dismay, I added, "It's OK. Just do as much as you can."

While the other students picked up their pens and got to work, this woman sat and sighed. She turned to her husband, and in full earshot of the class, said, "I can't do this. This isn't like antiques. Antiques was fun!"

I learned the fine art of grace under pressure that evening as I tried to explain the purpose of writing as a foundation for public relations work. But I kept hearing it—you know, how antiques was fun, and my class wasn't. I didn't need this on my first night. Besides, it wasn't my fault antiques got cancelled.

Well, I wasn't a bit surprised or offended when this lady and her husband moved to microwave cooking the next week. And I later learned that the other students got a charge out of her remarks just as I did.

Getting up in front of a room full of strangers and trying to please them all can intimidate anyone, especially the lonely freelancer who works independently most of the time. But don't let this fear of public speaking stand in your way. If I can conquer these fears, and deal with a bewildered student, so can you.

When I teach my classes, I prefer to sit at the desk in front of the room. We often arrange the tables or desks to form a circle so that we're all facing one another. I do this because it reflects my style and penchant for informality. I like to talk with my students, not at them. I encourage their participation. In fact, we probably get off on a tangent or two that other instructors might frown upon. But this is my style, and according to the evaluations, it seems my students prefer it.

"I treat my adult students as my peers," says Sandra Louden, who teaches greeting card writing. "We are all freelance writers dealing with various companies and editors. I may be a little farther down the career path than they are, but their ideas and observations are every bit as valid as mine." You can see that if you approach teaching from a give and take standpoint, you have much less to fear and more to gain.

This concept brings me to a common remark others make about my teaching. "Don't you worry that you're equipping the competition in your own backyard?" people ask me.

I must say that I don't see my students as competitors. I'm confident enough in my talents that any extra competition emanating from my teaching simply doesn't threaten me. By the end of our sessions, my students usually know which magazines I write for, but my editors refrain from directory listings and do

not solicit material. They prefer to work with a group of established writers, and I often tell my students this. But because my
class encompasses so much, I also know that each student's interest is different. Some want to write poetry. Some want to focus
on novels. Some want to write children's literature.

My job as instructor is to excite people to follow a dream,
giving them as much how-to information and realism as they
need to get the job done professionally and make lots of money.
It's my students' responsibility to translate my knowledge and
my writing interests into their own circumstances. Seeing that
fire ignited is another hidden reward of teaching. Instructors do
have the power to change a life, and when that happens, I'm
always very pleased to see my students succeed.

Once you put that competitive issue out of your mind, you
should make a point to include personal experiences and individual anecdotes from your writing career. My evaluations also tell
me that students enjoy the stories I share with them. I cite real-
life examples from client experiences, dealings with editors and
publishers, and the mistakes I've made along the way. My hope
is that they'll learn from my errors and prevent their own. Build
this kind of exchange into your teaching style, and chances are
good it will pay off for you too.

PREPARING YOUR LECTURES

Because of the approach I just described, I always format my
lectures rather loosely. I purchased a three-ring notebook with
pockets for storage. Using my Mac, I prepare my notes. When I
update a lecture, I just print out a new copy. I section off each
lecture in my notebook, placing my copies of handouts, answers
to quizzes and discussion items for any given week.

At the top of each night's lecture, I put in parentheses the
materials I'll need to bring to class. If I'm rushing out the door
(which I usually am), I don't want to stop and remember what
to take or risk forgetting important material. When we discuss
finding magazine markets, I take *Writer's Market*. If we talk about
greeting cards, I make sure I take a stack of cards and a couple
of mail-order catalogs. If I plan to read a passage out of a favorite
book, I write down the title and author's name.

To guide my students and myself, I type out a syllabus to hand
out the first night of class. This gives students an idea of what

we'll be doing, week by week and gives those students seeking a different kind of educational experience the chance to withdraw or choose another class.

On this sheet, I also list the homework assignments, which are usually minimal (and kind of fun), requiring students to study newspapers, magazines, card counters or whatever we're discussing in the next class. I keep one of these in my notebook, but I also list each week's assignment at the end of my lecture, just to remind the students and encourage their participation.

One last word about preparing your lectures: Don't write out every word you intend to utter. Nothing bores students more than the instructor who lacks animation and the ability to ad lib. If students wanted to read a good book, they'd spend their money on it rather than your class, and they could read it in the comforts of their own home. Write your lectures loosely, just as you would a good speech. Put key words or phrases down on paper so that they'll jog your memory, but don't plan to recite every word verbatim.

WHAT FLIES AND WHAT FAILS

Trial and error will be your best guide in knowing which teaching techniques succeed and which should be retired this semester. I've already covered the informal approach which I believe in. I've learned over the years that just as readers require a strong writer's voice when perusing a nonfiction text, students want and need the instructor's perspective and knowledge when they enroll in a class. For that reason, I'd limit outside speakers. If there is a recognized professional you want to bring in, do it only for thirty minutes, certainly not more than an hour. Otherwise, you are seen as less of an authority.

If you want to point students in the direction of further education, mention other classes that these authorities may teach. Mention their book that students can purchase, but keep control of the classroom setting.

Instructors report that tape recordings — both audio and video — haven't gone over too well in class. One time, I used *The Elements of Style Video*, but I have to admit it dragged on after the first few rounds. A video featuring published authors, an editor and an agent was much more appealing. A friend tried a similar technique, offering a cassette with a message from an editor in class. Students didn't like it either. Again, the lesson here is: Keep control. Students want you, not someone else. Select audio/visual materials carefully.

Another instructor I know reads and dissects his published work in class and makes particular points about it. In some of my own classes, students evaluate each other's work during the last sessions. While I've seen some sad faces, others walk away having learned a great deal from the constructive criticism. They also realize that rewrites are inevitable.

In terms of written material, I have always focused my workshops and classes heavily on writing. In my classes, students spot sexist language, learn to correct the passive voice, and realize their spelling skills need some work. The way I see it, teaching a student to write without giving them the opportunity to do so in class would be the equivalent of driver's ed without ever getting behind the wheel.

One lady wrote on her evaluation that my exercises were juvenile. (No, this wasn't the woman who moved to microwave cooking!) But far more students have written that they pinpointed their strengths and weaknesses, and that has been my intention all along. If you're unsure about how much in-class writing to include in the curriculum, just remember that the word "workshop" implies work. Let the time limits of your course and the number of sessions be your guide. A 70:30 ratio of lecture to work is fairly normal.

SETTING UP SEMINARS

The primary advantage of teaching through a school system is that the school takes care of the location, registration and promotion. But they also take quite a cut for the services rendered.

If you've developed a successful teaching style and are looking for greater financial reward, you may want to sponsor your own seminar. Of course, with the potential for profit also comes the risk of cancellation and financial loss. When you sponsor seminars, you book the hotel, classroom or public meeting hall. You rent the microphone and other audio/visual equipment. You pay for the direct-mail campaign to promote your seminar. If you end up having to cancel, most of that money is lost.

But if you've found a need waiting to be filled, sponsoring a seminar may be that next step in your teaching career. Author and lecturer Gordon Burgett offers a cassette series based on his successful seminar experiences around the country. It's called "How To Set Up and Market Your Own Seminar." In this series, Burgett offers a helpful guideline to determine your potential for success. "The more basic the need, the more likely you are to attract registrants," he says. "If they feel the need rarely, that's weak grounds for a seminar. If they feel the need daily, they will be interested. And if they feel the need all the time, they'll be there an hour early to get into your program, to knock on your door."

Focus on a service orientation. Set out to make your seminar participants healthier, wealthier or wiser, and your idea stands at least a running chance.

The writers and communicators who will most likely make up your audience will expect a comfortable public meeting place. Contact the local Chamber of Commerce or Convention and Visitor's Bureau to find out the names of appropriate facilities. Schools, churches and libraries may be able to offer you the space you're looking for, for a minimal fee.

Like courses, limit your seminars to three or four hours or people may not care to participate. Other factors to consider in the initial planning stages include the weather and conflicting commitments. Seminars sponsored in November or December are too crowded by holiday activities to draw a sufficient audience. Students may also be reluctant to sit indoors on a bright summer day. Furthermore, snowbelt cities require you to take bad weather into account. Many people will not care to drive long distances during the evening hours when the roads could become treacherous. My pick for successful seminar months would be March through May as well as September and October.

Offering your own seminar creates questions regarding sales tax levied on product sales, whether you need to hire any additional help or offer food. If you sell products (more on this later), you'll need to obtain a resale number from your state taxing authority. You may want to develop a fictitious name for your business and make arrangements for credit card sales as well. And, if you do have product sales going on, or if you simply expect a large crowd, have another set of hands to register people and collect their money.

Food is another issue. If your facility has a coffee shop nearby or vending machines, I would not bother with food and beverages. However, if you're away from these conveniences, coffee and donuts (for the morning sessions) often wake people up and put smiles on their faces. I'd skip lunch altogether unless you plan a networking experience or need food service to get a lower room rate at some hotels. Food choices always increase costs and usually offend someone — vegetarians, meat-lovers, seafood haters or those on restricted diets. It's invariably a no-win situation.

INCREASING YOUR TEACHING INCOME

Students always appreciate it when instructors provide jumping off points for further study. So if you have authored a book on your subject or if you have other products pertaining to it, selling these on the completion of your seminar adds to your coffers. But, some colleges and universities have strict policies prohibiting the promotion of services or products. Frankly, it's unfortunate, for both the instructors and the students.

You can sometimes get around such restrictions if you build the cost of a book or newsletter you've published into your materials fee. If restrictions still hinder you, start your own seminar where product sales are almost always expected. In either case, I'd quote frequently from and display your products. Pointing to such references enhances your credentials and ultimately promotes the class.

Always offer more in your course or seminar than students can find in your materials alone. To do otherwise would be inconsiderate of your students' time and money, not to mention threatening to the livelihood you're creating from your teaching. Others could easily walk off with everything you've written, and offer it with their own twist. And speaking of financial protection, it never hurts (and often helps) to display the copyright symbol on materials you've created.

When offering courses or seminars, encourage people to sign up fast with a deposit. In your promotions, state that space is limited. If you have control over a self-sponsored event, a discount for early registration encourages people to act fast. Promote the tax deductibility of your seminar. In addition, when you register seminar or course participants, always get their names, phone numbers and addresses. Keep this information for future mailing lists, book promotions or teaching opportunities.

If you have input into the price of your course or seminar, know that any job-related workshop or seminar that can be billed back to employers can be priced slightly higher than those aimed at the avocational crowd. Unfortunately, most writers start writing as a hobby, and only after seeing their own success, begin to think of their pursuit as a career. You may need to remind potential participants that it takes money to make money.

Also, examine your primary goal for teaching. If it's for income, the fee charged is important. If it's to attract consulting clients or sell books, tapes or other products, then the fee is secondary. Some instructors are so confident of their product's sales potential that they can afford to teach for free. Overall, if you keep the benefits of taking your course or seminar high and the costs to yourself (and your students) as low as possible, you'll maximize your profit and make everyone happy.

WHAT YOU GET IN RETURN

Earlier, I discussed what students obtain from attending your courses, workshops, seminars or lectures. Obviously, you're getting paid (and paid regularly), and that's a wonderful benefit! But most writers I know who also teach reap a multitude of personal and professional rewards. Says Sandra Louden, "Teaching is an excellent foundation for writing a book because students' questions and observations often expose the instructor to points of view she never previously considered."

Teaching indeed stretches your own knowledge as you attempt to find answers to students' questions. You become more comfortable in your own work and accomplishments, and you also learn how to effectively promote your writing career.

Tom Clark, senior editor of *Writer's Digest*, teaches adult education programs through the University of Cincinnati, and he remarks that doing so helps him keep in touch with the magazine's target audience. "By examining my craft and how I approach it," Clark says, "I learn a lot and become a better writer myself. And that makes me a better editor."

Recalling my own teaching experiences, I remember the student who had reluctantly left her journalism degree behind and was working in a secretarial position. My course dealt with newsletters, and I encouraged her to start one at work. She did, and she wrote me a letter overflowing with excitement. I've also seen students who, after taking an employer-sponsored workshop of mine, kept in touch and paid their own money for my subsequent courses. Others have stopped me in stores and elevators telling me how they enjoyed my workshops. One student even told me she couldn't wait for this book to appear, and told at least three of her friends to take my freelance writing course. Those kind of comments make my day, but more important, they prove to me that my efforts, even if only three hours each week, make a difference in a person's life.

Don't be surprised if word of mouth travels well for you, too. Students may become clients. They may partake of your manuscript critiquing services. They may buy your books or newsletters. And others who hear of your teaching success will invite you to teach or speak before other groups. Just remember, the best courses and seminars are taught by active professionals who love what they do and make a living at it. Keep up the good work, and who knows what's in store for you!

HOW TO GET STARTED

 Teaching keeps the cash flowing while you work on harder-to-pay-off projects. With a good subject, a little bit of courage, and an articulate and friendly style, you can make a difference in the classroom.

• Obtain continuing-education course catalogs and seminar brochures by calling colleges and universities near you.

• Look at what is not offered. Think of possible courses you would feel comfortable teaching. Focus on improving your students' health, wealth, earning potential or personal fulfillment.

• Idea in mind, give a quick call to the continuing education department and discuss it with the director. In many instances, the secretary can be just as helpful and may comment on your suggestion's potential.

• Write specific goals, a brief (one paragraph) description and a week-by-week outline of what you intend to cover. Send this page along with your resume to the director.

• Double-check all details surrounding your class, including the dates, times, prices, materials fee and the length of the course.

Errors in the course catalog make you, and the sponsor, look bad.

- Set a maximum number of participants. Break the class into two sections, and you'll increase your hours and income!

- Self-sponsor your own seminar once you've perfected your teaching style and attracted a steady stream of registrants. Use the seminar to sell products and services.

- To obtain Gordon Burgett's "How to Set Up and Market Your Own Seminar," contact Communications Unlimited, Santa Maria, California, or call (805) 937-3035.

- Be willing to help your students succeed. The satisfaction of helping others can be just as meaningful as a steady paycheck, and word of mouth makes very valuable publicity.

WRITING FOR THE PUBLIC

Chapter Ten

Newspapers

When people ask me when I knew I wanted to be a writer, I often recall my high school days, when writing term papers and school newspaper articles seemed much more like fun than work. Adding journalism to my course load during my senior year really clinched the career decision for me. I imagine many other writers can look back on similar times when they first got a taste of reporting and writing for an audience, even if it was an audience of peers.

Newspapers, whether big or small, remain fertile grounds for establishing good journalistic practices and developing a consistent track record of meeting deadlines. That's why I strongly recommend to students that they get involved in campus publications — newspapers, yearbooks or other kinds of journals. College students can take that extra step of spending a semester-long internship at a large metropolitan daily paper. There's just no substitute for the experience.

So what, you say. You're past high school and college, and you need income — now. Well, there's still hope. If you live in a large metropolitan area, there are job advisory councils that arrange internships for adults, and some of these can be for pay (albeit low wages). Smaller, suburban newspapers will often take on newcomers if they exude a lot of enthusiasm and can demonstrate good writing skills.

The same goes for specialty publications. In Pittsburgh, we have a number of specialty newspapers delivering news, commentary and advice to select audiences. Among these are *In Pittsburgh*, an entertainment and arts weekly; *Pittsburgh's Child*, a monthly parenting publication; the *Pittsburgh Business Times*, for weekly financial news; and the *Pittsburgh Courier*, targeting the African-American population each week. Once you have your foot in the door, you can show what you have to offer and increase your skills (and your income potential) by becoming a prolific writer.

Working for a newspaper also helps you build the reputation as a specialist. Start your writing career at a small specialty publication, then capitalize on your expertise and clippings, branching off into the national newspaper or magazine markets. Throughout this chapter, you can read about the full-range of writing opportunities frequently available at most, if not all, newspapers. You'll be able to determine which assignments appeal to you and go about landing them.

WRITING FOR YOUR NEWSPAPER AUDIENCE

A quick review of chapter four (Journalistic Foundations) serves as a prerequisite for this chapter, for in those pages, we learned the essential questions reporters must ask (the five Ws and the H), how to select and interview your subject, how to write in the inverted pyramid style, and how to construct powerful lead sentences that will hook your readers into paying attention and finishing your article.

Lead sentences deserve a second mention. It's vital that you hone the skill of writing leads, in all different types and forms. While journalism professors like to use many names for leads, you really need to be concerned with two main types — direct and delayed.

Typically, for hard news items, readers want to get to the information right away. They will not appreciate the writer dancing around significant events or issues at hand. Therefore, the most common lead used for hard-news reporting is the direct one, as written here by Andrew Rosenthal, in *The New York Times*:

> WASHINGTON, Thursday, January 17, 1991 — The United States and allied forces Wednesday night opened the long-threatened war to drive President Saddam Hussein's army from Kuwait, striking Baghdad and other targets in Iraq and Kuwait with waves of bombers and cruise missiles launched from naval vessels.

You can't get any more hard news than the breakout of war,

and as you can see, the direct lead tells readers exactly what happened. Imagine your readers anxiously awaiting word about loved ones deployed overseas as part of Desert Storm. Imagine their frustration — and anger — if the reporter took his time getting to the point of the story. Hard news is no place to play around. Give it straight. Give it accurately. And move on to the other details readers need to know.

Contrast this hard news lead to the approach feature writers often take with stories that are unusual, odd, strange or somewhat whimsical. Writers of lifestyle and news features frequently opt for the delayed lead because they can have fun with it. They can tell a story slowly, pacing the article as a tale and often tempting the reader to guess at what's to come. Read the lead published in *The Pittsburgh Press* and written by Joseph Barsotti, and you'll see what I mean:

> Did you ever throw a weekend party and nobody came? Or worse, they came and guzzled all of your hooch, but left the keg of beer in the corner three-quarters full?
>
> If you don't have a refrigerator big enough to store it, or if you have to return it to the distributor on Monday to get back your deposit, then you are out of luck. Or are you?
>
> One thing to do is to invite the neighbors to bring pitchers or gallon jugs over for some take-home foam. If there is any of the brew left, save it. Not for imbibing, but for use in cooking.

In this example, questioning the reader works well. The lead poses different situations that many can identify with. But it takes several sentences to get to the real focus of the story — cooking with beer.

When I teach freelance writing, I like to read leads I've clipped out of newspapers, and I invite students to cite their own examples. One semester, I read the following lead crafted by sports writer Dave Molinari in the *Pittsburgh Post-Gazette*:

> Mario Lemieux dresses the part when he spends game nights in the owners' superbox at the Civic Arena.
>
> His suits are superbly tailored. They have classic lines. And they retail for about the same as a three-bedroom Tudor.

But stylish as his clothes are, Lemieux had been hoping to wear something different for the Penguins' game against the Edmonton Oilers tonight. Something he hasn't had on in a while. Something in a 66 regular.

Lemieux, you see, no longer is trying to stay ahead of his recovery schedule. He's intent on lapping it. Forget tracking his comeback from Hodgkin's disease with a calendar; an egg timer should suffice.

This sports page story caught my eye, as all of Pittsburgh was tracking Lemieux's comeback after a several-month absence. Sports articles require an interesting hook even more so than other soft news stories, because in many cases, readers already know the score and the outcome. If they are to continue with the story, it had better grab them.

Leads are essential elements in any article. If you cannot write them well, your story will not get past the editor's desk, let alone your readers' fingertips. Practice makes perfect as you try both direct and delayed leads.

BEAT REPORTING

Look in most newspapers, and you'll usually see one writer covering city council, another the court circuit, still another business and finance or lifestyles, sports and so on. These are all "beats," and each has a different writer. Reporters specialize sometimes because they offer considerable background and understanding (a college minor in one of these subjects, for instance) or simply because of the luck of the draw.

Certainly, you'll want to try to go after those beats that appeal to your education and personal interests, but if you're offered a beat that seems rather unappealing to you, don't necessarily turn it down. The experience covering any subject, day in, day out, will hone your reportorial skills and add additional experience to your journalistic resume.

REVIEW WRITING

Many writers begin their newspaper careers writing reviews of art exhibits, concerts, dance performances, poetry readings, symphonies, lectures, theater, television, musicals, books or record albums. They do this because it hardly seems like work. Imagine getting paid to read your favorite novelist's recent release? You had planned to read it anyway, so why not read it, get published and get paid.

You can find markets for your reviews at most newspapers. Just use an ounce of common sense. While a financial publication may not be interested in the latest theater production, its editor may need reviews of business books. The more prestigious the publication, the more credentials you'll need. If you have educational or real-life experience in the subject matter, let your prospective editor know this.

It's important, at this beginning stage, however, that you invest some time in writing sample reviews. Review writing has to be judged as a whole, so while you can query all you want, it's the finished article or the previously published clips that will lead to a check in the mail. Ask your editor about the pay structure for published reviews. At some papers, book reviews, for instance, are published without pay. The only compensation the reviewer receives is the book.

To find items worth reviewing, check your daily newspaper, especially the Sunday sections, which contain many more listings. Stay in close contact with bookstores, publicists, writers groups, colleges, universities, lecture series sponsors, concert promoters and public relations personnel. Alert television viewing clued me in that psychologist author Dr. Kevin Leman frequently included Pittsburgh on his author tours. So, I called his publisher when I read about his latest release. Indeed, several weeks later, he came to town, and I was able to interview him over a very pleasant lunch. Furthermore, I met his escort, and I learned that this woman arranges the logistics for many of the authors and celebrities that pass through town. She's a contact I want to keep!

The Reviewing Process

First, a few reviewing rules. Always read or witness the entire work you are reviewing. You can't do your job, and do it well, if you only listened to half of the artist's album or read only the first few chapters and jumped to the conclusion. You can't write from a news release describing the work or the book. You need to experience all of it. Not only will you write a better review, but you'll also please your readers, not to mention the author or artist. I learned that Kevin Leman enjoyed my interview largely because I was familiar with his books and could relate them to real-life examples.

To achieve such a familiarity with a book, reviewers find it helpful if they read a work the first time as a fan or novice. Then, they reread it as a reviewer, making notes, searching out details, and asking critical questions. Of course, this approach might not be possible if you are reviewing a limited-engagement performance or a live concert.

One of the critical questions I alluded to above is: What makes this worth a person's time and money? It's a question that deserves an answer no matter what kind of review you are writing. People read reviews because they just might spend their hard-earned money on the product or performance you're reviewing. While their opinion may be different, these people count on your expertise and recommendations. Therefore, let your integrity and honesty rule. If there's something that wasn't quite right, tell your readers. Don't lie to them.

If you're concerned about sounding too judgmental or opinionated, use quotes or excerpts. In the case of a book, reprint a passage the author wrote. In the case of a lecture, quote the speaker. If it's a lyric, cite a line from the song. This technique works well when there is a negative element you want to express, for it allows readers to draw their own conclusions, and it helps you, the writer, hold to the dictate of showing versus telling.

As you progress in writing reviews, increase your opportunities by keeping in touch with artists, writers and others who can invite you to sneak previews and send you copies of recently released books and records. Knowing that a museum exhibit is coming to town or that an author plans a stop on his six-city tour helps you convince your editor, ahead of time, to build a review or feature into the editorial calendar.

Send a copy of your review to the appropriate person you've been working with, along with an attached note that asks, "Was I on target? I hope you'll write back and let me know." In some cases, especially if you were not thoroughly complimentary, the answer may be "*No*, you weren't." But more often than not, those you review will appreciate the insights and understand that you're only doing your job.

Restaurant Reviews

As one writer I know says, if you have taste buds, you can develop the skills necessary to write a restaurant review. And you have to eat, right? So why not eat *and* get paid for it!

There are more markets than you might think of for restaurant reviews. The obvious one is the newspaper—suburban or major metropolitan daily. But food and beverage publications and airline magazines also need such articles, although some magazines choose to run restaurant reviews within the context of the travel article.

Contact the lifestyles department or the person in charge of the paper's magazine or Sunday sections. Ask who edits the food/restaurant reviews, and send this person some of your best clips. If you're just starting out, write a few sample reviews after visiting restaurants in your area. They don't have to be expensive places to eat. Sometimes the local diner that serves great food at a reasonable price is more appealing than a gourmet restaurant.

To help the beginning cooks, acquire a culinary knowledge from cookbooks or ask questions of chefs or even friends who spend a lot of time in the kitchen. Talk to your local butcher about cuts of meat; the produce department manager about what's in season; and specialty store owners about ethnic delights and gourmet secrets. Listen to famous cooks on TV. Some local newscasts feature cooking segments. All of these opportunities will help you learn the terminology you'll need to understand menus, cookbooks and chef suggestions. Weave what you learn into a few sample reviews (discussed earlier in this chapter).

It's equally important to keep abreast of food trends and dietary and lifestyle habits. Today, we're a lot more conscious of fat and cholesterol than we were ten years ago. It used to be that only the middle-aged and older folks made modifications in their diets. Now, we know that what we eat at age five can influence our quality of life at age fifty. Because of this, you may want to stick to restaurants that cater to current dietary concerns. But then, everyone can make an exception, here and there, for a sinful dessert or two, or for the latest fast-food hangout around the corner. Some people don't care where they eat, just so long as they don't have to cook, and for the freelance restaurant reviewer, that's good news, too.

Before you journey out on your eating excursion, ask about

payment policies at your publication. Many newspapers will not allow writers to accept complimentary meals; others have no problem with it. Ask your editor if you can file an expense report, and if so, are there certain limits? And, if you do accept an invitation from a restaurant owner for that free meal, it's best to book your reservation as a typical patron, visit and be served. Then, at the end of the meal, you can present your invitation, ensuring that you have received the same treatment as any one of your readers could expect.

Once you've gathered some culinary knowledge and kept current with the trends, you're ready to eat. There's no harm in taking along a companion to help pass the time or to avoid those curious stares that seem to say, "What's she doing eating alone?" In fact, dining in the company of a friend allows you to each order different menu items and share, potentially broadening your review.

At the conclusion of your dining experience, jot down your notes. Detail the decor, the service, the prices (including the a la carte items), the presentation and the quality of the food. Honesty should rule. But knowing how a bad review can wreak havoc or financial ruin on a restaurant, be sure you can back up your comments. If you've had a particularly bad experience, you might want to visit the restaurant twice, just to be certain the experience wasn't an exception to the norm. When in doubt as to how candid you should be, try the direct approach that simply states a description of the decor instead of using adjectives such as "tacky" or "dated." You could guide people to the more popular menu items, leaving out mention of those that were particularly undesirable.

While restaurant reviews aren't timely news pieces, they need the "news" hook to get your editor's attention. If you're having trouble convincing editors to assign reviews to you or commit to running them once they're written, remember the "news" angle. Look for opportunities that give you a reason to pitch a restaurant or book review.

I recently read a Mexican cookbook review and a recipe from a local Mexican restaurant in my morning paper. The paper published the review, not just because they thought it was a good cookbook, but because it coincided with the Cinco de Mayo celebration.

OPINIONS AND EDITORIALS

In any major daily, and in less frequently published papers, there are opinion and editorial columns just waiting for you to add your two cents' worth of advice and commentary. Most publications won't pay for brief contributions (like letters to the editor), but some may implement a pay scale for longer guest-written columns. Ask yourself is payment more important to you than publication?

The op-ed page (meaning opposite editorial) is much less formal in tone than its counterpart years ago. Today's readers are open to different points of view, including yours, so here's your chance to sound off on a subject, air your pet peeves and get paid, providing of course, that you can back up your commentary with concrete examples, first-hand experience and a professional writing style.

Probably the first rule of thumb to apply is my famous sixth W that I include in my workshops. That is: Who cares? If no one cares, beyond you and maybe your best friend, you won't attract the attention of most readers, let alone an editor. Focus your efforts on issues and ideas that have public appeal and broad support (or lack of it) in the community. To obtain these ideas, read widely. Different newspapers and many magazines should certainly be included in your search for an appropriate topic.

When you've found what it is you want to write about, illustrate your points with anecdotes, statistics, quotations and if possible, a gripping personal narrative. Including these elements will help you hook the editor, and ultimately, the reader.

NEWSPAPER STRINGING

Many publications have correspondents stationed around the country. It's cheaper to use these reporters to feed the occasional story to the publication than it is to open a bureau or pay a staff person to write from that location. This same rule applies to city outskirts or outlying counties. Certain areas may fall within your newspaper's coverage area, but the stories are so rare, that they don't warrant a full-time beat.

Enter the ambitious freelance writer who wants to get paid and get published in a large metropolitan daily or in a news magazine like *Time* or *Newsweek*. If publications don't already have correspondents in your area, get in touch with the bureau chief or editor. Send some clips, a copy of your resume and a letter outlining why you'd like to become a stringer.

If you know of a particular event or personality that will be making news in your area, jump on the chance to get your story in print. The president or a senatorial candidate may be visiting your tiny borough, touring a factory or visiting schoolchildren. A local sports hero may have won some medals in the Olympic Games. Contact your editor in advance to land assignments.

But more often than not, news isn't planned. It happens, and stringers must be prepared to get to the scene, complete their interviews, write their stories and file them within a matter of hours. Therefore, if you haven't honed the skills of writing and interviewing, quickly and accurately, stringing is not for you. Wait until your talent and track record warrants such assignments.

Most newspaper stringers are not salaried, earning income only from the stories that get published. Most write more stories than ever see publication. Your news stories may be of marginal interest to your editor and the publication's readers. But that's OK. Just don't expect everything you write to see print, and don't expect to get rich and famous. Do expect to add prestigious credits to your name, if you're in the right place at the right time. And do expect to work hard and fast.

COLUMN WRITING

Column writing is another newspaper area where working hard and working fast is forever the way of life. Indeed, good columns are easy to read. I rarely miss Dear Abby or Ann Landers. I like to read psychologist John Rosemond for his parenting advice and Ellen Goodman of the *Boston Globe* because I usually agree with her viewpoints. Try writing one of these columns, however, and you'll see just how hard it is to be prolific, witty and appealing on a daily, weekly or even monthly basis.

A colleague of mine, Lillian Africano, had gone to *Woman's World* to discuss other writing projects when an editor approached her to write an advice column. She has written the "Ask Lillian" column ever since.

Your effort to land that kind of column assignment will be completely different, I almost guarantee it, for this woman's newsweekly had a pressing need and met it right away. Usually it works the other way around. Writers must come up with the proposed column concept and seek buyers for it. You must have a viable column idea that appeals to the masses beyond your own community, and your idea must compel the reader to seek it out on a consistent basis.

"Either there's a niche waiting to be filled with your column or no one wants it," says Africano. "Your publisher will have a 'show me' attitude, and coming up with the concept will require a certain amount of entrepreneurial thinking on your part."

You must also have a vivid imagination, a lot of persistence, perhaps an expertise or incredibly sound judgment, and an enormous supply of staying power, as keeping your column fresh each time will be another challenge.

You have all these elements, you say? The editor you propose your column to *will* want to know this. More than likely, you'll have to prove these qualities by showing samples of your proposed columns, and a list of ideas that will carry your column through over the long haul. To prove your worth, as Lillian Africano did, you may have to invest many hours in writing columns on spec. Some of us simply cannot afford to commit this time to a project that may, or may not, be purchased.

Another question you must ask is: Can I be brutally honest? If your answer is unequivocally yes, ask: Am I willing to be called to task for my honesty? Can I take the heat for an unpopular stance?

If your answer is no, don't get in over your head. Columnists communicate what they think, and it's not always popular. Sometimes, it's downright critical of government leaders, popular icons, community figures and celebrities. Before you write a column, be prepared to back it up.

Column Crafting

Once you have the ideas, the staying power and the commitment to succeed, you'll need to write your columns according to your deadline. Many writers agree that spicing your columns with anecdotes from your personal life or from the lives of the people you're writing about helps to make points and maintain readership. People like to relate to what you express. They also like to learn through your insights, informed commentary and even a little bit of news.

Keep your copy conversational, as if you and a friend were sipping tea and you were sharing your innermost thoughts and feelings. And while it's perfectly fine to emulate the style of a favorite columnist, be yourself. Your personality needs to shine through, and by being yourself, your style will develop.

Syndication

Columnists are paid by the publication they originally write for, and also by the number of publications purchasing their columns in syndication. Syndication is a writer's dream. Who wouldn't want readers from all over the country, or perhaps throughout the world, to share in their thoughts, feelings and viewpoints?

If your column has sustained itself over the course of many years, perhaps you are ready to syndicate your efforts. But know that it's another tough sell, for few of the columns presented for syndication each year are chosen for the honor.

Usually, if your publication is behind you, these folks may approach one of the major syndicates for you. Otherwise, you may want to contact the syndicates yourself. *Writer's Market* and *Literary Market Place* each list news syndicates. Syndication companies act as agents on your behalf, packaging your columns, shipping them off to their customers and sending you your half of the 50-50 split on fees. One column sale in itself doesn't amount to much, but if you're fortunate to have dozens of papers carry your column, the money adds up.

If a major syndicate doesn't back you, try self-syndicating your work. On a small scale, I've done this with my parenting articles for *Pittsburgh's Child*. Some of my feature articles have been picked up by other parenting publications. But it's meant photocopying my work, packaging it and presenting it, plus mailing it. Then there has been the telephone follow-up when I've failed to hear back from editors.

One rule of thumb when it comes to self-syndication: Never overlap coverage areas. Be particularly careful of areas where several cities are clustered. For instance, don't send material to both Ft. Lauderdale and Miami newspapers. This would overlap your coverage area. However, targeting the Tampa and Miami papers would be fine.

HOW TO GET STARTED

There's no better place to hone your journalistic style than working for a newspaper, where you will be forced to ask questions, probe for answers, research and write — all on a tight deadline.

• Try writing different versions of the newspaper stories you're already familiar with. Use both the direct and delayed leads to see how the story changes.

• Build on a personal interest or hobby by writing reviews.

• Tie reviews of books, restaurants or speakers into newsworthy angles and timely topics. Visit a Chinese restaurant and write about it for Chinese New Year or review a good mystery novel in time for Halloween.

• Review the masthead of your favorite news magazines or newspapers. If there is no local correspondent listed, send a resume, clips and a detailed cover letter to the bureau chief and ask to become a stringer.

• Broaden your readership by writing columns the public can count on. Most editors won't go out of their way to seek additional writers and material, but if your column is an exception, the profits of syndication could be substantial!

Chapter Eleven

Magazines

Next to a novel that I can't put down, nothing comes as close to captivating me as an entertaining magazine article. I think of the times I've read a publication, sitting in a doctor's office or waiting for my car to be repaired. My name was called, only I didn't want to get up. I *had* to finish the article. It's true: Articles that engage readers like this sell more magazines. That's the bottom line in this business.

To hook the ever-changing universe of readers, most magazines rely upon freelance writers. An overwhelming majority of these magazines couldn't survive without them. In large markets, especially where magazines are distributed on a national or international basis, the competition among writers is fierce. So is the challenge to come up with creative approaches with broad appeal.

THE DIFFERENCE BETWEEN NEWSPAPER AND MAGAZINE WRITING

On the surface, these two types of writing may seem very similar. A feature is a feature, right? Not necessarily. Both newspapers and magazines are based on solid reporting principles. Each requires a captivating lead, a steady flow of facts and a strong, satisfying conclusion. But, magazine leads are often longer, as are many magazine paragraphs. Newspaper writers, by contrast, have mastered the punchy prose that fits into specified column inches.

A magazine's approach is more leisurely. Whereas newspapers pride themselves on their objectivity and factual approach, incorporating a minimum of opinion, magazines often take a stance.

Take airline magazines as an example. These often feature destination pieces emphasizing the routes the airline flies. The airline has a stake in the coverage and its presentation. When I wrote the Bahamas cover story for *USAir Magazine* some time ago, I knew my job was to portray this group of islands as best I could, calling attention to all the reasons travellers would want to run out and visit their travel agents.

Having said this, I'm not implying that writers check their honesty at the keyboard. However, it's essential that you produce what is expected. If you find anything you don't like about a destination, there's usually a way you can still put a positive spin on the subject. If a city is crowded by tourists, for example, you can simply say that it's a popular vacation spot. You get the idea.

Another factor that sets magazines apart from newspapers is the national scope and appeal of their articles. Newspapers go to great lengths to localize a story, citing nearby experts and statistics whenever possible. Magazines also have fewer beats than their newspaper counterparts do. But this is good news to the freelancer, signaling that fresh insights and offbeat angles are welcomed.

Finally, magazines have long lead times with deadlines sometimes months from assignment. But if you take six months to write every magazine article you're assigned, your profit potential will plummet. Your success rate (and income) improve as you become prolific.

WHO BUYS MAGAZINE ARTICLES

It only takes a glimpse through *Writer's Market* to know the myriad of publications accepting freelance contributions. But finding the right publication for your story is often another matter. There are ample opportunities in almost every subject imaginable classified into two groups—consumer and trade. Both types are bought at newsstands, subscribed to or received through a controlled circulation.

Consumer magazines are those produced for a general audience. Trade magazines (otherwise known as technical or professional journals) target a much narrower readership, and they represent hidden opportunities for the freelance writer. While trade journals may not pay as well as some consumer magazines, their editors are frequently more accessible than their consumer counterparts. Because they aren't as inundated as consumer magazine editors, they're quicker to respond to queries and submissions, and they're more likely to dole out repeat assignments to the writers who have mastered their narrow market. And by their very nature, trade journals tend to be more stable than some magazines that disappear from the newsstand.

But while writers' guide books are great places to learn of new markets for your work, so is a thorough and periodic scan of the local newsstand. In fact, it's how I published articles in two start-up magazines when I first began writing. Other places to discover new markets include libraries, offices, professional organizations and club memberships. Most motor clubs have their own publications. So do some municipalities. Major universities offer alumni publications, all of which need editorial material, and some of whom pay for it. Out-of-town newsstands and bookstores are great places to browse. Unless you're running for your plane, never pass through an airport without scanning the magazine rack. You never know what new home you might find for your work.

RESEARCHING YOUR MAGAZINE'S MARKET

Once you've gathered a handful of magazines you plan to target, hold off sending those queries until you've done a little research. Proper analysis of the magazine and its readership often means the difference between acceptance and rejection.

A cursory look through the magazine tells you a lot about the typical reader. The quality of the publication often speaks for itself. If it's full-color printing, there's more money involved, before you even look at the price. Look to see if the publication is photo driven, as photography increases production costs and enhances the magazine's perceived value.

Next, pay attention to the advertising. Is this an upscale audience or a budget crowd? If you see ads for Mercedes, BMWs and exclusive resort vacations, you have your answer.

Is the reader young, middle-aged or older? Consumer products will give you your clues. If you spot a string of ads for diapers, formula and toys, you have just learned something important about your reader. If, on the other hand, you find ads for denture adhesives, pain rubs and geriatric vitamins, you now have a very different reader profile.

You can tell much more than the age of your intended readers, determining their spending habits, their lifestyle choices (spotting smoking ads to diet fads) and their commitment to personal improvement (by witnessing things like foreign language tapes and self-help books being advertised). If you see a lot of time-saving devices pitched on the magazine's pages, your readers lead hectic lives. And if you see exotic travel opportunities, then you know they are an active crowd.

What the ads don't tell you, the magazine's media kit often will. Advertising sales representatives use media kits to sell the ad space. These kits often contain important demographic studies, editorial calendars, readership surveys, competitive breakdowns, circulation figures and more. If you work in advertising, or you know someone who does, request a media kit. If you can't do that, offer to purchase a media kit, which is usually available to writers for only a few dollars.

All of these insights tell you where your magazine reader is today. But as Peter Jacobi, author of *The Magazine Article: How to Think It, Plan It, Write It* (Writer's Digest Books), writes, "Teach yourself to be sensitive to what's ahead, to what will be on readers' minds six or eight months from now, to what people will be doing or talking about when the article is published."

Once you have a grasp of the reader, get to know the others who produce the magazine each month. Read the editor's column for tone and clues to the magazine's content. Search the table of contents. Review the masthead and check the bylines of the writers. This will tell you if the publication is primarily staff-written or freelance based. Read the short bios accompanying the writers' articles, for this tells you whether your background is similar to theirs. Review the articles other contributors have written. If you answer, "I could have written that," . . . well, maybe you could have. Finally, analyze the cover copy to determine where the magazine puts its emphasis. Cover blurbs say, "Buy me!" to the browsing eye, and if they do their jobs correctly, they make people pull out their wallets and plunk down several dollars for information they simply must have now.

Once you've studied your magazine's market, it's time to study the writer's guidelines, to understand the editor's preferences as well as dos and don'ts. Guidelines tell what kinds of articles are most sought and what material will be automatically returned, what kind of rights the magazine buys, the research required, and sometimes, the payment that's offered. With an SASE, these guidelines can be yours, free of charge.

WRITING THE QUERY LETTER

To query is to ask, and query letters have become the industry-accepted approach of contacting editors and pitching ideas. Query letters are your foot in the door to a particular publication. They represent your writing ability and challenge you to express your thoughts succinctly and persuasively. Mere summaries of your article they are not, for good queries excite an editor to learn more about your subject. They also inspire the editor to have confidence in your ability to handle a topic and carry through a marketable magazine concept.

There are excellent books on the matter of querying editors, with Lisa Collier Cool's *How to Write Irresistible Query Letters* (Writer's Digest Books) and Gordon Burgett's *The Writer's Guide to Query Letters & Cover Letters* (Prima Publishing) among them. Most professionals agree that queries need to hook the editor who has the power to assign or reject.

Remember my sixth W—who cares? If no one cares about the topic you want to pursue, you've got a problem from the start. So what's the point? Will the reader clip this article and post it on the refrigerator? Is there a service-orientation that draws the reader into this article idea—something that makes a person healthier, wealthier, wiser, happier or more attractive? In short, how can readers make whatever it is you offer useful in their personal lives?

Writers who have trouble portraying the service-oriented qualities of their ideas can propose visuals that may help the magazine's editors (and readers) grasp the material. If you feel that charts, photographs, illustrations, sidebars or subheadings would make your information clearer to all concerned, say so.

Another element of the query letter is the point of view or perspective that you bring to the subject you want to write about. Even though magazines are much more subjective than newspapers, you'll still need to cite examples and sources.

What are your qualifications? Do you have advanced degrees, personal experience or friends in high places that allow you access to the information and insights you'll express? Could any writer write this piece? If so, why should the editor assign it to you? And why should the editor run this article now (or in the next six months)?

In one of my queries to the *Saturday Evening Post*, I pitched the idea of Pittsburgh, its parks and its family-oriented attractions. It was an article that could have run at any time, but since one of the parks featured the only life-sized Neighborhood of Make-Believe, I suggested that the article run to coincide with the twenty-fifth anniversary of Mr. Roger's Neighborhood. The article was published and paid for much sooner with that timely tie-in.

And speaking of timeliness, any editor will want to know, "when can I have this on my desk?" Let your editor know that you can deliver in two weeks or two months. Keep the tone of your letter conversational, but remember who you're writing to. Don't be cute or overly familiar, unless you've struck a rapport with this editor through prior work. Finally, after researching your market and crafting your query, don't forget to actually *ask* for the assignment. Simply state, "If this idea fits with your editorial plans, I hope you'll assign the article to me."

Query letters must be accompanied by an SASE and clippings, if you have never written for the editor or publication before (or even recently). A few clippings should suffice. Certainly send no more than four, and try to send only those that relate to what you wish to write about.

Writers should reference anyone who referred them to the publication (if another staffer or contributor said to use their names) or where they originally met or spoke with this editor. Query letters should *not* mention why you have become a writer, what you'd like to be paid, your opinion about the magazine (whether good or bad), descriptions of courses you've taken, facts that bear no foundation or footnotes to the facts you cite. In addition, writers should not request critiques, demand unreasonably quick responses or advertise their lack of writing experience. Let's face it, if you were the editor and a writer said, "I've never written for publication before, but . . ." would that line instill confidence in you?

Once you've written the best query letter you can, type it on stationery, following the approach of a standard letter. Keep the query to one page, if possible, but do not go beyond two. You'll be sending clippings and an SASE in your package, so you'll probably want to use an 8½″ × 11″ manila envelope. Type a label and neatly affix it. Clip to your letter a business card, if you have one, and you're ready for the post office.

RESPONSES YOU'LL RECEIVE

Waiting the obligatory six to eight weeks for a reply will be your next big challenge. But if you want to maximize your profits, you'll put the query out of mind and move on to other money-making projects, including new and different queries to other magazines.

The day will come, though, when your mail carrier leaves that reply you're looking for. I know the feeling of uneasiness I get when I spot that SASE in my mailbox. My heart races for a brief second while I think, "Oh no . . . here comes another rejection." Indeed, that's the way it is sometimes. Editors reject ideas for all sorts of legitimate reasons. Know, however, that if your editor has taken the time to pass along a personal comment, a reason for the rejection, you should pay attention. Read it twice. Save it. And if your editor asks for more information, chances are good there's a level of interest you can build on. Your editor often needs to justify to other colleagues why he or she should go with your query. If there is such a note, it could very well be telling you "work with me on this one." Go the extra mile, with more research and answers to any questions.

On other occasions, I've been happily greeted with a go-ahead. Usually, I'll get a hastily scrawled note on my letter indicating suggestions. Sometimes these will be outlined in a more formal letter, with mentions of who takes care of expenses, what the word count and deadline should be and how the copy should be submitted. Sometimes, that handwritten note has appeared on a form letter, used for all replies to freelance writers. Still other times, my editor simply phones me, passing along important assignment information during our conversation.

If your editor has assigned the article to you, there should also be mention of a kill fee, should the editor deem your article unfit for publication. Especially in tough economic times, when magazines shrink on account of insufficient advertising, it's important to negotiate a kill fee. If it's your first time writing for the publication or this editor, however, it's best not to mention a kill fee if you're writing on spec.

WRITING FOR PUBLICATION

The essentials of journalistic writing (chapter four) apply to magazine articles, just as they do to newspapers. Hooking your reader with a clever angle or lead is the first step (see chapter ten). You can't write an engaging lead without fully understanding the intended audience and the magazine's concept. Next comes building a sentence structure that's varied, rich with active voice and lean on clichés. Watch your use of repetitive phrases or words and weed them out.

If you assume anything of your readers, assume that they know nothing about your subject. Check all facts, and be sure to show instead of tell, citing examples, quoting resources and including anecdotes whenever possible. Finish the sentence: "If there's one thing I want my readers to gain from this, it's _____?" You fill in the blank.

Chapter three of this book described the manuscript mechanics. Aim for clean, error-free copy. Even if a publication's guidelines allow for handwritten corrections, always type or print out a fresh copy. Your finished article should be as near letter quality as it can get. Sufficient white space attracts the eye so be sure to include at least an inch margin all around the page. Don't forget your name, address and phone number, just in case your manuscript gets separated from your cover letter.

EDITORS AND THEIR PET PEEVES

Writers need editors just as much (if not more) than editors need writers. We freelancers often lapse into thinking that we could get published so much faster without that wieldy red pen. Nothing could be further from the truth. Editors improve our work and offer valuable suggestions that help us ultimately create further sales. If nothing more, just getting to know them keeps us from committing a whole host of unpardonable sins.

Witness what falls on top of most editors' desks each day and you would understand why it's a tough sell to convince these publishing partners of our worth. For starters, writers often submit their work to editors having never read a word of the magazine they hope to write for.

During my brief stint as an editor of a subscription newsletter, I was continually amazed by people who would write with off-the-wall ideas. I had one writer who always sent me health articles. Another sent me a copy of his hitchhiking book. I published a communications newsletter! My subtitle indicated this. So did my guidelines and my listing in *Writer's Market*. These writers never studied a back issue, or they would have known.

At *Elegant Bride*, editor Jackie Barrett-Hirschhaut says, "What bothers me the most are queries and/or manuscripts that are laughably inappropriate for my magazine. These submissions are purely based upon what the writer perceives the title of my magazine and its content to be, and they are a waste of that writer's energy and my own."

Barrett-Hirschhaut also advises writers to avoid simultaneous submissions to competing publications. When questioning whether you should make submissions this way, ask yourself, "What if two editors would want this?" If they would, you will have wasted one more editor's time, and run the risk of offending each of them, severing all chances of publishing your idea.

If you've studied a publication, chances are good you've pondered a few of the competitors' magazines as well. Another mistake freelancers make is submitting a query or manuscript similar to one recently published by a competitor. Unless it's a hot topic that everyone's talking about, let some time lapse before sending in such a suggestion.

Querying by phone and submitting completed articles on spec (when query letters are preferred) are two more sins. Arguing with an editor is absolute nonsense. Editors know the magazine's readers much better than you do, and if they don't, you probably won't be talking with them twice.

Sending correspondence and manuscripts that aren't readable ranks high among the irritating factors, so dispense with the shiny paper and the gimmicky fonts. They'll make you look foolish. And for everyone's sake, including the employees in the magazine's mailroom, please get your editor's name right. A quick phone call to the reception desk will verify whether editors listed in a directory still work in these capacities, whether they have moved on to other jobs or whether they've been dead for ten years. If you can't be trusted to look up the editor's name and spelling, how can you be trusted to get the facts straight if you're assigned an article? Barrett-Hirschhaut receives a lot of computer-generated queries in which writers forget to change another editor's name. The trust factor surfaces again.

Finally, editors will not appreciate your sob stories. Not one of them wants to hear why you desperately need this assignment and what bills you have to pay. The following letter came to me while I was publishing my newsletter:

> Many of us who graduated from college in 1992 have spent many months either looking for that ideal position or inching along in a job we hate. I graduated with a journalism degree from Syracuse a bit unaware of the horrible economy I faced. So when the going got tough, I decided to leave the country!

What this says is that when the going gets tough, this writer quits. The young woman went on to tell me that she'd be working in Taiwan but since she wasn't settled, it would be hard to tell exactly what angle she would take. She wrote, "perhaps you would have specific ideas to fit a certain issue." You bet I did! They were focused, outlined and presented professionally. The letter got even better, as this writer wanted to learn my reaction and said *I* could reach her at the addresses and phone numbers she included . . . in Taiwan! As if I were going to spend money on overseas postage, plus come up with her angle.

In the end, this writer did one thing we freelancers aim for — she sent me a letter I'll keep in perpetuity. But I kept it because it made me laugh. Unless you specialize in comedy writing, trust me that this is not the effect you want to achieve.

CLIMBING OUT OF THE SLUSH PILE

Your goal is to keep your letter at the top of your editor's in-box, and since the market is highly competitive, you need every advantage.

Start by generating ideas worth reading. Newspaper writers aren't as dependent on the steady stream of ideas that magazine writers are. After all, what is news in any given day determines what they will write about. We freelancers, on the other hand, must keep constant track of our ideas, often looking at our own lives. In my career, I've written about wedding planning, pregnancy discrimination, nepotism, parenting, family stress and travel-related issues, and I haven't had to look far to research many of these. I jot these ideas in notebooks or on scraps of paper, later analyzing them for where they might fit. Make that match based on the idea but also the style and voice of the magazines you have in mind.

Second, read outstanding magazines. Read widely, for if you are to succeed as a magazine writer, you'll need money coming in from several publications, not just one or two. Note the structure these articles take, the length, anecdotes, transitional devices, resources tapped into and the angle taken. Ask yourself: "What made this article work for me?"

Once you've begun writing, ask what you could do to improve on your piece? Could photographs add to the appeal? Could quotes make it stronger? Would a different angle be more appropriate? Finally, be open to your editors' suggestions, remembering that she knows the reader's tolerance level. She knows what's a turnoff and what will make a person throw down the magazine in disgust (or cancel a subscription).

HOW TO GET STARTED

Magazine writing offers a breadth of opportunity that few other writing specialties have. For every writer's interest, there's probably a magazine to match it. By writing well, you'll build up a supply of impressive clips which will lead to future sales in better paying markets.

• Collect sample copies of recently published magazines. To keep your business expenses low, ask friends to save those they subscribe to. Visit your library to peruse this month's issue on reserve. See if you (or people in your family) are eligible for student or group discounts to the magazines you've targeted.

• Gain a market edge as you develop an intuitive feel for what the reader will be coping with six, nine or even twelve months down the road. Read back issues to know where the reader is now. Keep up with trends to predict the future.

• Keep your query active, convincing your editor to use you.

• Weave into your query or manuscript sources you'll cite. Use authorities and statistics that display a national treatment to your topic, not just local appeal.

• Be patient in your response from editors. Expect a form reply, not a "how've you been getting along" letter.

• Never sell all rights in your effort to get published. Watch to see if your work is reprinted in future editions. Even the most conscientious editor can forget to put through a check request for your reprints.

Chapter Twelve

Travel Writing and Photography

When I wanted to write magazine features, I remembered the old adage: Write about what you know. I loved to travel, planning family vacations years in advance. Travel writing soon gave me my start in freelancing.

Travel destination pieces provide reliable, useful information. They are indeed another example of service-oriented journalism, for they lend a hand, lead the way and conjure up images that people use to vicariously visit the places you have explored. Travel writing, however, requires a few more skills than the basic magazine or newspaper feature involves.

A sense of adventure is high on the list. If you return to the same locales, year after year, travel writing, as a specialty, may not be for you. Travel writers must be willing to venture into the unknown. Usually, the rewards are very high. If it hadn't been for my honeymoon travel writing, I would never have visited Mexico, Hawaii or Jamaica. These destinations were not high on my "must see" list. Now, seeing all that they offer for couples and families, I'm trying to convince my husband why we must program these destinations into our vacation schedule.

Travel writing requires enormous energy. Most people go away to kick back, relax and read a book, but the travel writer always wants to do more than time allows, seeing everything, taking notes and asking a myriad of questions. Here's where organization enters in. Without knowing what your story requires and what you're capable of cramming into a few short days, the travel may turn out to be useless and the writing painfully difficult.

You'll have to make decisions. You'll have to say "no," to yourself and to others who insist you see this or venture off to that. At times, you'll have to be assertive, and most definitely, outgoing. Imagine asking a gentleman if he'd kindly move out of your frame of view for the perfect picture or asking the waitress if you can keep the menu for your research. Imagine telling Aunt Millie and Uncle Harold you just don't want to spend a day at the beach, insisting that you must research.

Travel writing takes a bit of self-confidence. If you're low on this quality as you start out, rest assured it will increase as you complete each trip. Persevere. That's what it's all about. Editors will reject your ideas, as they will in any form of writing, but it doesn't mean your favorite vacation spot is no good. It just means it might be a harder sell.

That's why turning family vacations into salable travel articles isn't as easy as people assume. Yeah, it's nice to have relatives in California, Vail, Colorado, or right outside Orlando, but these destinations have been done. It's easy for editors to pass your ideas off as "just another California query." If you want to make a living at travel writing, count on becoming independent in your search for new and different locales. Ultimately, you may need to travel alone or along with a group of other writers to get to the places people want to read about.

TRAVEL MARKETS AVAILABLE

The glossy travel magazines are obvious targets for your travel writing talents, but don't limit your search to these. Take a look at camping, motor club and airline publications. Women's and men's magazines as well as parenting and bridal publications feature travel aimed at specific readers. Regional magazines like quick and easy escapes. Travel newsletters keep diehard travellers informed by telling where to go, where to stay and eat, and what the prices are. And while many newspapers supplement their Sunday travel sections with wire service stories, these editors occasionally look for the freelance piece to add to the editorial mix.

When the family vacation ideas have been used up, and you can't afford any more independent journeys write about what lies close to home. Your city, town or state might be of great interest to other would-be travellers. When Pittsburgh opened its brand new airport, I pitched articles on my hometown all year long. Several sales followed.

Don't overlook business travel either. If you jet off to Cincinnati each Monday morning or visit the nation's capitol every other month, write about these cities from different angles, starting with the business traveller or first-time visitor in mind.

If you love writing about travel, broaden your income base by writing marketing brochure copy or by handling public relations responsibilities for travel and hospitality clients. You'd be writing about the same topics, only on the client side (not as a media representative).

If you're comfortable speaking before a group and can offer excellent photography, travelogues also bring in extra cash. And if you have a certain level of expertise and extensive knowledge of one locale, guidebook editing could earn you even more money. Contact the editors at publishing houses handling these books (and review chapters eight and twenty).

LANDING TRAVEL ASSIGNMENTS

Travel writers submit a story on spec or query with their ideas. As we learned in the previous chapter, querying cuts out unnecessary work and leads to a better reputation among editors.

But when you query, don't just offer to write a 1200-word feature on Florida. Tell your editor what's unique about the destination (and yes, Florida will be a tougher sell). What's your angle? Why would readers like your article? Is it timely? If so, why? Whom will you interview? What can your readers expect to do or see that they haven't done somewhere else?

Keep your query letter active. This strategy helps maintain the momentum your editor will require just to sit and read your idea, let alone assign you a story. Research what the editor has recently run, what the editorial calendar calls for and which advertisers support the publication. If you need to review these skills, refer to the previous chapter.

Once you've established yourself with an editor, you won't need to sell him or her too hard. Sometimes a phone call will suffice when you receive a press trip invitation or your family plans to attend a wedding seven states away. I've often called editors I regularly work with to get a feel for their interest. If they've already assigned that destination to another writer or if they have no advertising to support such a feature, they'll tell me. I save querying time, and I spare them opening unnecessary mail. But only call an editor when you've established that kind of rapport.

ORGANIZED PRESS TRIPS

After I wrote some travel articles, an editor asked if I'd like to travel to Mexico — three cities, for a week, with all expenses paid. At first, I thought, "Who, me?" Then, my reply: "Of course!"

Next, came trepidation. What was a press trip? Who were these "other writers" going to be? I remember having lunch with a friend who allayed my fears. "You're ready for this," Tony said. "You'll do fine." And he was right. Like me, you might receive a call someday asking you to represent your publication; like me, you might have a lot of questions.

Similar to the "fam" or familiarization trips travel agents take, a press trip means travelling with a group of writers or media people. Such trips are sponsored by government tourist boards, their public relations firms or hotel properties, hoping you will visit a city, a country or a ten-story high-rise hotel. You are the link to their general public.

When it comes to making arrangements, you usually don't have to do anything more than open a suitcase as someone representing the client will call you, forward your airline tickets, send press kits and possibly packing information. The account exec should notify you what is and isn't complimentary. Some meals, taxi fares, beverages, mini-bar, room service charges and tipping are often left up to you. But, as glamorous, as easy and as inexpensive as these trips might seem, they are indeed work. They aren't free vacations.

Writing for a bridal magazine, I can't complain when it comes to the trips I'm offered and the places I visit. After all, people don't normally spend their honeymoons in cold, dark, desolate locations. They usually head for sunshine in some tropical locale. But on many of these press trips, I can remember seeing more hotel rooms than I needed to know about and driving past patches of pure white sand, where unlike everyone else taking the plunge into turquoise waters, I took notes. Talk about vicarious experiences!

When travelling as a group, each writer's requirements will

differ. Writers on assignment for travel agent publications need to tour all those hotel rooms the same as food critics need to sample restaurants. It seems like photographers stop at every point to snap a shot. This all takes time out of a limited schedule, so review your itinerary ahead of time to decide if the trip is right for you.

Press Trip Perils

A trip's success depends, in large part, upon those leading it. I've been on great press trips as well as terrible ones. Most hosts are extremely accommodating. On my visit to Peter Island, I warmly remember the general manager rising at an obnoxious hour to join me for coffee, say good-bye and see that I left without a hitch. But ask seasoned travel writers about their experiences, and many will blame the disappointing ones on the account executive or the client who made (or didn't make) things happen. I remember four days in Acapulco — four days I'd just as soon forget.

Writing for newly married couples, I usually need to experience the shopping scene, for my readers want to bring back special mementos. Some want to complete china patterns or purchase decorative accents for their first homes. Another writer sought to research a shopping sidebar, so the two of us spoke up. The client was willing to show us some of her favorite shops, but the account exec herded us into a van and insisted we visit a fort. Now, there are worthwhile forts in this world, but this wasn't one of them, certainly not one I would recommend to honeymooners.

Life those four days was a mad dash all over Acapulco. In the end, this young man ignored not only our professional needs, but made no allowances for the bad cold I was struggling with and showed a blatant disregard for the physical challenges of another writer in our group. By showing such insensitivity to us and our readers, he cemented a very negative impression when his job was to do just the opposite.

I tell you this story to give you the full spectrum of experiences you might run into. To avoid such mishaps, specify your needs ahead of time. Now, when I receive that first phone call I say, "I'd really appreciate a few hours to explore my reader's interests, but I don't want to inconvenience the group. Do you think that will be a problem?" By asserting my needs like this, I've found that I can get a lot more accomplished.

Press Trip Etiquette

I must balance the picture here. I know plenty of account execs who have their own horror stories regarding us writers. Some of our comrades can be downright unpleasant, even rude. I've seen writers show off and drink too much. One even stashed a native woman in his hotel room, and brought her along for a free meal with the group! Then, there is always the constant complainer or the lonely writer who spills out his life's story. One of my editors remembers a freelancer who appeared at an official grand opening reception dressed in shorts, T-shirt and a baseball cap, without even remembering her shoes. Not only did she forget footwear, but she was oblivious to the fact that government officials and tourism representatives were among the honored guests. Remember that you're representing your publication, whether you travel with a group or on your own. Word of such behaviors can always get back to your editor who will *not* be impressed.

As many account executives have told me, finding writers to take press trips is never a problem, but finding the right group of writers often is. When you accept the invitation to join the group, you are indirectly agreeing to attend dinners and meet with tourist board officials and hotel managers. Expect a certain amount of this on every press trip, but as I indicated previously, the better itineraries balance mandatory meetings with individual exploration. If your assignment is so specialized that it requires a totally independent experience, perhaps the public relations firm can help you arrange an individual trip (although travelling with a press group is usually a lot less expensive for you and your publication).

MAKING TRAVEL PLANS

Should you opt for the independent journey, keep the costs down by contacting the airlines and asking for complimentary airfare. Because requests from writers are so numerous, many airlines have policies against granting free airfare, preferring to work only with organized press groups. Others, however, will at least help you obtain the lowest priced airfare for that route.

Booking hotel rooms is a little easier. Most hotel managers will arrange for two or three nights to be "comped." You pay for any additional nights or you stay at another hotel for a few more. I've known writers who do this, and not only does it keep their expenses low, but staying in more than one hotel gives them a better overview of the choices their readers will face. Ask for complimentary admission to theatres, parks, museums and other establishments. Public relations coordinators at these facilities will understand your needs and go out of their way to help you. Write to them, send clips and introduce yourself.

When making plans, it's advisable to have your editor write a generic assignment letter, asking people in the industry for their assistance with your research. Send this along with your letters. Also, know your magazine's circulation and your article's approximate publication date. If you're covering the cost of the trip yourself, check to see if you can file an expense report. If so, keep careful receipts and keep expenses to a minimum. Your editor will appreciate your concern for the publication's budget.

THE SPONSORED TRAVEL DEBATE

Travel writing probably sounds great so far, and I hear you saying that a few meals and cab fares won't break the bank. But some newspapers and magazines (usually larger papers in metropolitan cities) won't accept sponsored travel. They view it as a conflict of interest, afraid you'll feel bought and render a less than truthful account of your travels. What's at issue, I think, should be the individual writer's integrity, not who paid the bill. A sponsored trip or a complimentary admission isn't accepted in exchange for a rave review. It's accepted as part of a writer's research.

I understand that my job as a travel writer is to produce favorable copy, but if I spot a serious problem with a product, I will not lie to my readers. I've seen children's facilities that weren't safe and attractions that were a waste of a consumer's money. While some judgments are a matter of opinion, I'm talking about those that blatantly stand out. I share these findings with my readers, steering them to better experiences. As a concerned journalist and parent, I once wrote a personal note to a ship's safety engineer, warning him of a potential hazard. Honesty is my job, and I take my responsibility seriously. Every writer should.

If you want to sell to a publication with policies against sponsored travel, negotiate a press rate if that's acceptable or ask if the publication can pick up your expenses. Barring these solutions, write the expenses off your business income, but do consult your tax advisor first.

PACKING AND PLANNING

If you think getting ready for vacation was a chore, just add the business element to your travel plans. Understandably, you'll need to pack a few extra things.

I always pack a carry-on bag with reading material, plenty of business cards, a travel office kit, a notebook and my camera equipment. I'm one of those people you never want to get behind at airport security as I always request a hand inspection of my film (multiple x-rays can destroy it). I also use a handbag that's big enough to accommodate my camera, just in case I'm in an area where I don't want to advertise it strung around my neck. Men can use a backpack or some other means of concealment, but I'd advise against the typical consumer camera cases most vacationers use. They seem to spell tourist, and we all know criminals seek these souls out.

I also try to stock up on film in the United States, as foreign prices can be outrageous. I always carry medications to combat stomach or intestinal ailments, especially when visiting countries with questionable water treatment. For sea travel, I recommend prescription patches to combat queasiness, and of course, plenty of sunscreen for tropical locales (and even snow-covered areas, where the sun's reflection can be harsh). If you're laid up with any kind of ailment, you miss valuable research time.

Finally, unless you live near a major gateway, you'll need to make frequent airline connections. I can remember flying from Pittsburgh to Chicago enroute to San Juan and Tortola. (Figure out that back-tracking!) The more connections you make, the greater the chance your luggage may get lost. Always pack a change of clothes and some toiletries in your carry-on bag. All travel writers should renew their passports and carry these with them (even though a birth certificate is acceptable for some destinations). At this writing, passports are good for ten years.

In the suitcase I check through, I often pack an extra piece of luggage, the collapsible kind, in case I have additional press materials or even purchases to carry back home. Other useful items include a handheld tape recorder, extra batteries, guidebooks, and of course, the appropriate clothing. Remember the story my editor told. If you're travelling with an organized trip, ask your account executive what clothing will be required. Otherwise, pack things to mix and match, items that don't wrinkle or those that can be washed by hand. Comfortable shoes are a must for travel writers who will spend a great deal of time on their feet.

TAKING THE TRIP

If you've packed well, organized the research materials and personal items you need, you're all set. Mentally record everything, and write things down when you can. Always carry your notebook and camera. To write about the richness and scenery that surrounds you, you'll have to observe and record what others take for granted.

Don't be afraid to ask questions, especially of certified tour guides, account executives or the clients themselves. Talk with other visitors you may encounter when shopping, eating or waiting around the hotel lobby. Pick up literature whenever it's available. Don't be shy.

Of course, travel safely. Don't venture into areas you know you shouldn't. Drink and eat in moderation, especially if you're not used to the cuisine or the water. And try as best you can to develop the spirit of mañana, whenever it's called for. There's a lot to do in limited time. In many areas outside America, life moves at a much slower pace. Do as the natives do and you won't risk being labelled the fussy American.

Above all, allow yourself to experience the destination you've come to discover. Sink your toes into the sand, shop at the local markets, try the native dishes, absorb the local ambiance and get all the facts right the first time. It's much easier and a lot less expensive than visiting a second time. Such pursuits are easier when you're on your own, but when travelling as a group, ask if some independent time will be a problem. Experiencing the destination as thoroughly as possible is sure to please the editor you're writing for.

WRITING THE TRAVEL ARTICLE

Write according to the wishes of your editor. That means sticking to the established word count and including any information and interviews requested of you. Of course, double-check all facts.

But beyond the basics, write with the goal of showing versus telling. Take the reader with you, using action verbs that put the reader in your shoes, careening down the last dip of that roller coaster, skipping along the waves in the catamaran or drowning yourself in the sun's rays on the Lido deck. Leave out hackneyed expressions and popular clichés (i.e., watch those similes and metaphors).

Steer readers away from disappointing experiences. If an incident was so bad it was laughable, laugh with it. Putting unfortunate incidents into a humorous light gets your point across without being blatantly offensive. After all, you want readers to set down the article and feel as if they've learned something significant.

Today, many editors require writers to include truly useful information within the context of their articles. Others prefer to see information such as restaurant and hotel options, airline gate cities, money exchange tips and customs allotments placed in a sidebar. Still other editors require the personal touch added to stories. Here, writing from press materials and guidebooks just won't do. These editors are looking for first-person experiences to shine through and add dimension to your work.

Finally, when you title your travel article, think of that title as a cover blurb. How will it play? Will it entice readers to buy the magazine? If not, work on it a little longer.

PHOTOGRAPHY PAYS

Not only does photography supplement your writing income, but it's also required by an increasing number of editors. Some editors will not even touch a manuscript that's not submitted with photography. Thus, crisp, clear 35mm slides or newspaper black-and-whites often clinch the sale.

Photography adds immediacy to your article. It conveys an ambiance that sometimes cannot be achieved through words alone. And photography provided by the writer saves the editor or art director a great deal of time searching for ways to illustrate your story.

Writing a travel article requires a certain amount of visual thinking to begin with. So if you can learn to think this way, you can turn this talent into a profitable side business selling photography. And it doesn't require hundreds of dollars to start out.

Visit a reputable camera dealer and check out the range of cameras available. Most travel writers prefer a single lens reflex (SLR) with interchangeable lenses, but I've known many writers who achieve equivalent sales using automatic 35mm models. These "idiot cameras" (as they're called by the pros) choose your shutter speed and aperture opening and frame the shot for you. If that's how you must begin, so be it. With time, your talents will improve and you'll grow to the next level of sophistication.

As you try to increase your photographic and sales potential, consider cameras you can add extra equipment to. While the basic telephoto lens suited me fine for family vacations, I discovered the benefits of a zoom when I began travel writing in earnest. If you take a lot of action shots, an automatic rewinder is a must. If you do a lot of indoor work, purchase fancier flashes. Analyze what you think you'll need, talk with other photojournalists and seek the advice of trusted dealers. Salespeople may try to charm you with more than you need, but if they understand you are a professional just starting out, they'll stand to gain a lot more by winning your trust. Convince them of this.

If you really want to delve into photography, enroll in a noncredit class instructed by a professional photographer. Here, you'll learn how to choose equipment as well as how to light your subject, frame your shots, and produce images that create a sense of place. When you buy your camera, it's a good idea to purchase a full-size book (to supplement the guide that comes with your camera) for it will provide plenty of tips.

But when you're winging it, without the help of a pro or the guidance of a reference book, remember a few basics. First, editors love color. Given the choice between a brown building and a bright red one, go for the red. It adds to the appeal.

Second, take action shots. Just as your words must show instead of tell, so must your photography. Avoid the images of people stiffly posed along the wall. Instead, photograph your subjects doing what comes naturally. If they work in an office, catch them looking over papers or chatting with a colleague. If they instruct parasailing, snap a shot of them in the air, not propped next to their parasail. Also, watch your background and keep it free of clutter that distracts from your subject.

Next, don't overlook variety. Take sufficient photographs from various angles and viewpoints. Invariably, when I show my travel slides to family, someone always asks why I've taken so many shots of the same thing. To the casual viewer, this may seem like an utter waste of film, but for me, it beats losing out on an important sale. So shoot as much film as you want, as it's better (and less expensive) than repeating your trip. Also, don't neglect to take a number of vertical slides. This gives the art director many options to choose from, and verticals are crucial if you want to be considered for cover artwork.

Provide captions and obtain releases to send with your photographs. *Photographer's Market* tells whether model releases are required. As a rule of thumb, if a person is recognizable, or if the shot would be used in advertising, you should obtain a release. Some photojournalists worry with releases only for U.S. citizens, but use your best judgment and your publication's guidelines to decide.

There are plenty of travel writing books, but my pick is *A Guide to Travel Writing & Photography* by Ann and Carl Purcell (Writer's Digest Books). The illustrations and color photographs don't just tell; they show you what's required every step of the way.

HOW TO GET STARTED

Travel writing provides an imaginary escape for readers and another source of revenue for magazine and newspaper writers. As in all types of feature writing, remember that while amateurs write and then sell, professionals do just the opposite.

• Look for a niche in the travel market that's waiting to be filled — from the single crowd to senior citizens. Approach editors with specific angles in mind.

• Avoid destinations that have been done repeatedly. Instead, venture into unfamiliar territory.

• Focus your queries on destinations that have sufficient advertising in the magazine or newspaper. Top priority is often given to queries that stroke the advertisers.

• Seek out the public relations contacts for the destinations you'd like to write about, introduce yourself and ask about up-coming press trips.

  • Network with others in the travel writing industry. Send to the Society of American Travel Writers (based in Washington, D.C.), and ask for an application packet and explore the benefits of membership.

Chapter Thirteen

Radio and Television

I f you live near radio and television outlets, writing for broadcast audiences may provide steady work and income. Radio and television stations, as well as cable companies, are in constant need of advertising copy and continuity. Any of these outlets may need you to write editorials, documentaries or public service messages.

Stations with active news departments require competent broadcast journalists, and as discussed in chapter five, radio stations frequently use freelance-written one-liners to fill the air during morning and afternoon drive times. Beginning broadcasters and freelance writers have a better shot at these opportunities in the smaller markets, but if you've got the talent, nothing should stop you from aiming for larger stations.

CONTINUITY—AT THE BASE OF BROADCASTING

In a broad sense, the word *continuity* encompasses all short, non-programmatic broadcast-related material. This description includes commercials, public service announcements (PSAs), program promotions, station identification, time/weather announcements and anything else that fills the air between programs.

At radio stations, disc jockeys are responsible for writing their own merges from one sound to another, known in the industry as segues. Without these fillers, dead air results. Dead air gets noticed fast as it interrupts the flow of music and voice that our ears take for granted as we tune in to our favorite stations. It turns legitimate radio into an amateur hour routine in the minds of listeners. For these reasons, every on-air personality or journalist seeks to avoid dead air.

At large commercial radio stations, much of the broadcast material is written in-house by the program director or other employees who may wear many hats at the station. The best way for a would-be continuity writer to break into the business is to give it a try. If you work at a broadcast station in a nonwriting capacity, volunteer to write copy or submit pretend pieces to demonstrate your talent. If it's used, you will have taken a load off someone else's shoulders and no doubt made a favorable impression. Freelance writers can use the same tactic, particularly in small markets where budgets are lean and staffs small.

Unfortunately, the copywriter's work often airs without attribution, something most writers desire. It's the price writers pay for job security and a steady paycheck, if they're lucky enough to land a full-time, part-time or retainer-type work arrangement. To beat the anonymity, you'll have to build a portfolio to make it in the broadcast business. If you have a good voice to supplement your writing skills, put together a demo tape displaying both qualities. In either case, devote some time to writing and recording speculative pieces to add to this collection, and you'll get your name known. Try your hand at jingles, stations IDs, time/weather segments, PSAs, advertising and other copy as a way of broadening your talents and income base. This is a competitive industry, but if you're determined and talented, you'll usually accomplish your goals.

WRITING ON-AIR COPY

If building a portfolio of broadcast-related material sounds similar to the clippings you use to seek feature writing assignments and commercial work for clients, you're half right. The idea is the same, but the way you go about it is very different.

Do writers have a hard time switching between print journalism and broadcast style? "All the time," says Kenny Woods, assistant program director at WWSW Radio in Pittsburgh. "It's pretty difficult to boil down what you want to say in ten or fifteen seconds. You're constantly editing your edits." Woods's station has gone through several format changes, but in each case the writing has gotten tighter, resembling a form of headline news in many respects. So how does the writer master the difference in style? If you can remember the four Cs of broadcast copywriting, you'll be well on your way.

Clear, concise, conversational and correct—these elements are vital to everything the broadcast copywriter produces. Whereas the reader of your magazine feature can refer to specific passages, savoring them over and over, listeners cannot. They have one chance, often a slim one of less than thirty seconds, to grasp all the material you present. So the writer must strive for clarity not only for the listener but also for the announcer interpreting the written copy. To create good copy follow a few rules:

Use punctuation as a major writing tool. Punctuation plays the role of stage directions where your words are concerned. Take the question mark, for example. Realize that any sentence topped off with a question mark elicits an upward inflection. Keep your questions short so that the announcer perceives the question and prepares to use the inflection in his delivery. The same goes for the exclamation mark. Use it sparingly, for special situations that call for that hint of excitement.

Commas function in broadcast copy just as they do in print. They indicate a separation of words or clauses. But more importantly, the comma adds a short breathing space that enables talent to read copy clearly and conversationally.

Semicolons come to the rescue when conciseness counts. Use semicolons between main clauses with a single thought, and use them to take the place of the word wasters *and, but, for, or.*

Quotations are generally used more sparingly in broadcasting than in print, and mostly, in news copy (covered later in this chapter). Avoid quotation marks when indicating dialogue by using the colon after a speaker's name. It's much easier to read aloud. Colons also signal that a long list of items may follow. Thus, announcers can pace themselves accordingly. Use quotation marks around nicknames or names of ships, planes or spacecraft, only when they aid in the announcer's understanding of the copy.

Dashes can also be substituted to set off quotations as these are more easily understood by announcers. For example:

Campaigning today, presidential candidate Ross Perot likened the federal deficit to—and I quote—that crazy aunt you keep in the basement—unquote.

Dashes have always indicated a pause, and in broadcast copy, this device is especially meaningful. Dashes separate single words or phrases and add an element of hesitancy when needed.

Since an ellipsis indicates a break, they should be avoided except when material has been omitted, and you, the writer, need to indicate this.

Underline words requiring special emphasis rather than using the visually distracting italic type. And whereas readers read information contained in parentheses as side notes, parentheses set off technical instructions or phonetic pronunciations for the announcer. In broadcasting, information contained within parentheses is *not* meant to be read aloud.

Finally, the period differs in its punctuation role as well. Imagine writing a sentence, an incomplete one, and ending it with a period. Wouldn't your English teacher cringe? Well, in broadcasting, this is the accepted style. If the sense and flow of a grammatically incomplete sentence enables it to be remembered, put the period after it and be proud of it.

But use periods with extreme caution when they can be easily misinterpreted. Announcers can easily get tripped up if writers aren't careful. For instance, "Dr." can stand for drive, as in a residential street, or a courtesy title of a medical or academic professional. That leads to the next dictate.

Avoid abbreviations. Never abbreviate a word if it's intended to be read in full. For instance, you wouldn't want the announcer to read:

Nov. 22, 1963—A Day Americans Wept With One Another

Instead, write out the word "November." The same applies to days of the week, military ranks, titles and states.

However, just as in print journalism, it's acceptable to refer to an institution by its recognizable initials upon subsequent references. While the announcer may first read "Central Intelligence Agency," she may later see "C-I-A" upon all other mentions. Notice the punctuation here, again, calling the announcer's attention to a deliberate separation of sounds with hyphens instead of periods.

When in doubt, write it out. Write as words one to eleven, with the exception of 10. Write as numerals 10 through 999 (except eleven). Skip the zeros and write out hundred, thousand, million, billion and so on. Air time is too precious to test your announcer's math skills. Any other numbers can be written as digits, or as combinations, such as "nine-million, two-hundred-thousand."

When dealing with numbers, write conversationally. For example, "sixteen-hundred dollars" sounds much better and is more easily understood than "one-thousand, six-hundred dollars." Round figures to the nearest hundred, unless being exact is crucial to the story. Don't write $92 if saying approximately $100 would give your readers an easier grasp of the amount.

For clarity's sake, never write "a million" as this can be mistaken for eight million. Write "one million" instead. Spell out any fractions. Use ". . . st" to indicate 1st, ". . . nd" for 2nd or ". . . rd" for 3rd.

Write titles and ages before a person's name. As you'll notice, this rule runs opposite from what you've been taught in print journalism. But in broadcasting, the listener needs to know such information upfront to make sense of the story he's hearing. For example, in a newspaper article we might read:

Neil Armstrong, former astronaut and commander of the Apollo 11 mission, became the first human to walk on the moon.

But in broadcast copy, we would write:

Former Apollo eleven astronaut Neil Armstrong became the first human to walk on the moon.

Make every word count. Just as you would in other forms of writing, weigh each word carefully as you write it. Never use a fifteen-letter word when a five-letter one will suffice. Not only does a longer, more complex word test the listener's vocabulary, but it also adds more syllables. Syllables take several more seconds to say, and as we know, every second counts in broadcasting.

Thus, if you're conversational, chances are you'll be concise in your word choice as well. Write "we'll" rather than the more formal "we will." Not only does this save space and time, but it promotes a personal connection between reader and listener (or viewer, in the case of TV).

Synchronize sight and sound. Obviously this occurs in television, but it's often overlooked by beginning writers. An announcer's words must match the pictures flashed on the screen. But while your copy should describe what's going on, it should not refer directly to it. Instead, the words and graphics should complement each other.

Avoid left to right descriptions. Don't say "the man in the left corner," except in those instances when footage will be frozen and highlighted for the viewers.

Writing broadcast continuity also requires that you vary your sentence length, time each piece of copy precisely and read it aloud. Reading it aloud helps get the time down to the second, and it tests whether you've achieved the conversational style you're seeking. If you write with a person in mind, using the word "you" whenever appropriate, you'll also master this style.

Finally, conclude your copy with energy so that the announcer's voice trails upward, not downward. This approach helps to heighten a person's attention for what's ahead. Listen to your favorite announcers—whether on radio or TV—and you'll see what I mean.

WRITING PSAs

Earlier in this book, I spoke of my three months of writing public service messages for a commercial television station. I truly credit that experience with teaching me how to write clear, concise, conversational and correct copy.

PSAs are written on behalf of nonprofit organizations, churches or causes. They aren't difficult to master. If you practice as much as I did during that summer internship, you'll get the hang of it too. Just remember a few pointers in the process.

If you're writing these on the client side, remember that stations prefer ten-, twenty-, thirty- or sixty-second spots. The briefer, the better. Stick to the ten-, twenty- and thirty-second versions, and you'll have a better chance of having your spot aired. Offer stations several timed choices to choose from.

Stick to one main point instead of trying to get your listeners to grasp several points. Keep the copy lively. Just as the writer of a news story needs an attention-getting lead, the writer of these messages needs to grab the listener and inspire some sort of action as well. Therefore, promise a benefit to your listeners, preferably something tangible or emotional—something that will tug at their heart strings, if you must.

Cite a reason this spot is important. If you stick to the service-orientation themes of making people healthier, wealthier, wiser, more attractive or more popular, you've got a good start. Of course, some subjects won't require too much educational effort on your part. You won't need to explain why ovarian cancer screening is important, but you may need to explain other social service causes.

To highlight these, focus on positive appeals rather than negative ones. If you find your sentences written with negative words such as "not," "don't," and "never," restate these into positive appeals. Besides, stating a sentence in negative terms requires additional words, and with public service messages, you want to be as concise as possible.

Testimonials, when appropriate, also add credibility and prestige to your PSAs. When a nonprofit client sought to produce a positive parenting appeal, we used our celebrity spokesperson — a children's recording artist. This man was known to thousands of Pittsburgh families. Having him and his four kids participate in the PSA added the credibility of a real father, the warmth of a caring citizen and the prestige of his celebrity status. Here was our thirty-second spot:

> Hi, I'm Frank Cappelli. As the father of four active children, I know that parenting isn't easy. Every family has different needs, hopes, fears — and challenges. All parents start out with a lot of hope in their hearts. Keep that hope alive in your family. Spend time with your children. Talk, listen, laugh and learn together. And reach out for support from other parents who understand. A message from Family Resources.

In producing this television PSA, I wrote the spot, ran it by both Frank Cappelli and the agency's executive director and set up a production time with the station that helped us produce it. We chose a family-like environment with a sofa, coffee table, a box of crayons and paper for the kids to look busy while on camera. It worked perfectly, and in our case, fulfilled the station's wish for more family-oriented spots.

When typing your finished script, be sure to double-space your copy. In a TV script, the copy column appears to the right of the page under the heading AUDIO. In the left column, under a

VIDEO heading, you can single-space camera instructions and set requirements.

With all PSAs provide a contact name and telephone number that works. There's nothing worse than a producer or public service director who can't reach you. If your matter is timely, provide a kill date, whereby the spot stops airing. Submit your typed script on your organization's letterhead or specially-designed news release stationery.

Finally, in your cover letter, ask about graphics that might be able to be used and indicate your organization's tax-exempt number. These numbers often need to be kept on file by the station to verify that you are indeed a nonprofit organization, eligible for public service air time.

CABLE TELEVISION SCRIPTS

If you live near a community access cable television station, chances are good that station management is eager for volunteers and writing talent. Well-written scripts are essential for local access channels. So the positive side is that you can find a way of getting your written scripts produced into actual television formats. The negative side is that you may not receive any monetary compensation for your efforts. But if you want to write for television, local cable access isn't a bad place to start. Most station managers won't mind if you dub a copy of the program to use as a demo tape or resume. Just work this out ahead of time, seeking permission before you turn over your script.

If the material you write is suitable for family viewing, does not smack of advertising or blatant self-promotion, fills a need in the programming line-up, and is of specific interest to your local area, your script stands an excellent chance of being accepted. Of course, you must master the essentials of broadcast writing and have a bit of knowledge regarding TV production.

Spending time at a local cable access channel could be beneficial for you. As writers, we can't produce effective copy if we have no idea how our words will be translated into the finished televised product.

Among the things you'll quickly learn will be to keep your visual requirements as simple as possible. Imagine writing a script that requires three different sets. Do you know how much work, let alone expense, is involved? The same goes for cast members and talent. Each set change, each new person to direct the actions of takes time. In television, time is money. A lot of money. So keep your production requirements as simple as possible.

To write appropriate camera instructions, learn the terminology—how to open, cut, dissolve, zoom, fade, dolly, truck, tilt and pan. Know the different shots that you can use such as the full shot (FS) or cover shot (CS), the long shot (LS), medium shot (MS), close-up (CU) and extreme close-ups (ECU or XCU), also known as tight shots.

Also, understand the functions of the switcher in the control room and the character generator (a typewriter-like keyboard that produces coded electronic messages). Many of these commands and pieces of equipment are referred to in scripts and on advertising storyboards.

Once you feel you've mastered the techniques, the writing style and the terminology, it's time to approach your local cable station manager and introduce yourself. Just as you would query before sending unsolicited manuscripts to an editor, you must scope out the needs of your station before sending scripts. Ask about the station's programming needs and submission policies. Often a quick phone call is all you will need to obtain this information.

If you're fortunate enough to land an assignment, be careful of the rights you sell. Usually, the cable company will own rights to the production, but if you work it out in advance, you can retain the rights to your script, freeing you to sell it elsewhere if it's a hit.

WRITING BROADCAST NEWS

While most radio and TV stations hire experienced professionals to write, produce and announce the news, there may be opportunities for this type of work, usually in smaller markets. As with all broadcasting positions, it's competitive.

When writing newscasts, the basics of broadcast style apply. There are a few more stylistic matters to keep in mind, however. First, try to write your news in the present tense. While not all news copy will require this (and sometimes you must use past tense for accuracy) the present tense adds action to your writing and lends that sense of immediacy that people look to broadcast stations for. Avoid the passive voice. Substitute the active voice, and you'll see that your copy reads quicker and is overall much more effective. (See chapter four for a review of the active voice.)

Avoid using questions in your lead sentences. Question leads smack of advertising, especially in broadcasting, where your listener doesn't have the written words in front of him. Quotations should also be avoided until you've had the chance to set these up. And even then, use quotations sparingly. There is little time for them. Besides, they tend to slow the pace of your newscast. Paraphrase when possible, and use quotes only when they pack real punch or add significant authority to your copy.

Transitions between news items are also very important. Look for that common thread that makes stories work with one another, and use these to your advantage. Group local, national and international stories with one another, and move from the local to the international whenever possible. Of course, if war is breaking out or if the president has just been harmed overseas, then these types of stories are obvious exceptions.

Finally, watch for any words that could be libelous. The broadcast style book that I keep on hand (published by United Press International) has a whole list of red-flag words that broadcasters should avoid. That fourth C (Correct) plays an important role here, as you should never go on the air with information you're not absolutely certain of. The truth is your defense.

Double-space your typed copy and indicate the end by placing the journalistically understood " — 30 — " at the bottom of the page.

HOW TO GET STARTED

 Radio and television outlets often need the services of writers who can produce advertising copy, public service announcements, video scripts, program promotions, station identification, time/weather messages and more.

• Because the industry is so limited in its outlets and competition is fierce, opportunities are scarce. Start in smaller markets. Learn more about the field by reading *Broadcasting Yearbook*.

• Volunteer to write PSAs for a nonprofit organization or work at your local cable channel to get a feel for the industry.

• Develop an ear for broadcast continuity and news copy. Listen to a variety of radio stations and television newscasts.

• Practice writing broadcast copy since there are differences between print and broadcast styles. Take a news story from the newspaper and rewrite it for on-air delivery. Write with an extra sense of immediacy and high energy.

• Read aloud anything you write. There is no other test to see if your copy will work in this medium.

• Time spots and messages precisely to the second.

COMMERCIAL WORK FOR CLIENTS

Chapter Fourteen

Advertising

W hile it's unlikely that you'll pitch advertising campaigns for your favorite soft drinks, athletic wear or consumer packaged goods, as a freelance writer, your chances of breaking into the advertising world increase if you're willing to work for a variety of advertisers. Large advertising agencies, with their seasoned, creative staffs, service prestigious clients. Small businesses (mom and pop shops) often have no one to attend to the advertising function — no one to create a concept, write copy, produce the advertising, and place it in the appropriate media.

MARKETS AVAILABLE

When looking for those first commercial clients, seek local businesses, large and small. Corporations and nonprofit organizations are targets for your talents as are department stores, retail operations and commercial art studios who may need writing skills to add to their graphics capabilities. In recent years, professionals — doctors, chiropractors, dentists, lawyers and independent consultants — have joined the bandwagon to pitch their services as well.

Printers that you work with on other writing projects may know of commercial customers in need of advertising copywriting and media placement. Ask them for client leads. The same approach works with newspaper, radio, television and cable advertising departments. Finally, don't overlook the advertising agencies who already have many clients on retainer. Small agencies, especially, are frequently overworked and understaffed and may welcome occasional freelance talent.

BREAKING INTO ADVERTISING

After you've found targets for your talent, you need to sell your services. Showing off other forms of writing isn't going to help at all, so leave behind the first draft of your novel and the feature articles and fillers you've written. What you need are samples of your advertising copywriting.

If you don't have samples you've created as class projects, internship assignments or demos for previous clients, write a few spec ads. Critique or rewrite existing ads, improving them with a new and different approach. And no matter how many or how few ads you've created, always keep them on hand to demonstrate your capabilities. Remember that advertising is a highly subjective field. What turns one client off might be exactly what another client is looking for. Show your clients a range of creative potential and don't prejudice them by weeding out the portfolio pieces you think are bad and including only what you favor.

When you have some samples, analyze the advertising market where you live. In a large city, there will be advertising agencies and full-scale department stores with active ad departments. In rural surroundings, however, the local newspaper might be the mainstay of the community's advertising. If this is the case, forget about the big leagues and concentrate on creating and placing advertising for small businesses, predominantly in the newspaper. Look to the future, trying to determine which clients may need extended campaigns with separate ads for radio, television, direct mail and newspaper. Be sure to pitch this concept and build the cost of additional work into your presentations.

The people you'll pitch to in large operations will most likely be in charge of an advertising, communications, sales and marketing or sales promotion department. In an agency, you'll want to talk with the creative director or the copy supervisor. Whatever the department, the manager may be willing and eager to work with newcomers if she feels you can help the department's efforts and that the two of you can work well together. At smaller operations, you'll deal with the owner or manager of the business. Call to arrange a meeting that's mutually convenient and introduce yourself.

Remain open to other communications opportunities as they arise, if you truly want to break into this industry. When I graduated from college and was making the rounds in the temporary help circuit, I applied at a major department store in my hometown. I listed my degree and desire to work in communications. Months later, I received a call from the employment office. Someone had spotted my credentials and asked if I'd help move merchandise for the store's Christmas catalog. Some job for a college graduate! But, I took it, at minimum wage, for two weeks.

Once I got my foot in the door, I told my boss about my previous experience and my goal to write. Before long, he introduced me to the copywriting staff and assigned freelance writing projects. Two weeks turned into four months of nine-to-five work. When that stint ended, several take-home projects followed. Equally important to the money and experience was seeing how the department functioned. It certainly wasn't glamorous work, but it was valuable.

By contrast, I've known of college graduates who aimed too high and settled for nothing less because they had majored in advertising, and that's the only writing arena they would climb into. Whether you're looking for your first full-time or freelance job, realize that no first position is the one you remain with the rest of your life. Communications is a highly competitive industry. Take a freelance opportunity in sales, public relations or newspaper reporting. Do your job well. Learn. Ask questions. Make your goals known to others. Write spec ads that may never see production and never earn you a cent. If you want to make a living as a freelancer, you'll often find that your services are easier to sell if you've put in a few months or years of full-time, part-time or even temporary experience. And while the job might not be the perfect one, you'll be earning money while continuing your real-world education.

Finally, keep abreast of trends. Advertising professionals read *Advertising Age*, which you can usually find in the periodicals section of most large libraries. Make it a point to read this publication as often as possible.

BEAR IN MIND SOME BASICS

Good advertising conveys a sense of excitement about a growing business that's meeting customer and client needs. Therefore, advertising makes a lot of sense when business is booming. Many people do not understand this. In tough economic times, advertising is either the first budget item to get slashed, or managers race to increase their efforts in an all out attempt to save their businesses. Few realize that advertising is most effective when a business is already running smoothly, and that it takes time for advertising to achieve its full impact.

Advertising is also one of those media that you and your client can control. While you have little input when it comes to news stories and other publicity featuring your client, in advertising, you get to determine the message. You can revitalize a dated image, correct misconceptions, educate your audience as to the need for a certain service and move the business into the future simply by giving your advertising a breath of fresh air.

Advertising can and should work with public relations and other promotional efforts. A business cannot advertise one mode of service and render another. Customers and clients will spot the discrepancies. But while advertising can bring about all of these positive results, it cannot fix a failing business operation. It cannot make up for lost time if managers have come up with excuses for forgoing an ad campaign or if they've channelled too much money for too long a time into the wrong media outlets. Therefore, take great care and time making advertising decisions with your client. There may even come a point in your discussions when you, the writer/consultant, must admit that advertising is not the best alternative for reaching potential clients and customers. Advertising isn't for every client, but when it isn't, you can frequently present alternatives in the form of direct marketing, public relations, newsletters and other options.

CHOOSING ADVERTISING OUTLETS

Just as feature writers research their magazines and newspapers, so must the advertising copywriter. You cannot write for a medium you do not fully understand.

Set goals and objectives for your advertising campaign. Do you seek to remind dormant customers of your client's existence? Do you intend to announce a breakthrough in product development or introduce a new service? Is there a special offer to persuade with? A seasonal sale? A hidden benefit that no one has thought of before? Or, are you building a new image or sharing important information?

Once you understand what you're setting out to accomplish,

you can select appropriate media to carry out that mission. Find out what competitors use as their advertising vehicles. Get to know your target audience and what the audience's preferences are regarding newspapers, magazines and television viewing. Magazine media kits contain demographic information, readership surveys, popular sections of the magazine, circulation figures and make this research much easier. What keeps customers coming back? Put yourself in the consumer's shoes. Why should someone buy your client's product or use their particular services? When selecting media, you want your client to get the maximum response for the least possible cost. So the investigation begins.

Newspapers are a favorite for business advertising. A subscription in one household usually carries multiple readers. Newspaper ads are published immediately, they have special interest sections for highly targeted messages, and they offer numerous formats to meet a variety of budgets. But, newspapers have a short life span; they are read once and thrown away. And you often cannot control where the ads will be placed on the page.

Magazines have a longer lifespan, and a much more extensive pass-along value. You can select magazines for targeting specific groups, and you can frequently specify where you want your ad to be placed on the page. Magazines offer high-quality reproduction, color and flexible formats. On the other hand, magazines require a long lead time, from one to four months, to get an ad in the publication after delivery of the artwork and copy. Magazine advertising is competitive and expensive.

Radio advertising is another quick-reaching medium. People listen to these ads in their homes, offices, cars and stores. Radio ads are less expensive than television advertising, but unlike print advertising, once the commercial airs, it's no longer available to refer to. It's gone. Furthermore, your creative options are limited as is the quality control of the sound (unless you are directly involved in production).

Television ads are more action-oriented. They depend upon sight and sound, making them more persuasive than radio spots. Almost everyone watches television and there are a great many more creative capabilities in TV than in radio. But television production and air time are extremely expensive. And, like radio ads, TV commercials disappear.

Other media choices include specialty publications, yellow pages, third-class circulars mailed to residential occupants, billboards and transit displays. If you have a highly targeted audience, a specialty publication might be right for you. If you're a service or product that people only need occasionally, a yellow pages ad might bring in business over the long haul. Billboards and transit displays have longer life spans but are limited to those who see them while travelling. Besides, there is a greater expense in printing and installing such advertising before you even think of paying for the space.

Small businesses also frequently use program support and give-away gimmicks. The former refers to ads in something like the high school bowling banquet program. The latter refers to pens, key chains, calendars, mugs, magnets and other attention-getting devices. These two types of advertising are often placed out of respect for an organization or cause and for reasons of community stewardship. With give-away items, just be sure you've selected an item that is consistent with your message, and preferably one that will last long enough to keep the message in front of customers. Calendars last at least twelve months. Mugs and magnets last years while pens, pencils, paper tablets and key chains are disposed of more frequently.

Regardless of the media outlet you choose, plan ahead. Many ads, especially billboards, transit displays and give-away gimmicks take time to produce. I rarely recommend billboards to my clients, even though the space is free for nonprofits. But there are hidden costs (including printing and installation), and given the time involved, the bother rarely pays off.

Remember that consistency counts. If you've invested a lot of your client's money into producing a television commercial, and can only afford to run it once a week, you're hardly getting a good return on your dollar. For advertising to truly succeed, the public needs to see it over a period of time. Repeat advertisers often receive a price break on consecutively run ads. So look into frequency discounts and take the long-term potential into consideration when selecting your media.

CREATING AN AD

Earlier in this chapter we learned the importance of knowing your target audience. Well, the same goes for your client. Is the client conservative or open to a few risks and adventures? You may come up with the most clever slogan in the world, but if it's too cutesy for your client's staid and traditional image, it won't work. It could harm.

Pick a theme and stick to it. Remember service orientation. If you aim to make consumers healthier, wealthier, wiser, safer, more attractive or more comfortable, you'll stand a better chance of them paying attention to your ad. Copywriters have a mnemonic (memory-building) device they like to use—KISS. This stands for Keep It Simple, Stupid, or more politely, Keep It Short and Sweet! This means you should use your words sparingly and build plenty of white space into the graphic presentation of your ad.

Headlines require an even more concise style. Make a word list, from which you'll pull words to create your headline. Avoid word wasters such as negative expressions. Negative words are also harder to focus on and they detract from the benefits you seek to promise in advertising.

Know what you should and should not place in your ad. Certainly the business name, address and phone number deserve mention as well as any special merchandise. Mention the name of the product and company in the headline, if you can.

Think, however, whether you want to date your ad copy with a specific price, or simply entice people into your store. And, consider listing store operating hours, especially if they're unusual. Don't waste the space if they're standard business hours, as every word must be meaningful. And you don't get more meaningful than referring to the reader of your ad. Try to incorporate words such as "you" and "your" in your headline and ad copy. These speak directly to your audience.

Broaden your selling vocabulary with *Words That Sell* by Richard Bayan (Contemporary Books), a handy reference for any copywriter. Consumers are much more sophisticated today and government regulations are also a lot tighter. You can no longer dupe people with words such as "sensational," "colossal," or claims to be the "world's best." You need to back up these statements since excessive claims are a sure way to lose customers.

In addition, you can't use words that don't accurately speak about the benefits of your product. In recent years, advertising has had to conform to standards when using terms such as

"light," "fat free," and "heart healthy." Avoid excessive claims
that make people's eyes roll in distrust. Jargon also confuses people. Aim to communicate, not impress with lofty language.

Also, add fulcrum phrases to your advertising copy. Envision
your words sitting on a seesaw. Each thought is constructed in
such a way that the midpoint is obvious. It's metrically balanced
on each end. When I was in college, the phrase we learned came
from a Fuller Paint commercial. It read "a century of leadership
in the chemistry of color." Picture a seesaw with "a century of
leadership" on one end, "in the chemistry of color" on the other.
Fulcrum phrases are intrinsically pleasing to the ear, and like any
rhythm, easy to remember. A lot of advertising slogans use them.

Finally, track your advertising by inviting customers to mention the ad or bring it with them. Coupons work wonders this
way. If you provide a mail-in response, use a department and
two letters to track which publication generated the additional
business. This information will come in useful when you go to
revamp your ad campaign and consider future media buys.

ADDING ARTWORK

As a freelance writer, chances are you may not concern yourself
with the graphic design of the ad. But, if you have desktop publishing equipment and advertise these services, you may need a
few pointers.

Artwork has three main functions within your advertising. It
explains or demonstrates your client's product or service. It grabs
the reader's attention. And, it improves the ad's overall appearance, making consumers more receptive to it.

Photographs work well in your ads when you need the real
thing to sell your product or service. For those professionals advertising their services, photos establish credibility and make
them more than just a name. Check with photographic studios,
newspaper photographers or art schools who could help provide
this if you need it. Illustrations are appropriate, if done well and
used sparingly. Professional artwork services supply pages of in-
dexed illustrations which can be clipped and used in your advertising layout. But some of these can be cost prohibitive for the
small business owner or the freelance advertising copywriter and
consultant.

For television ad scripts, you'll need to show a storyboard

presentation (video description) of your ad. Unless your art skills rival your writing talents, you'll need a graphic artist or professional illustrator to help with this task. Storyboards show, scene by scene, what happens throughout the duration of the commercial. To be certain that your visuals and words are synchronized, review chapter thirteen on radio and television writing.

COOPERATIVE ADVERTISING

Co-op advertising, as it's known in the industry, is a cost-saving advertising vehicle for many small businesses. Manufacturers and retailers share the costs of the advertising and both benefit from the business generated. But the paperwork can be bothersome. Find out if there are restrictions as to the type of media you can use. Ask the percentage or dollar amount the advertising will cost. How and when will reimbursement be made? And, what proof does the manufacturer require before reimbursing you? It's best to have a lawyer look over any contracts you're not sure of before entering your client into one of these co-op arrangements.

HOW TO GET STARTED

 Advertising enhances images by conveying a sense of dependability and credibility. It informs, persuades, reminds, announces and breathes life into a worn-out business operation.

• Research the advertising opportunities near you. Look in the yellow pages or ask the Chamber of Commerce for names. Contact department managers, small business owners, retail stores and advertising agencies.

• In your search for clients, don't overlook professionals who may need to promote themselves in today's competitive marketplace.

• Show spec samples or other pieces you've produced, all carefully displayed in a professional-looking portfolio. (For tips on portfolios and self-promotion, refer to chapter three.)

• Be prepared to sell not only your services but the concept of advertising. Show how you'd increase sales and awareness with an ad campaign.

- As you put new spins on old products, educate your audience, creating a need for what you sell.
- In your ads, don't forget to ask people for a response — a written reply, a phone call, a stop in the store or a product purchase.

Chapter Fifteen

Public Relations

S ince running a full-page ad in a leading magazine can cost in the six figures, it's no wonder that businesses have sought less expensive ways to get their messages across. Enter public relations, a rather intangible but nonetheless effective method of reaching potential customers for your commercial clients.

PUBLIC RELATIONS DEFINED

Isn't public relations just a nice write-up in the newspaper, you might ask? Not at all. Public relations indeed includes newspaper coverage, from a mention in a column and a quote in a major news story to a photo with an accompanying caption and a credit on the op-ed page. But public relations is also the manner in which telephone inquiries are handled, personal contacts, direct mailings, audiovisual presentations, newsletters and broadcasts. Effective public relations is all of these things put together, and then some.

As you can see, public relations is all around us. Today, it's a function most nonprofit organizations, companies and corporations, schools, libraries, government offices, hotels, parks and other facilities require to stay in business.

Public relations is not advertising because you don't pay for the time or space involved. Clients pay a staff person, an established public relations agency or a freelancer/consultant like you to earn them coverage through timely, professional and informative exchanges. But herein lies the problem. Because of its intangible nature, public relations continues to be a hard sell with decision makers. People can point to an advertisement and readily see how their hard work and money have paid off. Public relations efforts simply aren't that easy to track. You'll never know the exact number of people who read the mention in the paper or who heard the teaser on the air. You may never know how many recipients read your newsletter or tossed it in the round file. Certainly, you'll never completely understand what the public relations role entails until you try it for yourself. It's one of the most popular client activities for freelance writers, and if you can sell its importance to prospective clients, your income potential has no limit.

ESTABLISHING A PR PLAN

Here are a few questions to obtain background information on your client. Why and when was your client's organization formed? Who played an important role in its development? What's being done now? What are the organization's current goals and objectives? Who is active in the organization (i.e., board members, volunteers, notables or celebrities)? How is the organization perceived by others? What would you like them to think of it? And, how will you bring about that change between what is and what could be?

What is your aim in setting up a public relations plan? Do you seek to publicize a special event or do you seek some sort of recognition? Do you wish to enlist volunteer support or further public awareness? Do you hope for added prestige or do you desire additional program participation or product support? Which audiences are more important than others?

Once you know your objectives, you can solicit the opinions of others within your client's organization. Many nonprofit groups have established public relations committees or boards of directors to help you. Rely on their expertise and interest. Brainstorm for public relations ideas, eliminating no idea in this initial stage. Upon second review, carefully weed out those suggestions that aren't realistic. Work within a budget. While public relations (as opposed to advertising) is free, there is a cost of materials and creative time. Whatever you decide, make your plan workable and be open to outcomes you may never have considered previously. Some of your decisions may include the following public relations efforts.

ENLISTING MEDIA SUPPORT AND COVERAGE

Media placement remains one of the best known methods of obtaining good public relations. But to do this, you must first compile lists of current media — separate ones, especially for your client's public service efforts and news-related coverage. Since my client is a member agency, I've often built on the media list provided by the United Way office. I periodically double-check these listings to see who has left a particular newspaper or station, and who has replaced the former contact. In addition, I've maintained separate lists for community groups and schools, when appropriate. For one nonprofit client, I've targeted about a dozen corporate newsletter editors around Pittsburgh, as some have reprinted our newsletter articles with attribution, giving us an extended reach that's been very beneficial.

If you have national clients, and it's not easy to make hundreds of long-distance telephone calls, rely on national directories such as *Bacon's Publicity Checker, Editor & Publisher International Year Book, Standard Rate & Data Service, Inc.* and *Gale Directory of Publications and Broadcast Media*. Your library may have at least one of these resources.

Lists compiled, it's time to begin establishing relationships with media representatives. Reporters rely on public relations personnel to make their jobs easier. Therein lies an important rule of thumb: Be a help, not a hindrance! Meet deadlines, return phone calls promptly, be familiar with a reporter's beat and know what story suggestions are appropriate to pitch and which would be considered absurd. Be respectful of a reporter's time. Don't ask to see stories before they're printed, and don't play favorites. It's a surefire way to increase your enemies.

A NEWS RELEASE—THE STANDARD PR TOOL

If you already read chapter four on journalistic foundations, you have a working knowledge of news writing. Preparing a news release is very much the same. Before you begin, however, make sure that what you have to offer is really newsworthy. If what you need is coverage, use a "Request for Coverage" rather than a news release. I use this format, which is very straightforward and very effective for producing coverage. On news release stationery, I feature the words *who, what, when, where, why* and *how*. Tabbed across from each word is the appropriate information—exactly what busy editors need to decide whether they can or will cover a specific event.

In a news release, however, include the information—the who, what, when, where, why and how—in the lead paragraph. Write in inverted pyramid form, funneling to the less important information midway through your release. Stick to the facts. Adjectives and sales pitches belong in your sales literature, not in your news releases.

When writing, cite names and titles accurately, and use quotations whenever you want to attribute something with impact. Avoid all industry jargon, even if your client urges you to keep it in. Keep your writing clear and concise. When ending, use a brief summary paragraph that states who your client is, the basic mission and anything else that could educate media representatives who are unfamiliar with your client.

In the upper left corner, date your release and indicate "For immediate release" or "For release after 10:00 A.M." You get the idea. Across from that, in the right corner, provide a contact (usually yourself, as consultant) and a phone number where you can be reached or have messages left. Type your news release on your client's (or your PR company's) news release letterhead. Regular stationery will do if you don't have separate paper already printed. At the end, use the "—30—" symbol to indicate you're finished.

Mail your news releases a few days ahead of time to daily media (a week or two in advance for weekly publications; months ahead of time to monthly publications). Address it to the appropriate editor, referring to the media list you've created. Don't call to see if your release will be used. Editors don't know what each news day will be like, and they cannot commit to coverage. So sit back, wait and pray that a major news event doesn't erupt, preempting your chances of any media coverage.

If an event is involved, call that morning or the evening before to offer any last-minute details. Offer to fax a copy of the release or request for coverage if the editor is unfamiliar with it and would like to see it. Again, don't be a pest.

NEWS CONFERENCES

Many public relations personnel send out releases to gain attendance at their client's news conferences. But before you rush to stage such a show for the media, make sure you really have something newsworthy to offer. Remember your role as a public relations consultant. It's to make a reporter's life easier, not more complicated. Invite a reporter to your news conference when you could have arranged the same or better coverage by personal appointment or telephone interview, and you will irritate this hurried journalist. Most will want to have one-on-one interviews anyway. For only a handful of media, you could arrange personal appointments to disseminate your message.

On the other hand, if you expect a large level of interest, go ahead with preparations for a news conference. I've found it's best to hold such events in the morning (but not too close to the noon news deadline) or in the early afternoon (well away from the five and six o'clock newscasts) as these are less hectic times for media people.

Make sure you or someone else is on hand to direct reporters to coffee, restrooms and telephones for filing stories or simply to meet any special requests. In selecting your location, make sure your room has enough lighting and electrical outlets for cameras and tape recorders. It should be large enough that people can move around comfortably. Conference rooms work well for this purpose.

Avoid too many talking heads at the front table, and offer the diversion of charts, slides or other information. While news conferences can be elaborate, yours doesn't have to be costly at all. Perhaps you won't require visual displays. Just make sure that your spokespersons are knowledgeable and are comfortable being questioned and photographed. Allow for one-on-one interviews after your main presentation concludes.

Finally, assemble press kits (explained below) and distribute these as your reporters leave the news conference. Occasionally, you'll need to hand these out before the presentation. A standard rule for any type of public speaking is to avoid passing out literature that could distract attendees from the speakers' comments, but sometimes reporters need to be briefed with the material in the press kit to have a better grasp of the subject at hand. Some reporters will arrive early and expect a press kit to look over while they wait. Every situation is different. Use your best judgment.

Press Kits

Also called media information kits, press kits are the staples of the news conference or media event. They are neatly organized folders featuring side pockets. Affixed to the front is an imprinted logo or label bearing your client's name.

Inside the press kit is at least one news release, background or fact sheets, biographies of key participants in your presentation, feature stories that have been written about the organization, charts, logos or graphics that illustrate your information, brochures pertaining to your client's work, suggested questions, and photographs (with a label affixed with the appropriate caption). Not every press kit will contain the exact same components, but these are several of the options you will have when constructing the kit.

Press kits are convenient to have on hand when reporters (or freelance writers like yourself) call to obtain information. Just be sure to update them frequently. Also, provide information that's appropriate for various media. Some writers will not require photographs, charts or graphics while newspaper reporters usually will. It's perfectly acceptable to issue different kinds of kits — those for magazines, newspaper and broadcast. In fact, this often saves your client money.

TALK SHOWS

Have you ever wondered how certain guests got booked on *Oprah Winfrey, Donahue* or *Good Morning, America*? Sure, in some cases, program producers find these guests. Other times, however, public relations people seek out the producers, booking their clients as guests and prepping them for the interview ahead. The shows you contact may be locally produced but the advice here remains the same.

Just as you would research a newspaper column or magazine you're pitching ideas to, you must watch or listen to the talk show to understand its format, audience interaction and ratings appeal. There may be some shows you'd rather steer clear of because the subject matter isn't appropriate, the host is abrasive or the time it airs is wrong for your intended audience.

Address a one-page letter to the program's producer, suggesting a specific angle for a segment and telling of your client's availability as a guest. You might even provide convenient dates.

Remember to cite important statistics and background, answering that question in every producer's mind: "Why should I book this guest?" Provide news clippings on the topic or person you're promoting and offer sample questions.

Follow up with a brief phone call two weeks later if you haven't received a response, being prepared to pitch the idea verbally if necessary. Should the producer like your idea and book your guest, ask for confirmation in writing and by phone, closer to the actual taping. You should also come to an understanding if there are any expenses involved and know who takes care of what.

To prepare your client for this guest appearance, ask him or her to watch or listen to some of the shows. Think ahead about questions that might be asked and prepare some responses. Instruct your client to dress appropriately, avoiding patterns that appear busy on camera. As a rule, solid colors are best. White appears too washed out on camera while black conveys a harshness and shows no detail. Red ties look good on men. Noisy or flashy jewelry is taboo for women. And watch accessories such as matching scarves, socks, hosiery and handbags.

Posture, mannerisms and speech habits play an important role in audio/visual presentations. Talk to the camera and audience, not your host. Help your client become a master of the twenty- or thirty-second sound bite, a political tactic to get on the evening news that works just as well for any other talk-show guest.

Skin tone and overall appearance also count a great deal. Remember the Kennedy/Nixon debates and what Nixon's appearance without make-up cost him. In television, make-up is for everyone, including men. It eliminates glaring shine on the skin and adds color under the intense lights. While some stations provide make-up assistance, others do not so seek out advice from an image consultant if your client must regularly appear on camera.

OTHER PUBLIC RELATIONS OUTLETS

Outside of staged events, news conferences, personal interviews and talk show appearances, you may use your writing and promotion skills to compose letters for your client. One type of letter you should learn to master is the letter to the editor, otherwise known as the op-ed piece. (See chapter ten for more information on opinions and editorials.)

These are excellent devices for commenting on the business or industry your client is involved in. Actually, letters to the editor receive a higher readership in many newspapers than staff-written editorials and syndicated opinion columns. So, put your best thoughts into clear and concise form. Letters to the editor are not tirades. They state opinions, provide supporting facts and suggest action items when it's appropriate. They always conclude with a signature, title and name of an organization. Newspapers verify the authenticity of such letters before publishing them, so it's best to provide a telephone number and address for your client.

Wire services may also be of assistance when you want to send news releases, requests for coverage or other urgent data. Most major news operations subscribe to at least the Associated Press or United Press International. In your area, perhaps there is a public relations wire service available as well. Most are listed in the telephone directory.

Annual reports and newsletters are two additional vehicles for public relations, but these will be discussed in chapters sixteen and eighteen, respectively. Special events and fund-raising will be featured in chapter seventeen. And you can apply the information about talk-show appearances and writing speeches (chapter sixteen) to establishing a speaker's bureau for your client.

Every public relations professional should be familiar with several different methods of assisting their clients or should be able to work with other professionals and freelancers who specialize in these areas.

CLIENT CONFLICTS

If you do your job well and conduct yourself professionally throughout your client relationships, conflicts may never arise. But then, you are only half of the consultant/client relationship.

I've had clients who were not so agreeable to work with, most of whom didn't remain clients for very long. I do the best job possible for my clients, putting any ownership of the work I do aside, knowing it's their project. They, not I, must be happy with the results.

While there's truth to the saying that "the client's always right," there have been times clients wanted me to proceed in ways I knew were counterproductive, like going to print with incorrect information just to get the job completed or divulging information about other clients that should remain confidential. When this happened, I stood my ground. The way I see it, my professional reputation is being risked with flagrant errors as much as the client's is. And, if I breach a confidence to benefit them, I'd be likely to do the same to hurt them someday. Therefore, I don't breach any confidences, and everyone remains happy.

Sometimes the nature of your client's work is at odds with effective public relations. One of my clients went to great lengths to protect the identity of families using its services. That's the way it should be. However, when the media come knocking at the door, they always want living, breathing people to go on camera. It's a struggle, at times, to balance the agency's work with its desire to create name recognition and not offend the media.

Other conflicts may arise if you use spokespersons or others to represent your clients. Since one client sought to strengthen families and prevent child abuse, image control was extremely vigilant. We couldn't afford to become aligned with anyone who could be called into question for their behavior or actions. Thus, when a sports team sent us a player, known by fans as the team fighter, we were not pleased. While he signed autographs and couldn't have been more polite, we had to deal with the contrast between his and the agency's image. The very next night, a board member's child witnessed him in a brawl on TV. Because of the contrast, I chose not to publicize this player's appearance. After all, our message was against violence. This man displayed violence, even though it was in the context of a contact sport. The team's public relations officials weren't so understanding, but I stand by the agency's convictions on this one, and as you work with your clients, you should be prepared to navigate tough waters from time to time as well.

Understand that public relations is frequently a hard sell to most commercial clients who want to see immediate results. You may never be completely satisfied with the job you do, as you strive for more coverage and a better image. You probably won't receive a byline for much of what you write, but you will add important pieces to your portfolio, and you'll be helping to build a better organization.

HOW TO GET STARTED

Effective public relations strategy is built upon speed and communication, plus maintaining a network of contacts that can be mobilized quickly. If you can master these skills, public relations can provide a base income, especially when you can arrange a retainer with clients. This allows you to work on other, more speculative freelance writing projects.

• With image at stake in every business and organization, start your search for clients by consulting the Chamber of Commerce in your area, browsing through the yellow pages and asking business owners. Contact your United Way for nonprofit referrals.

• Establish realistic, achievable goals and objectives. Form a public relations committee at nonprofit organizations, asking others actively involved in business and industry to volunteer their time and input.

• Let clients know how much advertising space costs in the publications you submit editorials to. Your client will soon see that continuing public relations efforts (and a consulting relationship with you) is the better bargain.

• Develop media lists and keep these current. They will come in handy for news releases, public service campaigns, newsletter mailings and much more. Prepare your lists so that they can be photocopied directly onto mailing labels.

• Develop personal relationships with reporters, learning how you can work together to help each other.

• Subscribe to *Public Relations Journal*, published by the Public Relations Society of America (PRSA) in New York City.

Chapter Sixteen

Business and Technical Assignments

One avenue you ought to explore to keep the cash flowing fast is business and technical writing. Corporations need to communicate. Without such efforts, they cease to attract new clients, customers and government support. Someone has to write all of this material, and with the trend to cut back on staff, the freelance writer stands to gain opportunities if she seeks them out.

When writing for commercial clients, you're free to take on as few or as many assignments as you like. You won't have to spend hours thumbing through files, waiting for inspiration to strike as your clients will likely originate the subject matter you'll write about. All you must do is persevere and implement your writing skills in a professional manner. There's little need for extensive outside research.

The drawback is that there's no byline. In fact, your writing will frequently be attributed to someone else who may get the glory, and much of what you write will be completed under a work-for-hire agreement, meaning that you cannot copyright your work, use it for yourself or implement it with other clients. In a work-for-hire arrangement, there are no royalties or future reprint sales down the road. Simply put, there just isn't much prestige.

But there will be plenty of interpersonal contact. Plan on attending several meetings (perhaps more than your share) as you decide on goals and objectives, learn your subject and review project drafts with your clients. For the lonely, isolated writer, these meetings can be a blessing. The other primary advantage is the fast rate of acceptance. Whereas you may wait six months for acceptance or payment on publication at a major magazine, you'll often know the status of your business assignments, sometimes the day of delivery. And except for the occasional slow-paying client, you'll receive payment on a monthly basis.

MARKETS FOR YOUR WORK

Business and technical assignments require just as much cerebral challenge as other writing genres. A good writer will rely on his ability to grasp many details, research and interview, organize his thoughts, convey them succinctly and conversationally, and meet deadlines as they're set. These skills are necessary whether you write commercial reports for insurance companies, annual reports for stockholders, corporate histories, financial presentations, collateral materials and business manuals, executive speeches, feature articles for executives, technical literature, video scripts or work produced for creative agencies.

You'll find many of these projects at small and large businesses. In small towns, where executives are not as inundated with sales calls, they may be more readily accessible. Write to them, citing examples of your work. Set up an appointment to show your portfolio. Ask what the company's writing needs are, and seek ways to match them with your skills.

Creative agencies, especially those that do not place large amounts of media advertising, concentrate more heavily on producing collateral materials for their clients. These agencies may also be more receptive to freelance talent. And if you previously worked for a business or industry, knowing the inside track and who the decision makers are may be your best bet for breaking into the business writing field. Capitalize on your contacts.

ANNUAL REPORTS

Each year, public corporations and nonprofit organizations must produce an annual report for stockholders and contributors, respectively. These reports, while sometimes slick and glossy, are being produced with an increasing consciousness toward budget. As businesses grow leaner, employees, stockholders and community members do not want to see money lavished on four-color printing, loads of expensive artwork and pompous presentations.

What they do demand is an honest account of the business. They want to know where and how the organization has helped others, what makes the company special, what makes it better than others in the industry. The public likes to learn this year's success stories, how major problems were tackled and whether the company was a good steward of public and private money. Finally, people want to know what's in store for the future, and this organization's place in that larger picture.

Keep your goals and objectives in mind when producing an annual report. Know whether you're reporting growth, change, competition, industry advances or a general accounting to stockholders, members and donors. Often, you'll be doing some of each. Your annual report should take these questions and goals into account. Sometimes, they also include company histories, employee profiles, features on philanthropy and corporate initiatives on the environment, education and health care.

As a rule of thumb, annual reports begin with an engaging cover that shouts "Read me! I'm important." If you forget this important point, the months of hard work to create your report will end up in someone's round file. In fact, annual reports are largely design driven so be sure to have your graphic elements in place before you begin any text.

Next, proceed from general information and work to the specifics. This way, readers can decide for themselves how far to plunge into the written material. Some will devour the entire report. Others will scan it and file it away.

After meeting with the insiders (your clients), write for the general public. Avoid industry jargon, or if you must use it, explain it for the layperson. After all, most annual report readers comprehend such matter at around a ninth grade reading level. Write above this threshold, and you'll lose them for sure. Attractive graphics and pictures also enhance the reader's understanding of difficult concepts.

When choosing photographs, include one of the chief executive officer, executive director or whomever is in command. This allows the readers to put a face with a name. Other photos should be selected just as carefully, with a balance of ethnic populations, men and women.

BUSINESS MANUALS

In today's information age, manuals introduce new products to us, testing our limits of knowledge and teaching us about today's technology. Manuals tell us how to assemble, use, maintain or

repair all sorts of products. They provide training and staff information, outline various jobs and specify operating procedures at
particular companies. We use them at home and at work. While
fellow professionals may come and go, manuals hang around
forever (if we remember where we put them!).

As a freelance business writer, you can use your writing skills
to produce these handy references. If you have any educational
or work-related expertise, that background will help you secure
those initial assignments.

The first step you'll take is planning for the project. Here,
you'll work with your client as well as artists and designers to
create a format that you're all comfortable with. It should be a
format that works for everyone involved — client, artist, writer,
and ultimately, the consumer.

Next, gather product information, outlining the main points
of what you want to say. Remember, the goal of most manuals
is to teach. Write the manual's text following the outline and the
principles of good writing. If you've mastered clear and concise
writing and added a conversational tone, you're off to a good
start.

In manual writing, consistency counts. Whereas word choice
and diversity are assets in other projects, manual writing requires
repetition. Don't be afraid to repeat the same word or phrase
you've used throughout your copy. In fact, alternating between
words and using synonyms only confuses the reader. Whenever
you introduce new terminology, you're implying that there's a
new idea or new information.

Cut any words that don't further the reader's understanding
of the concept at hand. Keep your copy short, opting for small
words and selecting brief sentences. Don't say "beverage" when
"drink" would do, or "minuscule" when "tiny" suffices.

Write using the active voice with imperative verbs that clearly
state a command, such as *move*, *place*, *rotate*, *press* or *turn*. Don't
create illegal verbs by adding the " — ize" suffix. Consult a dictionary whenever you're tempted to do so and verify that the
word exists. Finally, be objective. Manuals are no place for your
opinion. Just the facts, please.

When you've finished your first draft, be prepared to revise
and test what you've written. Double-check the accuracy, usabil-
ity and clarity of the instructions. Is the reader progressing with

each new step? Is she confused? Can she find information she needs without an exhaustive search? Is your material still too technical or have you gone to the other extreme of being too simplistic? Did you get off on tangents?

EXECUTIVE SPEECHES

Ask anyone for their list of secret fears, and public speaking often pops up toward the top. But a lot of businesspeople spend their lives speaking in public. For the skilled writer, drafting remarks and public speeches for business leaders and executives can provide steady income, especially if you live near major convention centers and hotels that host conferences. Politicians are also prime candidates for your writing talent.

Admittedly, writing executive speeches may seem years into your future, but I've found that professionals and business leaders come to rely on writers for such tasks. Even if you work in a full-time public relations capacity, don't be surprised if your boss comes to you for a little help with speech writing. Many people simply don't feel comfortable or confident writing these themselves.

Remarks are generally made in less formal settings while speeches elevate a person to a level of leadership where they can impart information or entertainment—sometimes both. When your client speaks before a group, he or she has an unmatched opportunity to lead through the power of words—words you'll provide to impress, persuade, sell, entertain, advance a cause or further a career. Rest assured, there's a lot riding on what you write.

Begin by meeting with your client and finding out a little about the person. There's no sense drafting a series of humorous remarks only to learn later that your client isn't comfortable with comedy. Find out their comfort level and what your client wishes to get across.

Next, learn a little about the program and audience. Is it a formal presentation or a round table, panel discussion? Who will speak before and after your client? How much time is allotted for each speaker? Will there be a question-and-answer session? What's the program's ultimate goal? Why has your client been asked to speak? Will there be a lectern or podium, a stage or audio/visual equipment?

Similarly, will audience members be casting their devoted gaze toward your client the entire time or will there be a meal before, during or after the remarks? Will the audience be made up of professionals, fellow workers, people with less experience or more experience than the speakers? Will there be spouses in attendance? What's the average income and educational background of the audience?

All of these questions will help you draft appropriate remarks that speak directly to the audience, not around, above or below them. If there is a formal presentation involved, don't be afraid to consult a photographer or a commercial artist for photographs, charts or graphics that can help communicate your message.

When drafting the speech, find out if your client prefers a word-for-word draft or a summary of notes to speak extemporaneously. If you choose the fully written approach, be sure to instruct your client with presentation pointers, as the audience will want to be spoken to, not read to. If your words are conversational in tone, you'll help achieve this result.

You'll need to grab the listener's attention by quoting meaningful statistics, asking a question, introducing a shocking item or telling a humorous anecdote. In the body of the remarks, move from general information to more specific. Conclude by wrapping up all major points, answering questions you posed, filling in the blanks and finishing all stories you began. Here is where the "ask" comes into play. If there's a desired action you hope will result from your client's remarks, ask for it. Ask for the donation. Ask for the order. Ask for careful consideration. Just be sure to ask.

Avoid esoteric expressions, as well as those that could offend people. Obviously, sexist, racist or ethnic references do not belong in any remarks, even in joke form. Refrain from using big words when smaller ones will communicate just as well. Sprinkle the remarks with appropriate anecdotes or personal experiences as this helps to build bridges with the audience.

Finally, when giving your client public speaking pointers, remind him to restate any questions that are asked before proceeding with an answer. This benefits those listeners who didn't hear the question to begin with. Should microphones go dead or interruptions result, instruct your client to go with the flow. Introducing a humorous response often puts the others at ease and lessens the speaker's embarrassment.

Should humorous remarks fail, have him say something like "I'll never use that joke again," or "Boy, that was a real show-stopper." Don't repeat punch lines either, as this interrupts the rhythm of the remarks. Generally, if your client is at ease with himself, the audience will pick up on this, and the entire speaking experience will be a successful one.

TECHNICAL WRITING

Can you read a blueprint or a technical drawing? Understand computer lingo? Do you have a knack for translating esoteric engineering instructions into everyday English? If so, technical writing could provide additional income, especially if you live in areas with emerging technology.

Governmental and military facilities as well as private industry frequently require the services of technical writers. These industries include engineering and construction, automotive and aerospace, electronics, biotechnology and robotics firms, computer hardware and software companies and scientific research and development facilities. If you already work in these areas, but perhaps in a nonwriting capacity, volunteer to take on technical writing assignments and prove your skills.

Break into the field of technical writing with practiced inter-personal, interviewing and organizational skills. The ability to think logically and grasp new concepts quickly comes in handy. You'll also need to think and communicate visually, writing in a clear and concise style. College-level training in engineering or computer science is also extremely helpful. This proves that you understand the terminology and have a base of knowledge. Barring a degree or such college-level study, enroll in continuing education courses available at most community colleges and at some vocational-technical schools. If you want to work in government or military offices (or for those who do such work), you may be required to apply for a security clearance.

Defining terminology and eliminating jargon are two essentials of technical writing. Write with a reader in mind and provide examples that he can relate to. Use the present tense, the active voice and specific descriptions. Again, when a short word will do, use it. Use lists when necessary to make your thoughts better understood. Finally, avoid turning nouns into verbs, especially by adding "ize." Programmers are particularly prone to this vice.

SURVIVING AS A BUSINESS OR TECHNICAL WRITER

No matter what industry or aspect of writing you work in, there are common concerns among all business writers. Finding and keeping clients is often the first hurdle. Look to the industries near you, consulting the yellow pages, high technology councils, a Chamber of Commerce or the Small Business Administration.

Seek reasons to keep in touch with your existing clients so that they don't fall into a dormant cycle. It takes much less effort to sell a previously satisfied client on a new writing job than a customer unfamiliar with your work. Send correspondence and clippings your clients might appreciate and schedule lunch meetings periodically to discuss your client's changing needs. Give progress reports when working on particular projects, and without divulging any professional confidences, share what you're working on for other clients. What works for one company might be just what another one needs. (See chapter three for additional self-promotion tips.)

While one client may occupy a great deal of your time and boost your bank account sufficiently, don't become too dependent on him. I've seen self-employed professionals do this, and they've had to scramble when those clients have cut back or changed consulting arrangements.

To protect your credit rating and cash flow, never carry a client's expenses. Have invoices for specific services billed directly to the client. For tax-exempt nonprofits, having them pay the bills works to their financial advantage. You'd have to pay sales tax.

Setting fees is another tough call. Some clients will mistakenly believe they should pay you the hourly rate their regular employees make. If this happens, you'll have to persist in negotiating more money. Point out that you carry your own medical and disability insurance, provide vacation time, retirement accounts, tax payments and your own office and supplies. Charge fees commensurate with the work time and talent required. If you substantially lower your rates, you lower your work's perceived value. Offer to work with the client to price assignments individually (at a project rate) or hourly (by keeping careful track of your time). If hourly figures seem too high, estimate the hours and quote a project rate, but be sure that you agree to the estimated hours. Otherwise, you may find yourself taken advantage of and lose money on the job. Build in a loophole so that you can earn additional income if the job runs longer than expected. To keep cash flowing in, bill monthly (not at the project's completion) and demand payment within thirty days. You reduce this risk even further if you stipulate that one-third of your fee is payable at the start of a project, another third upon completion of the first draft, and the remainder upon final approval.

HOW TO GET STARTED

Business and technical writing requires the same self-motivation that all freelancers need for survival. Those who come from reporting or feature writing backgrounds have learned to meet deadlines, check facts and write clearly and concisely, but any writer can start out in this field. Since business writing can be rigid and the formats very structured, expect a lower level of creative input, but steady financial rewards as well.

• Begin in an industry you're already familiar with. Seek potential clients using telephone directories, building a list of names. Ask satisfied clients for recommendations.

• If you want to write annual reports, collect the ones you receive as a stockholder. If you aren't one, call corporations and ask for this year's edition.

• Writers who are willing to continue their education and work with their previous employers on a freelance basis, often have the best beginning in a business writing career.

• Maintain your reputation in this field by sticking with your writing business over the long haul. Stopping and starting your efforts, only when cash is tight, is not wise. For corporate clients to take you seriously, you must remain committed to business and technical writing.

Chapter Seventeen

Fund-Raising and Special Events

As government funding dries up and private contributions tighten, nonprofit organizations, churches, hospitals, museums and galleries, colleges and universities, public broadcasting stations, community causes and special task forces all rely on the strength of the written word to reach prospective donors.

To market your writing skills in the fund-raising field, make a list of the community-based and social service agencies near you. You'll find these in your telephone directory or at United Way. Someone in the communications or development office often will know of organizations that need fund-raising services. They'll also know which agencies have in-house personnel or those who might employ consultants or freelancers.

Write to the executive director or president of the organization you're referred to. You'll impress this person with a powerful resume focusing on the results you've achieved, specifically how you've increased pledges or operating funds. One cover letter I came across early in my career made reference to "raising funds and friends." That savvy business attitude not only got the candidate an interview, it got her the job!

But what if you don't have experience raising funds and friends? Well, it's never too late to begin cultivating contacts and learning the ropes. Volunteer your efforts. There's not a church around, nor a nonprofit organization for that matter, that wouldn't welcome another set of hands when it comes to serving on the fund-raising committee or helping with capital campaigns, annual fund or membership drives, or direct mail solicitations. Once you've gained some hands-on experience, move on to more structured agencies with more formal fund-raising efforts in place.

WRITING AN APPEAL

In fund-raising, there are generally three activities that you'll most frequently pursue: direct mail appeals, grant proposals and special events. Who hires direct mail writers? Essentially, anyone who promotes products or services through the mail, so the opportunities are endless. Effective appeals consist of a blend of fact and emotion. Communicate the major accomplishments undertaken this year (or since the agency's inception). What community need does the agency (your client) serve? Whom does your client serve and how? Who delivers the services (i.e, volunteers or paid staff)? Can public demand or support for your client's cause be demonstrated? What are the agency's short-term and long-range goals? Are these goals consistent with the organization's mission and service track record? What are the current funding sources? Finally, is your client a good steward of contributed money? Potential donors want and need to know all of these things in order to feel confident about donating their hard-earned money.

Since direct mail is by far the most prevalent method used for raising funds, you must hook your reader, being persuasive and tugging a little on the heart strings. Feature real people in the forefront of your written material to convey this. Show people's success stories. If you start with people, almost pretending that your prospect is sitting across from you, you'll write with the customer's needs in mind. Then, you can turn to the product you're trying to pitch.

Give examples of why your client's services work. Show that your client has been a good steward of public and private funds, and that these happy faces are the result. Carefully chosen photographs can often tell these stories better than even your best written words.

In most agencies, the highest response from a direct mail campaign comes from previous contributors. Therefore, keep your examples and photographs fresh. Potential and previous contributors also respond better when presented with specific projects their funds will help. A broader appeal doesn't generate the same level of giving. Also, offer your readers specifics in terms of contribution amounts and the problems at hand. To say "countless children suffer . . ." doesn't hit as hard as "many thousands of children suffer . . . ." Give a date that concludes your campaign.

Your appeal letter or direct mail solicitation has very little time—literally seconds—to get noticed. You must attend to every detail of the overall written package, from envelope to letter. In his book *Successful Direct Marketing Methods* (NTC Publishing Group), Bob Stone writes, "The outer envelope, or carrier envelope, has one job: to get itself opened." Stone adds that this envelope can dazzle, impress, tease or excite the reader's curiosity, but that whatever it does, it sets the tone for the entire appeal. Finally, phrase your direct mail appeal carefully. Some words speak more powerfully than others. For instance, "buy one, get one free" speaks louder than "50 percent off."

RESEARCHING GRANT MAKERS

Many nonprofit organizations spend a great deal of time searching for grant money as a source of funding. Grants are given in return for promised actions and designated purposes. They can be renewed but sometimes are not, so learn the basics of tracking down these funding sources and persuading them to donate funds to a particular program.

With so many agencies chasing so few funds, the competition is much tougher today than it used to be. Grantors are more discerning, and the criteria they've set, much more explicit.

To write a convincing proposal, learn as much as possible about the grant makers in your area. Ask your librarian for help. Turn to the yellow pages, Chamber of Commerce, United Way or other business leaders who have valuable connections. In my hometown, the business newspaper publishes a book of lists that can be helpful in tracking down industry leaders and appropriate grantors. In addition, the Carnegie Library of Pittsburgh is another resource. It's an affiliate of The Foundation Center, a national clearinghouse for information on philanthropic giving, headquartered in New York City. There are other affiliates across the United States. Perhaps there is one near you.

Consult the *Chronicle of Philanthropy*, the newspaper for the nonprofit world, the *Non-Profit Times* magazine, the *Federal Register* and other government publications that announce available grants and application requirements. The *Foundation Direc-*

tory lists funding sources that comprise over 90 percent of all U.S. grant dollars. On a smaller scale, the *National Data Book* lists smaller foundations. Grant writing professionals should consider joining the National Society of Fund Raising Executives (NSFRE) in Alexandria, Virginia.

Above all, don't waste time chasing a funding source when it's evident your project doesn't meet with the goals, objectives and philanthropic mission of the funder. You'll be off to a running start with your proposal if you follow the information you learn from these publications and send for the grantor's funding guidelines and annual report.

WRITING GRANT PROPOSALS

Be realistic about the money you request. Unrealistic requests will lessen your chances of securing the necessary funds. Know that many grantmakers expect to be consulted in the early stages of a project's planning. Weave their thoughts into your written proposal.

Focus on positive appeals rather than negative ones. Don't plead for funds to avoid a deficit or keep doors open. Present your client's organization as a community asset, carrying forth a mission. Key words that convey a positive message include *achievement*, *accomplishment*, *performance* and *success*.

In formatting your proposal, include a brief cover letter and a proposal summary—a one-page abstract that explains the amount requested, the total project budget and purpose, and the results you hope to achieve. Don't inflate the project's budget, but don't underestimate it either. If the agency does receive the grant, it will have to make up the difference somehow. Underestimating costs sets the agency up for failure in the worst way.

Provide an introduction to the organization, with history, mission, goals and objectives, significant accomplishments, service area and population served. Don't assume that the foundation knows anything about the organization.

Reiterate your goals and objectives. Address the project's staffing requirements, with highlights from resumes, job descriptions, recruitment attempts and training plans. Provide a method and schedule for the project's implementation. State how you'll evaluate the success, manage the budget and seek future funding. Foundations want to know how the program or purpose will continue when the grant concludes. List specific sources of revenue instead of vague "additional donors."

Your written narrative should not exceed approximately three pages (this doesn't include actual appendices such as the project's budget). Supporting documents include a tax-exempt status letter, listing of your client's board of directors, an annual report, current operating budget, audited financial statement and letters of support and appreciation from concerned citizens as well as news clippings, if these are requested per the grant maker's guidelines.

Finally, don't beg. Persuade with a professional writing style that gets to the point quickly. Heart-wrenching, emotional stories or examples of service are often more effective when told during a subsequent visit or conversation. And remember, foundations are not simply buildings or large institutions. They are made up of people — people who give grants. These people want to feel that they're investing in an organization, not just giving their money away. Earn their respect and trust. Should the grant be awarded, be sure to express your gratitude.

OTHER FUND-RAISING TIPS

No one person can raise funds and make friends for an organization. It's a collective approach. Raising funds and friends starts by getting rid of the age-old notion that institutions are entitled to charity. In today's economy, organizations must earn their funding. It's a natural arena for writers who must show rather than tell about their client organization.

Put together a core of individuals with influence and connections. Attract those volunteers and board members who can contribute funds themselves. Aiming for 100 percent participation among board members is not an unrealistic objective. Use these contacts to network, adding other influential names to your client's database. Build on those relationships. Remember that the highest percentage of response in a fund-raising effort comes from previous contributors. Make the most of these relationships and financial resources.

SPECIAL EVENTS PLANNING

The third area of fund-raising, and one that many writers frequently overlook, is the special event, whether it be a black-tie dinner, community outreach picnic, public or media open house or any other type of event. Indeed all of those groups that raise funds, make friends and heighten awareness are often interested in hosting special events. So are businesses and corporations, retailers, food product companies, bookstores, publishers and professionals. Sometimes, retailers in the same mall or shopping plaza will band together to form an association. In doing so, they pool their resources and work for the common good of all merchants.

Effective writing (and sometimes desktop publishing) is needed to create news releases, advertising, invitations, program booklets, flyers and feature articles that support these fund-raising special events. In addition, if you know how to mail-merge your databases, you have another marketable skill that will help you boost your writer's income.

If your freelance work requires you to wear the consultant's hat, select a special event that has the potential to make money (if that's a primary goal) or one that will attract a lot of media attention, thus increasing the public's awareness. Put careful thought into the type of event you'll host, making sure that the event and the mission of your client work well together.

In one client's case, we worked with a bank-sponsored jazz festival for children. We and another agency set up tables, distributed literature and collected donations. We had thought of hosting an ice cream reception immediately after the concert, but when we saw the catering price, we decided to forgo any food. Even for a menu as simple as ice cream, it would have cost ten dollars per person. The concert was free and attracted families from all socioeconomic levels. We didn't feel it was right to set up an event that children would want to attend and families couldn't afford since our agency's mission was dedicated to helping parents handle stress.

Learn to collaborate. My public relations clients have participated in arts festivals and the jazz concert I cited. Other nonprofits pool resources with hospitals, nurses or physicians, adding a medical component to provide health screenings. Sometimes, a multiple effort works better than an individual one, and it helps to keep the costs down as well.

Plan your event early. A year or two in advance, especially in major cities, is not too far ahead to set a date and reserve a site.

The year before, or at least ten months prior to your special event, prepare a large calendar covering everything that needs to be accomplished.

It's vital that the event and your client's organization tie together. Choose a concise and memorable name, something with a snappy ring to it. Ride the wave of national events, like "Adopt-a-Cat Month," if you're working with an animal rescue agency or "Child Abuse Prevention Month," if you're dedicated to children's welfare. By talking with others and learning about their successful fund-raisers, you may be able to put your own particular spin on an event that already works. As it's said, if it's not broken, don't fix it. Such is the wisest approach when pulling off a special event.

If you want added appeal, line up celebrities who might be willing to promote your cause. (Review "Client Conflicts" in chapter fifteen for additional concerns about working with celebrities and sports greats.)

Events usually come about more smoothly if you appoint a committee and coordinator early on. No one can pull off a special event alone. It must be a concerted effort, drawing upon the expertise and people power of many individuals. If you have difficulty recruiting volunteers, look to senior citizens, youth groups and student organizations (e.g., fraternities and sororities) to get involved with your client's cause. You'll need a cadre of volunteers throughout your planning, from stuffing envelopes and invitations to serving as ticket takers and gophers at the event itself.

If you plan an outdoor event, make sure you have contingency plans for inclement weather. Designate a rain date so you won't be stuck fielding phone calls at the last minute. Have this date printed on your tickets and on all literature you produce. Also, if a keynote speaker is involved, have a back-up speaker ready to go at a moment's notice, and of course, secure all agreements for speakers and entertainment in writing. As the date draws near, plan to invest at least as much effort and money in promoting and advertising your special event as you did funding its entertainment.

HOW TO GET STARTED

 Virtually all charities, hospitals and higher education institutions seek to raise funds and friends. You may be called on to write direct mail appeals or grant proposals, or plan special events.

• Develop a list of charities, nonprofit organizations, colleges, universities and hospitals. Contact The Foundation Center in New York City to see if there is an affiliate near you.

• If you lack experience, join a fund-raising committee, capital campaign or membership drive.

• Collect direct mail material you receive from publishers, financial service providers, mail order companies, ad agencies and others. Turn to these samples for inspiration and ideas. Successful appeals are those you receive repeatedly.

• Enlist a core of volunteers to help with special events. Even the best-laid plans need back-up support, usually when you least expect it and at the last minute.

LONG-TERM
INVESTMENTS

Chapter Eighteen

Newsletters

They greet us on our desks and in our mailboxes. They tell us when the next meeting will be, what interest rates might do or what the minister has to say. They are newsletters, and in today's information age, they come from nearly everyone.

This is no exaggeration. In any given month, my church sends me news regarding special events, births, deaths or changes of address within the congregation. My financial planner's newsletter advises us and reaffirms my commitment to save for my children's college education. (Newsletters are very good at kicking us into gear once in a while!) Even our former real estate agent sends us monthly tips helping us decorate our home and accent the yard. The same goes for my travel agent, favorite charities and companies whose products I've used. Someone has to plan and put together all of this information. Why not you?

If you've honed the skills of effective writing, you already have one of the skills you'll need to turn newsletter writing into a profitable side venture. Perhaps you'll begin with newsletters for clients. In time, you might self-publish one of your own. The basics apply to beginning all varieties of newsletters.

THE DESKTOP REVOLUTION

Today, a great majority of published newsletters are created with desktop publishing (DTP). Paul Brainerd, president and founder of Aldus Corporation, coined this phrase, envisioning computer systems that could perform the functions previously accomplished by expensive typesetting and layout. With the advent of DTP, writers became instant newsletter editors, capable of combining text and graphics and making up camera-ready pages with the click of the mouse.

I have only a cursory knowledge of graphic arts. Actually, I can't draw a straight line, even with the help of a T-square or ruler. But with desktop publishing, I'm free to set up an attractive, eye-catching format complete with graphic lines and design elements. In addition, I can import a client's logo into my documents plus take advantage of the increasing amount of clip-art and illustrations available on diskette. These computer capabilities allow you to maintain a family look in your client's publications, tying the newsletter's design to that of stationery, brochures and other collateral materials.

Purchasing a DTP system is easier than you might think. Most personal computers are equipped with enough memory to operate the popular page layout programs like PageMaker or QuarkXPress. But be certain of this. Ask questions and do a little research prior to purchasing (and review the sections on selecting computers and printers in chapter two).

Don't be discouraged. I can hear you saying, "I don't have a computer, and purchasing one, let alone software, is out of the question." You can still make money from newsletters, relying on outside services to produce the finished product. With good organizational skills, it can be done.

Having your own desktop system, you're free to do everything yourself. Without one, you can still gather information, plan each issue, write and edit your stories and the contributions of others, select clip-art from catalogs and complete or oversee the typesetting and paste-up of the camera-ready artwork that will eventually go to the printer.

SELLING THE CONCEPT

It's essential that you know how you'll tackle a newsletter before you sell the idea to a prospective client or to subscribers. After all, you've got to convince these people to spend money on a new product. If the client already has a newsletter, you still must sell them on giving you a chance. What can you offer to make the newsletter better? An attractive format? A more sophisticated look? Better content? A crisp, new writing style?

Put yourself in your client's shoes. A newsletter, particularly one started from scratch, must be worth the resources everyone will be investing. Your job as writer and editor is to convince your client that the newsletter will bring in more customers or additional donors. In short, it must make money. You also might need to emphasize the importance of keeping employees or members informed. Newsletters, done correctly, are wonderful, highly targeted public relations vehicles, promoting goodwill to all who read them. Done poorly, they can become a joke and a waste of time, money and effort.

On the brighter side, marketing newsletters to clients is much easier than selling them on other forms of public relations work. That's because they are tangible. When you're finished writing, editing, producing and printing a newsletter, you have a product to hold up to those who have paid you, and you generally have a mailing list that guarantees a certain level of readership and interest in the information you've imparted.

DETERMINING FREQUENCY

In the beginning, you need to establish some basics. The decisions you make at this juncture will guide you throughout every issue. Determine how often you will publish your newsletter — weekly, semi-monthly, monthly, bimonthly, quarterly, semi-annually or annually. Most newsletters require at least a quarterly frequency or better to establish the comfort level readers must have for the publication to prove successful.

Analyze your budget. Artwork, illustrations, photography and colors increase the costs of each issue. It's easy to get carried away with your initial enthusiasm. I once was contracted to edit an employee newsletter from scratch. We identified a reporter in each department of the organization and secured the commitment of the executive director to write a column for the weekly publication. The first several issues were filled with more than enough material. Then, the process began to drag. We all had other job-related priorities and once the initial excitement wore off, it got to be one more chore each week. So we made the decision to publish semi-monthly — a decision we should have made in the very beginning.

NAMING YOUR NEWSLETTER

Choose a word or phrase that quickly and clearly identifies the newsletter and its content. A good name helps position your newsletter. It should be easy to pronounce and remember. However, in trying to be lively, avoid titles that sound too cute. Aim for something with impact, a powerful word or two to make just the right impression.

This is especially important if you're publishing a newsletter for personal image building. Self-employed consultants and professionals often use newsletters to turn dormant clients into active ones or to obtain media exposure. For this, consider using that individual's name in the title.

Other newsletter names often build on words that convey a sense of communication—words like *almanac, briefing, digest, forecast, outlook, notes, spotlight* or *update*. Newsletters I've produced have used the words *connection, direction, reporter, resource* and *quarterly* in their titles. Brainstorm all the alternatives. If you need more than one or two words to convey your message, consider using a subtitle. For many years, I published a subscription newsletter for communicators, students and working professionals. It was called *Perspectives*. But when I created it, I knew that title alone wouldn't do the job, so I used the subtitle *Concepts for a Career in Communications* to explain what the publication was all about.

If after sketching a few rough drafts of your newsletter's name-plate, you're still not satisfied, turn to one of many books devoted to newsletter production, such as *Editing Your Newsletter* and *Newsletter Sourcebook* (North Light Books) both by Mark Beach and *Newsletters From the Desktop* (Ventana Press) by Roger C. Parker. All of these books contain attractive examples. By reviewing their formats, you can pick and choose which elements you feel work best for you.

DECIDING ON A FORMAT

A three- or four-column approach yields the most professional look. There's maximum flexibility, and it's perfect for photography. A two-column approach is still good and easier to read than a one-column format which looks like a typewritten letter. A one-column format is the easiest to do, but it can get boring after a while.

No matter how many columns you choose, remember that format is the framework of your newsletter. Make it workable, issue to issue. Use lots of white space to avoid a crowded view of the page, and be consistent.

To graphically break up pages, consider boxes or tool lines, photographs, clip art and pull quotes. All of these attract the reader's eye, pulling him into the story. Using reverse type or screened elements is acceptable, but use these sparingly. And if any of your artwork needs an explanation alongside, then it isn't working for you.

If there's one rule to adhere to in layout, especially when it comes to desktop publishing, is that using less is preferable to using more. Put a novice, with little graphics expertise, in front of a computer. Watch his eyes light up at the sight of bold-faced type, boxes, lines and other elements, and you'll see what I mean. Give this person fifty different fonts, and he'll use them—all in the same document!

Another element factoring into your format is your newsletter's mailing requirements. If you intend to mail the newsletter in an outer envelope, all the page space can be devoted to editorial content. However, if you create a self-mailer, then you lose space and must build a self-mailing portion (that meets postal requirements) into your format.

CONSISTENCY IS CRUCIAL

No matter what you decide in terms of frequency, names or formats, be consistent. We're all drawn to our favorite sections in newspapers or magazines knowing exactly what to expect from them. We enjoy opening up to standard columns, finding our favorite items in the same place issue to issue, often reading these sections first. But move the funnies from the entertainment page to the sports section, and you could interfere with someone's evening, and more important, you'll lose readers. The key here is comfort. Give your readers consistency, which builds such a comfort level. By doing this, readers will keep your newsletter. They'll read it, devour it, clip it, post it and love it.

If you fail to provide this level of consistency, your newsletter may appear amateurish. When a client's new staff member took over the newsletter I had created, the format changed. In time, the agency's executive director shared with me the new look, which admittedly he was not too pleased with. Where we had created standing columns, continuation of text from other articles now appeared as well as boxed items that looked sorely out of place. Where we had established appropriate margins, extra lines of type now crowded the graphic design. The newsletter and its new editor didn't progress, and the task of editing and designing each issue soon fell back to me. Lack of consistency killed this newsletter's overall appeal.

DEVELOPING A WRITING STYLE

Have you ever received a holiday newsletter? Or shall I say, a book? You know, the newsletter from self-absorbed sister Sally, that after rolling your eyes, you file away intending to read, only you never get to it and maybe don't want to anyway!

Newsletter writing is a skill worth honing. It will carry you far in your writing career, for if you know how to cram six pages into two, people will actually read your writing. You'll stand a better chance of making good impressions, and ultimately, finding work as a freelancer. My rule of thumb is: If your newsletter is placed on the "to be read" pile, it isn't doing its job.

A newsletter's format is tight and very capsulized allowing for timely information or trustworthy commentary. Look at the grandaddy of them all, the *Kiplinger Washington Letter*. This newsletter has been circulated weekly to clients since 1923. Notice that "news" isn't a part of the title. That's because the editors are selling commentary to an audience already well informed about current events. They are selling advice and analysis, what some might call "news you can use." And if you asked faithful subscribers why they keep mailing their checks in, they'd probably tell you that the easy-to-read format and helpful writing style is definitely a factor.

Knowing this, write your copy with the quick hit in mind, telling the reader everything she needs to know in as few words as possible. As with other news writing, structure your stories in the inverted pyramid form, with the most important details — the who, what, when, where, why and how — in your lead paragraph. Then, if you must cut to copyfit, you won't be sacrificing important details as you chop the story from the bottom up. Of course, always provide a lead, a strong middle and a satisfying conclusion, only in a more concise form.

Using the active voice will also convey the sense of immediacy newsletters are known for. Edit yourself after you've written a first draft. For a list of handy reminders, turn to chapter four, and review the "summing it all up" section. Finally, read your copy aloud to determine whether it's conversational. Remember, you're aiming for comfort and consistency.

PRODUCING CAMERA-READY ARTWORK

Your job will be easier in the long run if you use any of the page layout software packages. Initially, it might take several issues for you to produce the finished product with relative ease. Your desktop skills will improve with every newsletter you produce, so practice is essential. Allow yourself plenty of time for delivering the first issue.

For those using the more traditional paste-up and layout method, you'll need a few, less costly, supplies than the desktop publisher. A light table (or small portable one) is perfect but not essential. A drawing board or flat surface will work in a pinch. You'll need artboard for laying out a lot of graphics, but simple white paper will suffice if you only need to paste-up an occasional graphic. Apply acetate over the blocks where photos will go. Glue down everything with rubber cement, checking for proper placement with a T-square and triangle. Apply a fixative to avoid smudges and secure a tissue overlay on top where you can write any markings to the printer.

If you use this paste-up and layout method, a basic graphic arts book would serve you well. The same applies to DTP where numerous books are devoted to the subject of page layouts and makeovers. If you're ever in doubt as to how you should prepare camera-ready materials, ask your printer. These professionals can guide you not only in terms of mechanical preparation but also in paper selection, ink supplies and more.

In fact, with a little ingenuity, you can make your newsletter more sophisticated with little additional cost and effort. "Use a different screen percentage of a single color to create a tint that gives the effect of a second ink color," writes Mark Beach in *Newsletter Sourcebook*. In addition, create scalloped columns whereby you hang all columns from atop a horizontal line, leaving the bottom of the text uneven.

When developing camera-ready artwork, I use newsletter stationery I've previously created with all the standard items like title, subscription information (if there is any) and standard tool lines. I print a fixed quantity of sheets in a particular color ink on a grade of paper that ˙allows no show-through. My supply usually lasts for months. Tell your printer if you plan to feed your paper stock through a photocopy machine or laser printer. It will make a difference in the finish on the paper and in the ink used. I always allow for this flexibility, ordering laser finish stock so that my client or I can print extra copies if we need to. By printing stationery ahead, you only have to plug in the items that change each month, usually in black ink. These items include the date, the volume and number, and of course, the information.

SUBSCRIPTION NEWSLETTERS

Readers pay for information, not fluff. With subscription newsletters, keep graphics and artwork to a minimum or don't use them at all. When I sat down to write *Perspectives*, I always tried to focus on ways my readers could get ahead in their careers and make money — universal objectives for just about everyone in my diverse audience. Keep satisfying reader's needs, and your financial needs will be fulfilled as well.

Of course, money is one of the perks and perils of self-publishing a newsletter. You can earn a sizeable income if you do your job well, but with newsletters, there is a constant turnover among readers. People cease to need your publication (or so they believe) or they need it more than ever. Tapping into this changing market requires promotion, and plenty of it. You'll need to reinvest much of your earnings to attract continual attention to your newsletter, thereby securing additional subscribers. As president of the Newsletter Clearinghouse, Howard Penn Hudson wrote *Publishing Newsletters* (Mcmillan in 1988; also available through Newsletter Clearinghouse in Rhinebeck, NY), a book filled with a multitude of ideas for generating additional income from subscription newsletters. Frederick D. Goss details his view of the business side of publishing and managing newsletter properties in *Success in Newsletter Publishing, A Practical Guide* (Newsletter Publisher's Association, Arlington, VA). Goss's nonprofit organization, the Newsletter Publisher's Association, is another valuable resource for self-publishers.

CHURCH OR CLUB NEWSLETTERS

When working with church groups or community organizations, the value is in content, not in slick design or expensive paper. If you're ever at a loss for ideas, try a brief tease for the next sermon or featured speaker, a calendar of events for people to plan around, birth announcements and obituaries, financial information or excerpted material.

In the case of reprinted items, you'll have to seek permission first, but I've found most people are flattered to have their work reproduced. Just be sure to cite the source, and if possible, give people a phone number or address to contact the article's author for more information.

With church and club newsletters, people profiles facilitate getting to know one another. Highlight a member of the month. Design a crossword puzzle with members' names and clues so that people in the organization learn a little about the others. Say thanks when it's appropriate to do so, and you'll build more goodwill than money can buy.

COMPANY NEWSLETTERS

For employee publications, newsletters may often be the only communications link between management and staff and back up again. Actually, your aim should be lateral communication, in which both sides feel they are getting something. Use your newsletter to build morale, concentrating on the positive, while reporting the facts as they are. Avoid selling the management line and becoming too preachy in tone.

For the marketing newsletter, provide readers with practical information they can use. And while your goal is to keep the product or service in mind, you can wander off to related subjects. The real estate newsletter I receive does this by providing an occasional recipe or tip for household safety.

DOLLARS AND SENSE

How much income you earn depends a lot on where you live, whether you work with nonprofit groups or money-making concerns, and whether there is significant demand for your services. Newsletter writing and production could earn you anywhere from $25 to $2500, not subtracting the cost of necessary equipment and supplies.

In setting your rates, estimate the time it will take to write, edit, revise, layout and work with the printer to achieve the finished product. Then add at least two hours to your bid. First issues and start-ups will always take longer—I guarantee it. Your client will most likely want this changed or that moved, and you'll want to be compensated for all the design time it takes to strike a final format. If possible, charge separately for the set-up or explain that the first issue will cost more than subsequent ones. Also, watch those issues with the occasional insert. If you're expected to write and typeset this insert, let alone coordinate the printing of it, add an extra cost to your invoice.

Finally, always ask printers, paper suppliers and other vendors to bill their services directly to your client. Nonprofit organizations are tax-exempt, so it works out, in many cases, in the client's best interest. Besides, not having to pay miscellaneous invoices frees you to produce more newsletters and keep the cash flowing into your writing business.

Other ways to save money include keeping a strict schedule (printers charge more for rush jobs), shopping around for the best prices and professional services, and completing as much of the newsletter in-house as your talent and time will allow. By far, editing every word, sentence, paragraph and page eliminates unnecessary material from your newsletter, cutting back on time, space, paper, printing and distribution costs. I've always tried to copyfit the text I create into the allotted space. This has consistently saved time, and time is money.

HOW TO GET STARTED

 Newsletter writing can be lucrative. It can keep the income flowing when editors are slow to pay for other assignments or when writer's block gets you down. Besides, turning your attention to another type of writing can recharge your battery for other projects. And newsletters are certainly creative outlets for your desktop publishing talents.

• Decide how you will produce the newsletter. Desktop publishing indeed makes production much easier.

• Take time in developing the nameplate, format and standard items your newsletter will feature. Charge an extra, one-time set-up fee to compensate for the many hours you'll put in creating just the right look.

• When writing, keep your style capsulized. If you wouldn't

send a six-page newsletter in seven-point type to friends for the holidays, don't send it to clients throughout the year.

• Before your newsletter goes to the printer, prepare a printer's dummy showing how the finished product will look with the self-mailing portion and other graphic elements. This eliminates costly errors.

• Know that as a newsletter editor you'll likely hear about the missed information or typographical error someone found rather than the pleasure and knowledge they derived. Realize you've done the best job you can, and take criticisms in stride.

Chapter Nineteen

Lyric Writing

When thinking of long-term career investments, lyric writing quickly comes to mind. Unlike writers of books or articles who receive fees upfront or on completion of their work, lyricists labor long hours uncertain of payment. Only after a song has been recorded will the writer earn any royalties, and even these are divided among all those who own a share in the work's profits — lyricist, musical or songwriting collaborators, recording artists, music publishers and record companies.

Jingle writers are frequently paid a flat fee, called a buyout, from the advertising agency commissioning their work. When aired nationally, these jingles may earn their writers residuals based on when and how often the jingle airs. Bear in mind, however, that jingles can be resold into other music markets with new lyrics attached to them. One piece of music has the potential of earning much more over its lifetime, depending upon the creative energies that develop it.

While payment in the music industry may seem like a serious drawback, rest assured there is money to be made in songwriting. Children's music is a particularly viable option. "Unlike the pop record business where, if the planets or cards (or whatever you believe in) are aligned right, you can make a lot of money in a relatively short time, the children's market is slow but sure, and doesn't burn out overnight," writes John Braheny in *The Craft and Business of Songwriting* (Writer's Digest Books).

Teaming up with another songwriting partner also pays off in the music business. Fans worldwide will always remember John Lennon and Paul McCartney for their contributions to music history and the 1960s, in general. Twenty years later gospel-turned-contemporary artists Amy Grant and Michael W. Smith successfully collaborated on numerous songs, singing and touring together on occasion, until both catapulted onto the Top 40 charts as artists with their own separate efforts.

HOW LYRICISTS MAKE MONEY

Another advantage to becoming a lyricist is the ultimate control you have over the use of your work. As the song's creator, you determine how your material will be used. Often, this matter of choice opens up new and substantial income opportunities, including licensing for records, compact discs and cassette tapes, commercials, television programs, movies, radio or advertising jingles, video games, even toys. Remember, songs are bought outright, and a song makes money each time it's used.

Three organizations in the United States are responsible for collecting license fees from radio and television stations, the networks, bars and restaurants. ASCAP and BMI are the two largest performance rights organizations with SESAC ranking third. These organizations distribute the fees to their members, according to complicated formulas and contractual splits. John Braheny explains the four major income sources of songs—mechanical, performance, synchronization and print royalties.

A beginning lyricist would be wise to keep track of their song's usage and make sure that it's properly documented (providing this is possible). A&M recording artist Frank Cappelli made his mark in children's music with *Cappelli & Company*, a half-hour program produced by WTAE-TV of Hearst Broadcasting, and later syndicated to the Nickelodeon cable channel. In the early days of the show, Cappelli realized the importance of reviewing the local station's ASCAP surveys and turned in his own ASCAP records. This resulted in fewer discrepancies and increased income.

SONGWRITING COLLABORATION

"A good marriage between the words and the music of a song is what makes a song succeed," says Paul Zollo in the *Beginning Songwriter's Answer Book* (Writer's Digest Books). In a lot of cases, songwriting requires collaboration with a musician who can give the lyrics a musical structure. After all, some people are gifted with words while others understand the qualities of melody, harmony and rhythm. If you're a writer blessed with both talents, consider yourself lucky.

You might also be the kind of person who dislikes the idea of a partnership. According to Sheila Davis, author of *The Craft of Lyric Writing* (Writer's Digest Books), typology is most definitely a factor. "Introverts prefer to work alone, and they often want to do the whole song," she says. "The extroverts love collaboration, bouncing ideas around. There isn't any one right way. Each writer has his or her own style."

If writing is your strongest suit, and you need a collaborator, don't dismay. Songwriting organizations in your area may know of musician members who seek writing services. Attend workshops at music schools, colleges and universities. The National Academy of Songwriters in Hollywood, California also has a Songwriter's Network, published in each edition of its *SongTalk* newspaper. Any member of NAS can use this service, regardless of where you live, to seek collaborators.

In choosing the songwriting partner you'll work with, seek someone with similar goals and motivations for writing songs. Your musical tastes needn't be identical, just complementary. Interpersonal communication and a healthy sense of respect for one another's talents is essential. In short, there should be personal chemistry between the two of you. Distance need not be a major factor, but perhaps it is a minor one. While collaboration can occur through the mail, it's probably more efficient to work together in person, at least occasionally.

Once you've found a partner, it's time to formally agree on the business aspects of your collaboration. You say this smacks of distrust? Well, maybe. But remember, songwriting is a business. Questions of authorship or artistic differences may occur, especially upon the death of one partner or upon the dissolution of your collaboration.

Label your agreement "Songwriter's Collaboration Agreement." Identify all parties by name, address and social security number. Title and name all compositions you create together, making note of who writes the lyrics and who is responsible for the music (or if both contribute equally in these areas). Designate the exact royalty percentages and know who is responsible for particular expenses incurred. Should one party be out of town or impossible to reach for an extended period of time, provide for power of attorney so that the remaining partner(s) can convey the copyright. This requires notarizing the agreement.

In addition, provide a means for arbitrating disputes, through another individual or through NAS, making the arbitrator's decision binding on all collaborators. Finally, date and sign the agreement.

These suggestions should serve merely as a guide to beginning writers. If your collaboration requires additional stipulations and provisions it would be wise to seek legal assistance in drafting an agreement. Beware of offers that seem too good to be true. They probably are. There are companies preying on lyricists anxious to have their words put to music. The best collaborative effort makes money for each partner when its songs earn royalties. Never pay a collaborator in advance, out of your own pocket. The business just doesn't work this way.

WRITING FROM WITHIN

There are a lot of suggestions when it comes to writing lyrics and music, but perhaps the overriding one is to write from within. If you write songs based on what you think will sell in the marketplace, your lyrics will be empty, devoid of emotion and feeling.

But what makes it in the marketplace does matter. Some lyrics don't play as big a role in certain forms of music as in others. For instance, lyrics aren't as essential to rock 'n' roll as they are in a country western ballad. Some words just don't sing well either. They don't work easily when set to music. So steer clear of these. Also, the typical popular song lasts no more than three minutes.

The basic lyric needs meaning, brevity, a rhyme scheme and a good use of sound. While some writers believe that rhyming dictionaries are totally unnecessary, others use them as a tool to combat writer's block. Use your own judgment. Most writers agree, however, that lyricists need notebooks in which to record key phrases or lyric fragments, including idioms and turns of speech. If you're fortunate enough to have a computer, you'll find it handy to store these phrases and fragments under specific categories for retrieval at a later date.

Writers who intend to make money from their songwriting know what people want to hear. In popular songs, sex and love are good choices. Death, politics or emotionally charged issues are taboo. That's not to say that the exception won't sell, and sell well, but in the beginning, you're best to stick with what's proved successful for other writers.

Formula songs have better chances of achieving commercial success because there is risk involved, from the publisher's perspective, in undertaking the unusual. What's your primary motivation for writing? Do you want to say something in a way that's never been expressed before or do you want to sell your lyrics as quickly as possible? There are two distinct schools of thought on this matter. Either motivating factor is valid, and you needn't apologize for it. There will always be those musicians and writers who disdain suppressing artistic vision in favor of economic reward, but since it's *your* career, *you* should make the determination.

MUSICAL STRUCTURE

Beyond the type of lyrics you will write, it's helpful to know the fundamentals of a song's structure. Structure, in the music business, refers to the arrangement of the song's components — the verse, the chorus, and the bridge. The two most common structures heard today are the verse/chorus structure and the verse/bridge structure. Many songs use all three elements — the verse, the chorus and the bridge.

The word "verse" derives from the Latin word "turning," and it's a word used in poetry as well. Verse refers to the metrical line of language, or a stanza. The verse usually opens the song and has a pattern that's repeated throughout, with different words each time (i.e., turning). While the metrical pattern and melody repeat, the words of a verse change (turn) each time.

As a writer, think of your beginning verse as a lead paragraph. It sets the scene, hooks the audience and presents the basic information — main character, situation and time. Your verse will put the listener in a happy, sentimental, pensive or funky frame of mind.

Chorus is the section of the song that repeats both musically and lyrically. The chorus focuses the listener on the song's true essence or meaning, usually with a simple and succinct, easy-to-remember phrase. That's why this section of the song almost always contains the song's title, usually in the first or last line of the chorus. In children's recording that predictable repetition in

the song is even more important. In Cappelli's "Pass The Coconut," see how the chorus incorporates the title:

> Calling out, "Coconuts," my friends
> Hear what I have to say
> Gather 'round, gather
> 'round, my dears
> Here on the half moon bay
>
> Oh, the seed of the coconut tree
> Travels the salty sea
> Washing up on a distant shore
> The start of another tree
>
> (Chorus:)
> Pass the coconut to me
> It is so sweet to eat
> Pass the coconut to me
> Oh, what a lovely treat
>
> It is a plant oh so kind to man
> No branches but oh so tall
> Very large leaves, swaying
> in the breeze
> And then the coconuts fall
>
> The fruit is a drupe covered with a husk
> Ah yes, the husk is strong
> The nut is a seed with a sweet white meat
> Come on, and sing along
>
> (Chorus)
>
> Growing up next to the bright blue sea
> Swayin' in the tropical breeze
> Fall to the sand, roll out to the sea
> Growin' to be one more tree
>
> No one is sure where the nut came from
> The coconuts find a way

They travel over the bright blue sea
And grow by the half moon bay

(Chorus)

Often, the verse melody leads up to the chorus, building tension that's released by the chorus. "Pass The Coconut" does exactly this. In this song's lyrics, the melody and structure are the same each time but use different lyrics while the chorus remains the same each time and is repeated after the verses.

The Beatles' classic "I Want to Hold Your Hand" is written in the verse/chorus structure, but there's also a bridge added, starting with the line "And when I touch you, I feel happy — inside . . . ." A bridge, in musical jargon, functions the same way as bridges we drive across in our cars, linking land to land. A bridge connects verses with verses, verses with choruses or choruses with choruses.

A musical bridge breaks the boredom when listeners begin to tire of the melodic repetition. A bridge detours us to new material, both musical and lyrical. The beat may shift. Instrumental portions of a song may take over. But any way you cut it, a bridge is a diversion, and one that is entirely optional to the songwriter. Next time you hear your favorite songs, listen closely for the verse, chorus and bridge structures.

WELCOMED FEEDBACK

Mention feedback to a musician, and you'll elicit a grimace. But here, I'm referring to friendly feedback, the kind you receive to boost your songwriting career.

Once you've written your song, you'll feel an overwhelming sense of accomplishment. You'll be proud of your efforts, and rightly so. But resist that urge to marry your work. Set the song aside until you can look at it again with a fresh perspective. Analyze the lyrics. Which parts of the song work and which are weak? Analyze the song's melody in much the same manner. If there are portions of your song that prove to be particularly bothersome, rework them. Yes, the dreaded rewrite is an inescapable part of the lyricist's life as well. Zollo's book contains a handy checklist to guide you in this rewriting effort.

To help you achieve the constructive criticism your songwriting efforts require, join a critique group composed of beginning songwriters like yourself. These organizations aren't merely for musical aficionados who sit around and talk about their tastes in music. They are for serious songwriters who seek to fine tune their skills, learn songwriting as both a business and a craft, and ultimately, place their creations in the catalogs of major music publishing companies.

In my hometown, the Pittsburgh Songwriters' Association meets monthly to offer support and suggestions to its growing list of members. To find a similar group in your area, contact music stores and schools, colleges and universities for recommendations.

RISING IN THE INDUSTRY

Songwriters survive in much the same manner as other writers. They strive to make as many professional contacts as possible and always keep an eye toward networking. "There's no set way to go about this," says Cappelli. "Try to create opportunities, and once you have, take advantage of them. Early in my career, I sang at the home of Michael Landon, participating in a fundraiser for an environmental cause. While there, I had the opportunity to meet Robert Lamm of the group Chicago. Those kind of contacts are great to establish and keep up with."

If you're considering other writing outlets besides lyric writing, you might try doing music or concert reviews. If you're lucky, you might be granted an interview with an artist you admire. Ask questions, listen and learn from the comments offered.

PUBLISHING POINTERS

Music publishers seek songs and work hard at finding artists to record them. While the writer is the creator of the song, and has every right to represent his own material, many choose to use the services of a music publisher much like writers and authors choose to use literary agents to further their careers.

Those who prefer to set up their own publishing companies find the process of doing so is not difficult at all. "I'll never forget hearing, years ago, about how the Beatles and other successful composers got some raw deals when they first started in the music business," recalls Cappelli. "When I started researching children's music, I decided to start my own publishing company. I don't think anyone really realizes how easy that is to do. A federal law requires ASCAP and BMI to accept anybody as a publisher. Write to them and tell them you want to become a publishing company, and you just pick the name. After all, when a song is recorded and sold, the publisher and the writer split everything. If you're both, you increase your income."

Cappelli turned down offers by recording studios that offered to publish his songs for him, knowing that this business strategy would pay off over the lifetime of his career. If you seek to establish your own music publishing company, the licensing organization you choose may charge a nominal application fee. In some parts of the country, you'll have to file a fictitious name statement. To find out what steps to take, call the office of the Secretary of State in your state of residence. You'll have to officially join one of the performance rights organization — ASCAP, BMI or SESAC — as a publishing member. When undertaking such an important business step, it's wise to seek legal counsel just to make sure you're not overlooking any important details.

But if you decide that you don't want to be bothered with the administrative and sales work required to place your songs, put together a demo package to send to a publisher. Your package should include a cassette tape with no more than three songs, clearly labeled on the front of the tape itself. Be sure to put your best song first.

Use the copyright symbol with your name and the current year on the label. Label the back of the tape with your name, address and telephone number. If your tape is separated from your typed lyric sheet, a publisher will be able to return the material to you.

A lyric sheet should be prepared for each song. Make sure this is double-spaced, with the choruses always indented. Use upper- and lowercase letters when typing your lyrics.

While your material has to speak for itself, you should include a brief cover letter, typed on professional letterhead. Here, you should introduce yourself as a songwriter and outline the contents of your demo package. Publishers are busy people, and they will not appreciate learning what moved you to write your songs or what your friends think of them.

Always be sure to enclose an SASE large enough to return all of the material. Wrap the lyric sheet around the cassette tape and secure it with a rubber band. Now you're ready to head for the post office.

When you hear back, a publisher may ask if he or she can hold onto the song and try to place it. If the publisher is successful, a contract will follow. Sometimes, the publisher may offer an exclusive one-song contract immediately. If this should happen, you cannot approach any others with the same song. Or, a publisher may ask you to sign a nonexclusive, one-song contract, meaning that he has the rights to try and place the song, but you, as writer, are still free to pitch the song elsewhere.

HOW TO GET STARTED

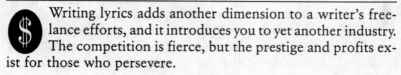 Writing lyrics adds another dimension to a writer's freelance efforts, and it introduces you to yet another industry. The competition is fierce, but the prestige and profits exist for those who persevere.

• Team up with a collaborator if you need help adding musical structure to your lyrics. A successful collaborative effort combats bouts of writer's block as another person's fresh perspective adds dimension to the song.

• To learn such structure yourself, listen to your favorite songs, and with the lyrics in hand, chart the verse, chorus and bridge, witnessing and learning from the pattern.

• Don't write off formula songs. Listeners find the predictability in formula music reassuring and somewhat comforting. Before you move into uncharted territory, master the tried and true.

• Join a songwriting association and build your network of contacts in the industry. Learn from anyone who is willing to offer constructive criticism and advice.

• Follow the accepted submission procedures for submitting lyric sheets and demo tapes. Always provide an SASE.

• Start your own publishing company if you want to maximize your income potential. Seek legal advice when establishing such a business venture.

Chapter Twenty

Books

C an you see yourself writing a book? If you're like many writers, the answer to that question will change at some point in your career. It did in mine.

Two and a half years into my freelance career, I attended my first writers conference, held in my hometown of Pittsburgh. I remember that day vividly. As I sat down to my assigned seat at the networking luncheon, I remember thinking to myself, "I'm not sure how valuable this discussion is going to be." Most of the other writers were beginners, and I had already cracked major magazine markets, represented my publications on several press trips and was at work on a pet project—a contemporary romance novel. But just as the waiters began to serve, one of the two literary agents invited to the event sat down in the only available seat—the one next to mine.

While others immediately jumped on this poor woman, pitching their novels and ideas, I waited my turn. When the conversation turned my way, I mentioned my writing for bridal and travel markets. Her response: "I'd love to represent a honeymoon travel book." Not only had I found an agent, but I also walked away with the idea for a book I'd never even dreamed of—one I knew I could write, if only it were to sell.

Unfortunately, the market wasn't as receptive as either of us had hoped, despite her persistent efforts and my own. She turned the proposal back to me. But I tell you this to prove that someday you may find a book within you, and it will often be when you least expect it.

The Book Industry Study Group, a publishing trade organization, predicted that book sales in 1993 would exceed $17 billion, and that the industry would grow at a 7 percent pace that's expected to last well into the 1990s. Bookstores are cropping up everywhere, with superstores abounding in areas where people have a real passion for reading. But while 45,000 to 50,000 new titles are published every year, a staggering number of proposals and manuscripts will be rejected, and only about two hundred of those published may become best-sellers. The odds are not stacked in your favor.

Still, lots of writers dream of becoming authors, but many allow the pursuit to end. Others make the dream become a reality. That's the difference between a published author and a want-to-be. All authors require the ability to conceptualize a larger-length project, work hard at its completion and persevere in the marketplace. But clearly, some writers have advantages over others in cracking the book business.

Those authors with famous last names frequently bring their celebrity status to the printed page. Politicians, public figures, military heroes and Hollywood legends are primary examples. Experts see publishing as a viable option. Business leaders like Lee Iacocca, transplant pioneer Dr. Thomas Starzl and pop-psychologist Dr. Kevin Leman have all done so. And famous names such as Danielle Steel and Stephen King have become literary franchises to their publishers.

Other writers who have the right connections move ahead in their careers because of ghostwriting opportunities, good agents or access to privileged information. Frequently, writers who have spent years earning a solid journalistic reputation from magazines and newspapers see books as their next logical career step. And finally, those with financial resources often self-publish their works, leading to additional success as publishers.

THE PUBLISHING INDUSTRY

Publishing is a business like any other. The product is books comprising many different genres and even distinctions within those genres. There are the featured books that publishers launch every spring and fall, the ones that promise to lure the crowds into bookstores in hot pursuit. There are also midlist books, those that are new but not in the same category as the publisher's best bets. Finally, there are the backlist books. These books were published months or even years ago, but prove to be consistent sellers. Therefore, publishers continue to print, revise and update these editions.

Major publishing houses have not escaped the wave of mergers and acquisitions that pervaded the 1980s and 1990s. Companies are looking for tighter profit and loss margins, and thus, are very careful in the projects they acquire. Today, because of downsizing and streamlining of operations, editors wear many hats, acquiring properties, developing and editing them plus seeing to the business details of their departments. With this tremendous workload, it's as if they're looking for reasons *not* to publish a particular project. Those that make it beyond the query stack or out of the slush pile had better prove themselves worthy of an editor's consideration, and fast.

So what do publishers and editors look for? First, it's imperative that writers do their research. Visit bookstores and libraries. Read. There's no other way to gain a sense of history about books, knowing what's been written and which books have sold. By doing this research, you build a storehouse of literary knowledge, adding to your understanding of writing styles and commercial successes. Try, as publishers do, to look ahead two years, making an educated guess as to what the reading public will demand. Sooner or later, you'll find a topic you can call your own.

Also in demand is service-oriented nonfiction. Book buyers don't just read to pass the time or chuckle at a few well-developed phrases. They want something for the effort they invest in the reading process. They want to become healthier, wealthier, wiser, more attractive and popular or better established in life.

In addition, readers (and editors) don't have much disposable time. Men and women both work. Frequently, college and high school students do too. We're now seeing an entire generation that was weaned on television and the capsulized formats of *USA Today* and *CNN Headline News*. Thus, tight writing is essential to your success.

Finally, editors require writers to bring something vital to their projects. There must be a new twist, a hook, an angle. It could be serious or humorous. In fact, it could be both. I think that Kevin Leman's success with parenting books has stemmed from his ability to tackle the awesome task of raising a child with a strong sense of humor.

All of this information leads to some soul searching. Before you propose a book idea, ask yourself: What's the take-away value of the book I have in mind? What will my readers walk away with?

What do I add to the subject that's not currently found on the bookshelf? Is it my new insight, fresh perspective or a sense of humor sprinkled on an otherwise dry subject?

Can I sift through prodigious amounts of research, organize my thoughts and carry this process through several chapters? Remember, we're not talking about a long feature article here; we're talking about a book that may exist longer than its author.

Finally, can I pull off this project alone? Or, do I need the assistance of a famous name to draw an audience? A co-author to share in the completion of the manuscript? Or an agent to represent me?

DO YOU HAVE AN AGENT?

Attend any writers conference, and that's the question you'll hear one aspiring author ask another. But what writers ought to be asking is: Do you really need an agent, and if so, are you truly ready for one?

Writers frequently feel they need an agent to see them through the writing of a particular project, but really, the time to seek representation is upon completion of the best project you can possibly write. For novelists, this means completing the entire draft. For nonfiction authors, it means a well-written proposal and perhaps some sample chapters.

Agents can serve a lot of purposes for writers, far beyond mere representation. Agents are authors' advocates, interceding on their behalf. They take on projects, sell them to interested publishers, negotiate contracts and strike the best deals possible. They can guide your career, shape your work, champion your causes. An agent/author relationship is a true business partnership that, if successful, will last throughout your writing career.

An agent is one of the few people who will give you honest feedback. Why? Because an agent works on commission. He or she has a real incentive to see you succeed. If you don't make money, neither does your agent. Thus, it's in an agent's best interest to wrangle as much money as your writing can command. Agents can also ensure that you'll get a fair read from an editor.

This certainly beats wading through the slush pile.

Agents, however, cannot sell manuscripts or proposal ideas that are not salable to begin with. An agent can shop a project around, but there are no guarantees that it will sell. At this point, your talent and original idea must stand alone, and there must be a market for both.

Agents also cannot command outrageous sums of money — or even a lot of money — for beginning authors, so forget the notion that you can retire after selling one book. (Yes, there are those rare stories that end up in *People* magazine, but I'm being conservative here.)

An agent cannot promote your book, be your best friend, lend you money, or solve your legal affairs or personal crises. There are other experts for these, namely publicists, attorneys and psychologists.

Finally, an agent cannot sacrifice great amounts of time on unpublished writers. Pattie Steele-Perkins of the Elaine Davie Literary Agency asks writers to understand the agent's food chain. At the top, she says, are advances and royalty checks; underneath are editors, contract negotiations and completed manuscripts sent in by published authors. Further down the chain are multibook authors, completed manuscripts with potential, nonpublished authors whose books have been at the publisher for a week, nonpublished marginal authors and unsolicited manuscripts. As a beginner, do you see where you fall?

Since agents must navigate the slush pile as often as editors do, rejection letters find their way into many writers' mailboxes. Agents don't sit around thinking of cruel ways to fend off starving artists. After all, they face rejection every day as well. Keep this in perspective, and know that the competition to find representation is stiff. Agents cannot handle everything you write. They will not take on articles, greeting cards, and poetry. You must sell these smaller projects.

But the question remains, do you need an agent? Perhaps you can successfully market your work and strike suitable deals yourself. I know novelists married to attorneys who look over their contracts, and nonfiction authors who never use agents. Some writers like the excitement of the sale, and they've developed the business acumen to negotiate agreements they're happy with. Only approach an agent if you're convinced one can help your cause, and then, only when your work is polished, your attitude professional and your expectations realistic.

FINDING AN AGENT

If you've practiced that favorite question—who is your agent?—then you've already discovered one way of finding an agent for yourself. Recommendations from published authors is one of the leading ways to seek representation. Of course, you should never use an author's name unless that person has given you express permission to do so.

Another way of finding an agent is to meet one at a conference, as I did. In fact, this is probably the most helpful of all. People connect with other people. Only then do they get turned on to ideas. Your best shot at finding representation is to discuss your writing and your career goals face-to-face with an agent.

If neither of these options is available to you, try using directories that list agents and their areas of expertise. *The Writer's Digest Guide to Literary Agents & Art/Photo Reps* is an excellent resource, as is *Literary Market Place* (R.R. Bowker) and the *Insider's Guide to Book Editors, Publishers and Literary Agents* (Prima Publishing).

If there's a book that you particularly admire, call up the publishing house and ask who represented it. If you're already published, but remain unagented, perhaps your editor can suggest agents for you to contact regarding future projects.

When making your agent decisions, resist the urge to sign with the first agent that comes your way. Find out the agent's area of specialization. Don't waste your time with agents who deal only in fiction if you're trying to market a self-help book. Ask for a list of recent sales and for a client list, if one exists.

Inquire about policies and fees charged, if any. Will the contract cover one project or all of your writing for a stated period of time? Some agents charge reading fees and others do not. Directories usually list these two types separately. Most agents will expect reimbursement from clients for expenses they incur representing their work. These fees include heavy volumes of photocopies, messenger services or overnight deliveries. Whether to sign with an agent who charges a reading fee, however, is at times hotly debated among writers. Agents who charge such fees do so to cover the overhead costs of running their businesses. Others frown upon the practice. Whomever you choose should be a person you feel comfortable with. Steer clear of anyone who annoys you or who you don't absolutely trust.

FIRING AN AGENT

As in all relationships, two parties join together with high hopes. Agents want to make authors successful, selling each project they take on. Authors want to work with, not against, the advice of their agents. But sometimes there are signs that the agent/author relationship is (or should be) coming to an end.

Seriously consider making a change in representation if your agent does not respond to your queries, submissions or phone calls, within a reasonable period of time. The key word here is reasonable. Agents cannot spend time hand-holding their clients. Unfortunately, this is exactly what many beginning writers demand. Reporting to you too frequently uses time, energy, letterhead and postage, which all could be better spent marketing your work to editors and publishers.

But if you haven't heard back on queries or submissions after four to six weeks, it's time for a polite reminder in the form of a short fax or a courteous letter. At the two-month mark, perhaps a brief phone call is in order. If your communication efforts continue to fail, and no legitimate reason is offered, you have a right to question the relationship.

Other reasons for agent dismissal include failure to pay advances and royalties promptly or undue pressure to pay for elaborate editorial or rewrite services that guarantee a sale. There are no guarantees in this business, and even though such agents are rare, they exist. Steer clear of disreputable editorial services that prey on unsuspecting authors.

While there's no great way to break off the agent/author relationship, it's best done professionally and in writing. Refrain from airing any dirty laundry. Withdraw your work from representation and thank your agent for the time and energy devoted to your work, even if you think these efforts were lacking. Politeness lasts forever in all businesses, even in publishing.

COLLABORATION

Plenty of people have salable book ideas, but no time to write them. Or, perhaps they have the time, but not the talent. Look at many of the best-selling how-to books or autobiographies penned by celebrities, business leaders, government officials, politicians and local personalities. Many list an "as told to" author.

William Novak, the writer behind *Iacocca: An Autobiography*, Nancy's Reagan's *My Turn* and Tip O'Neill's *Man of the House*, earned the title "king of the ghosts." But Novak never expected to become a ghostwriter. In fact, he added a contract clause that allowed him to decide, upon completion of *Iacocca*, whether he could accept cover credit (which he did). Publishing history records that he made the right decision!

You may be just as hesitant as Novak was entering into a collaborative arrangement, but if you're accustomed to refining other people's words, playing the part of the ghost might very well add to your writing income. And while the term ghostwriting was once frowned upon, it's now been replaced with a significant rise in respectability as well as a semantic shift to "co-author" or "collaborator."

To find opportunities, let your agent, writer friends and publishers know of your availability and interest in collaborative projects. If you have a particular client in mind, write to the person directly. Pay attention to the advertising in *Publishers Weekly*. Also, run ads in professional journals for would-be authors who might seek a writing partner. If the book you co-author becomes a best-seller, you can be fairly certain that your name will get around. One success could lead to better contacts — and contracts.

Other arrangements have been established between friends, family and fellow writers. Cousins June Casey and Joan Triglia write under the name June Triglia. While June lives in Southern California and Joan resides in Pittsburgh, the two have collaborated on many novels, including *Flowers of Betrayal*, *Bound by Blood* and *By Her Own Design*.

Holly Miller, who has built a successful career as a travel writer and editor, combines talents with Dennis Hensley, another noted writer and *Writer's Digest* correspondent. Under the pen name Leslie Holden, they've co-authored three novels and two nonfiction books. The two live a hundred miles apart.

If you're looking for a collaborator, don't pick a clone of yourself, advises Miller. "Look for someone who brings an added dimension to a writing project," she says. "Dennis and I are completely different: gender, age, background, interests. However, it's important to choose an equal talent so that one isn't hanging on the coattails of the other." Miller adds, though, that she and Hensley take turns being the "lead writer"—the one with the authority to make a final decision on any given project.

Through collaboration, you may have the opportunity to meet influential and inspiring people. You'll spend a lot of time with your client or co-author so the skills of cooperation, flexibility and listening are crucial. Since some personal contact might be necessary, you might limit your search to your local area, at least in the beginning. But, as the above examples illustrate, long-distance partnerships can be profitable.

Remember to keep your own ego in check. When serving as an as-told-to author, the book is your client's, not yours. So if you haven't written that first book yet, you may want to wait until you get the creative issue under control. Authors who have already written under their own names have an easier time giving up control to someone else. Of course, your primary goal is to portray your client in the best light possible. Find an individual you can work well with—someone you believe in as much as you believe in the mission of the book. You'll go through many drafts on your way to the completed manuscript. "The best advice I ever heard was that *ninety percent* of writing is rewriting," says Novak. "I don't expect to get it right the first time."

To write a biography, read everything that's been written about the person, for this can uncover all kinds of questions to pursue. Spend as much time in person with your subject as possible. Get your conversations on tape, transcribing them yourself so that the subject's voice becomes a part of your writing. Flag important words or phrases that you'll want to reference later.

If your subject hits a memory block, ask if there are others who might be willing to share their recollections. Interview these people to find out additional details, and then return to your subject to verify the information.

To keep your income high and risk low, work only on those projects that have firm contracts and commitments. Avoid speculative work. If you don't, you may never be paid for your hard work. A lot of people outside the publishing industry have little, if any, knowledge of the publishing process, the work involved and even the style of communication required for commercial success.

Collaborators are sometimes paid a flat fee, which can be much lower than the actual book advance to the celebrity author. In other cases, you share in the advance and get 50 percent of the author's royalties. When authors self-publish, an hourly rate, chapter rate or page rate is more likely. To protect your financial interests with self-publishers, arrange to be paid one-fourth in advance, one-fourth upon the halfway mark, one-fourth when the project is 75 percent completed and the remainder upon the book's completion.

In *How to Write With a Collaborator* (Writer's Digest Books), Hal Zina Bennett and Michael Larson encourage aspiring collaborators to seal all agreements in writing, and they give examples you can use to develop your own.

Writing with a collaborator can further your career and income potential. It can also be an uneasy alliance. Consider the option if you wish to pursue a career in book publishing. Don't let a lack of expertise close the door to a great idea. Build that idea into a book, even if it takes one or two others to help you achieve that goal.

BASICS OF BOOK PROPOSALS

Whether you choose to write with a collaborator or go it alone, you'll find that nonfiction frequently takes less time to sell to book publishers. Nonfiction books begin as proposals. There are plenty of books devoted to proposal writing. Michael Larson's *How to Write a Book Proposal* (Writer's Digest Books) has guided me in the proposals I've written, including the one that sold this book. Agents, authors and editors agree on a few key components essential to every proposal.

Begin with an introduction to your book project. This is called the overview, or brief description of your idea. Here is the hook—the selling line. Conceive one sentence that summarizes the book's mission. Then, expand that selling thought into two or three paragraphs. Focus on the book's purpose, approach, organization and content. In essence, answer, "Why this book?" Why do people need, or think they need, your book? And if there is a why, then answer, why now?

Will your book require a foreword or introduction? If so, alert your potential publisher to anyone who could contribute this portion of the book, especially if this person's name would be a valuable cover credit. Continue to think through the project so that you can write a paragraph regarding your book's back matter. This includes the index, glossaries, appendices, or other relevant information. If there are any legal or technical considerations that may need untangling, be sure to address these.

Editors will also want to know that you've done your research. You should have a clear understanding of the marketplace, knowing who will buy this book. Include these groups under the heading potential markets. Devote a page, or at least a paragraph, to the competition surrounding your book. What will make readers reach for your book instead of the others already stocked on bookstore shelves?

Promotional outlets is another heading and an area that deserves mention. Your idea could be the best one ever, but if it can't be effectively marketed to the reading public, it won't do you (or your publisher) much good. Discuss ways you can innovatively sell your book and speak before groups to heighten consumer awareness. If you know of experts, celebrities or others whose endorsement would enhance the salability of your book, include these.

If your book requires costly research, you should include a page of resources needed to complete this book. Use this only for extraordinary expenses such as travel, excessive and long-distance telephone interviews and surveys you may need to conduct. Write off incidental expenses as your own costs of doing business.

A page devoted to your credentials follows. This portion about the author highlights pertinent facts about yourself—previous jobs, special connections, years of experience or education that make you stand apart from the pack of other writers seeking to write such a book.

Some publishers will require that you submit one to three sample chapters to get a feel for the calibre of your writing and the form the material takes. If the publisher's guidelines or your agent suggests writing these, give it all you've got. That first chapter will hook readers, inspiring them to read further, or it will send them searching for their TV remote control. Convince an editor of the book's worth from the very start, even if it takes some additional writing on spec.

Finally, you'll need to submit examples of your work. For a nonfiction writer, this usually means articles, columns, small booklets or commercial projects.

When all of these materials are written and gathered, assemble them in a neutral colored two-pocket folder. Writing samples go in the left pocket along with reviews or endorsements of your work. In the right pocket, place the proposal contents including any sample chapters. Your introduction (overview, competition, potential markets, promotional outlets, resources and author bio) should be roughly one to four pages, double-spaced. On the outside of your proposal folder, use a plain white label that's centered with the proposed title of your book and your name. I like to purchase the folders that feature a built-in space inside to insert a business card. I think this adds a professional touch.

WRITING YOUR NONFICTION BOOK

There's no one way to write a book. Some authors like to dictate content; others sit down to the word processor or computer. Still others, write their drafts longhand and use typing services to complete their manuscripts.

In writing this book, I often curled up with a clipboard to begin various chapters and sections. Once I had the thoughts flowing, I dashed to the keyboard and continued entering material as it came to me. At first, I thought I'd begin writing those portions that I felt most comfortable with, but I began with the first section and ended with the fifth, writing my way through each chapter until the first draft was completed some seven months later.

Like other writers, I found that immersing myself in recent books my publisher released helped me master the style my editor was ultimately looking for. If your publisher doesn't automatically send some of these, be sure to ask for a few recent releases. Students in my writing classes shared their questions and insights from the perspective of the beginner, and this was also extremely helpful in writing this book.

"In writing a 'how-to' book, as I did, the author must remember that many people reading her book are novices and need not only the basic facts, but constant encouragement," says Sandra

Louden, greeting card writer. "If a book makes the reader feel she can accomplish what is set forth in the text, she will probably recommend it to others. An author doesn't have to be an expert in the field, but she does need to bring a unique point of view to her subject that hasn't been explored before."

Break a manuscript into portions, accomplishing small goals along the way to the project's completion. Set artificial deadlines for yourself. Force yourself to complete so many pages every week or a specific number of chapters each month.

This book was finished far ahead of the year my publisher allotted for its writing. First, I loved writing the book, and was anxious to explore other book-length projects. Also, two months after signing my contract, I realized I was pregnant with my second child. That served as an added incentive to get the job done. But I've always encouraged writers to develop a healthy work ethic for their own economic survival. If your publisher gives you a year to write a book, try to do it in less, but never rush through a project. Turn in only your best work. If you finish ahead of time, you can move on to other income-producing projects.

Once you've written a portion of your manuscript, resist the urge to marry it. Mail it off to your editor for comments (and to prove you're not just squandering your advance!) and move on to the next few chapters. Seek permissions along the way as these must be turned in with your completed manuscript. In fact, beginning writers may want to keep the number of permissions to a minimum since it's often the writer who is responsible for paying for these. Check and double-check facts along the way as well. If you wait until the end of the book to begin such tedious work, you'll have to scramble. Don't overlook the introduction, appendices, and the index, if you're responsible for these segments of the book.

Finally, if after several months of intensive work, you feel like you're ready to throw your computer against the wall, take a break. A week or two away from the project won't slow you down that much, and it might result in the boost of renewed energy you need to tackle the rest of the manuscript. (Yes, we freelance writers do deserve an occasional vacation, too!)

Again, at the project's completion, put some distance between you and the book before you give it that final review. And with all the hard work you've poured into your book-length manuscript, be sure to save a copy or two on a diskette. In fact, get into the habit of saving to disk after each work session. I kept a diskette in my safe deposit box, and updated it after several chapters. I simply was not willing to take any chances.

Future Editions of Your Book

If your book sells well, and your publisher decides to go to a second printing, you'll probably receive a call asking for your input. Perhaps you've found errors in the book—incorrect facts, facts that need to be updated, type-os. You'll want to make these corrections now, but realize you'll be limited in the amount of changes you can make. "It's very tricky," says Arlene Eisenberg, who with her two daughters wrote *What To Expect When You're Expecting*. "It's not like rewriting the book. You can't add a page here or there." Indeed, if you add one item, you must delete something else, almost like fitting together the pieces of a puzzle.

A revised edition, on the other hand, requires significant changes. Often, the author negotiates a new contract. Most publishers insist that authors rewrite at least one-third of the text in order to release a revised edition. Eisenberg points out that many books, especially medical textbooks and references, are outdated by the time they're published. Savvy writers would be wise to insist upon a contract clause allowing for frequent revisions, if their books are of a critical nature. These editions not only benefit your readers but also bring you additional income over the lifespan of your book.

WRITING FICTION

While nonfiction writers go about their work with the advantage of facts, interviews and history at their disposal, the urge hits many writers to create fiction. These writers rely primarily on their vivid imaginations with the aid of some research. After all, good fiction entertains, but it also must inform. It weaves important information about the world (as it was, is or may be) as it tells us about the make-believe story the author has created on its pages.

The opportunities in fiction are many and varied including short stories, screenplays, romance, mystery, horror, adventure, western, or science fiction novels, and children's literature, each requiring skills peculiar to the genre.

All fiction requires imagination and a capacity for storytelling. While the nonfiction writer aims to create a life of ease with the how-to, service-oriented book, the novelist strives for just the opposite. As a fiction writer, your job is to build suspense, create curiosity and foster a sense of worry about what is to come. Without these essential elements you will not produce the page-turner that editors, publishers and readers require.

These elements are too complex to cover here, but you can find many excellent books in stores and libraries that explain how to write great fiction. Some of the best ones include *Writing Fiction* by Janet Burroway (Little, Brown), *The Art of Fiction* by John Gardner (Knopf), *The Art and Craft of Novel Writing* by Oakley Hall (Story Press) and *The Complete Guide to Writing Fiction* by Barnaby Conrad (Writer's Digest Books).

Genre Fiction and Formulas

There are many genres of fiction which beginning writers select — romance, mystery, suspense/thriller, horror, action/adventure, western, fantasy, science fiction and the literary novel — far too many to examine within the text of this chapter. But before you decide to concentrate in one area and ignore another, learn as much as you can about the different genres, the formulas required for successful publication and an editor's expectations. Fiction, as a rule is much harder to sell than nonfiction, but if you start in specific genres, you might increase your chances, at least in the beginning.

Romance. I can't tell you how many people I've met who scoff at the romance novels by Danielle Steel, LaVyrle Spencer and various Harlequin authors, yet these books make money. It's estimated that romance novels account for over one-third of paperback sales.

What makes these escapist novels so popular? When the typical working woman returns from a day at the office, she wants to be taken away and told a story.

Romance novels offer a sort of Cinderella story, yet they have progressed far beyond the bodice-ripping tales that sold twenty years ago. Today's heroines reflect modern life. They work in successful careers. They're independent and strong. They have children. They struggle with issues. So if you think you can churn out a few sizzling sex scenes and create a starry-eyed young woman for your romance novel, think again. In fact, the challenge to writing good romantic fiction is creating the necessary sexual tension that carries the characters and the reader to the book's conclusion. Passionate encounters are far easier to write than the tension is to create.

Research is another important element (and no, I don't mean research of the love scenes). You, as author, must offer substance. Your hero and heroine coexist in a historical, gothic, regency or contemporary context. Select the subcategory that you enjoy reading, and send for a copy of the publisher's guidelines, which contain added tips including the degree of sensuality the imprint calls for.

Before weaving your own romantic tale, know that many romance authors are required to write under a pseudonym since publishing houses see their authors as valuable assets. Alluring names on the book's cover sell better too. Immerse yourself in the romance genre, reading several per week to get a feel for the publisher's tastes. Romance novels are sold at newsstands, drug stores or through mail order, but most are remaindered after one month. Still, the worldwide reach is incredible. Your story just might be translated into several languages and sold in numerous countries!

Mysteries. While all good stories offer elements of suspense and intrigue, mysteries deliver these in much higher doses. Mysteries puzzle us. They challenge us. Like romance fiction, there's nothing too cerebral regarding their content. However, with mysteries, readers must draw on their deductive reasoning to figure out the solution from the clues you've left along the way.

A well-written mystery — whether it be a cozy, a detective story, a crime novel or a classic whodunit — challenges your readers, arresting their imaginations so that they keep reading, keep deciphering the information as it unfolds. It's your job to untangle that which has gotten twisted.

Pay attention to details. Know the setting you've chosen, learn about human psychology and why people act and react as they do. Read accounts of everyday crimes that occur and talk with law enforcement officers to bring a level of authenticity to your fictional tale.

Violence is fairly minimal in a good mystery. So are subplots that can easily distract the reader. Just be sure to conclude your mystery with a final scene explaining how the solution came about—how the puzzle was put together.

Science Fiction. Traditional science fiction literature has projected the technology of the future. Writers with backgrounds in scientific fields often combine their technological knowledge with their active imaginations. But what was once fantasy (like space travel and robotics) is now reality. Thus, science fiction stories are growing more sophisticated, more discerning.

If you want to crack this popular market, know that many other aspiring science fiction writers have literally grown up on the genre. If you aren't familiar with science fiction, find magazines that publish short stories, conventions that attract science fiction fans (such as the Star Trek gatherings around the country) and books by various publishers. The advantage to writing in this genre is the endless reach of your creative ability. Whatever you can conceive, with skill, you can convince your readers to believe. While other fiction areas focus on characters, here the situations you create are the driving forces in your stories and novels. But to bring such elements to the page, you must spend ample time researching and planning. Know everything about your futuristic or fantasy world before you sit down to the keyboard.

Other Genres. Romance, mystery and science fiction tend to be the most popular genres for beginning writers, but there are others. Deemed the escapist novel for men, action/adventure books are the man's equivalent to the romance. The stories are relatively simple—good versus bad, going to battle over a problem and lots of fast-paced action.

Writers often choose action/adventure because they aren't able to carve believable science fiction details. They sometimes use current headlines to inspire viable ideas dealing with action, especially if they can create a page-turner that ends with the reader wanting more. Indeed your chances of successful publication and greater financial reward improve if you can propose a series for your action/adventure character who survives the weapons and warfare.

Other genres are more difficult to define. These include fantasy and horror, each a close relative of science fiction. A writer aspiring to break into these markets should study publisher's lists, analyzing the books on it and how that particular publishing house defines the genre. Horror, for example, can be the battle between good and evil. Or, it can be about the things that scare us. Editors do not want to see tired clichés or hackneyed characters (such as vampires, ghosts, bogeymen, possessed children and serial killers). A good litmus test is: If it's been done before, steer clear of it! Rethink it until a new, fresh concept springs forth.

If you have what it takes to wrestle with the darker side of human nature, and can combine this with strong emotional writing (a read that makes you shudder), chances are you can weave a potent dark fantasy or dark horror manuscript. While some of these genres are more difficult than others (there's a limited hardcover market for fantasy, for instance), give your first fictional attempts your best shot and begin networking with other writers who can help you develop your craft.

Children's Literature

When we think about the books we cherished as children, we often think about those that touched us. There's no doubt that children's literature can last for generations. Unfortunately, many writers who wish to share their talents this way start out embracing all the wrong ideas about the industry and the requirements of children's literature.

Myth number one is that writing children's literature is easy. The reality is a $2 billion industry that continues to grow. Competition is just as fierce as it is for writers hoping to sell genre fiction or that great American novel.

Myth number two suggests that because children make up the target audience, they aren't as discriminating, the hidden thought being "I can write whatever I feel like, and these kids won't know the difference." If this sounds like something you're thinking, rid yourself of the notion, for while children enjoy the books, parents buy them. These purchasing decisions are often based on recommendations of friends and librarians.

"What makes it harder in a sense is that there are so many critics and reviewers who take the time to look over the three thousand new books for children every year," says Colleen O'Shaughnessy McKenna, author of Scholastic's "Murphy" novels. "Make your writing worth the purchase of a school's librarian."

The third most popular myth: If a writer has children, he can write children's literature. Wrong again! Having a child (or dozens of them) isn't a prerequisite, although being around youngsters fosters a healthy understanding of a young child's concerns and world.

"Erik Erikson once said that the best books are written by authors who love their readers," says Fred M. Rogers of public television fame. "I think the biggest challenge for a children's author is to love and respect the inner drama that a young reader brings to a book."

Beginning writers frequently base their children's tales on their own son's or daughter's antics, but what may appear hysterical or cute at the family picnic won't necessarily play well in print. That's why editors advise against translating your family experiences into the pages of a children's book. Instead, use the humorous incident to inspire a more in-depth storyline. But before you begin thumbing through baby books or family photo albums in search of that special memory, take time to explore children's literature and learn from those who have succeeded in the craft.

All of the elements discussed earlier—hooking your reader, creating conflict, reaching a climax and closing your story—play a part in children's literature. Relevance is particularly important whether you're writing a picture book for kids or a teen romance, and since very young children have even shorter attention spans than most readers, your hook had better be even quicker. Young readers are much more interested in what is happening now, tomorrow or next week than they are in what took place in the past. Use literary devices such as the flashback and time lapse sparingly since they grind the action to a halt.

Relevance also requires that you write at a child's level. Editors ask children's authors to experience situations from a child's perspective. How would you feel if you always had to look up to a person towering above you? Or what if you could never reach what others around you could easily retrieve?

"Often many authors are writing out of their own unresolved conflicts," says Rogers. "Scary biting mouths, for example, may not be the most appropriate image for young children who, at that time in their lives, are working hard on trying not to bite and who need to find other outlets for their angry feelings." Rogers credits his mentors in child development—people like Erik Erikson and Dr. Margaret McFarland—with helping him listen to and understand children, and he encourages other writers to find knowledgeable people to learn from.

The words you choose for children must also be relevant and within their range of experience. *The Children's Writer's Word Book* (Writer's Digest Books) by Alijandra Mogilner provides word lists for various reading levels. While checking word choice, eliminate sexist or racist language as well.

Understand the tremendous impact your work will have. Use your talents to their fullest potential in order to enrich a youngster's world. Open that world to different cultures and races. Extend societal expectations so that children see men and women both as nurturers and strong, independent thinkers and doers.

As you're writing, keep the focus on children or young adults. Beginning authors often allow adult characters to intrude on the plot. No child wants to read about the sage grandfather who wields all the power and wisdom, and comes across as the story's hero. Given a choice, this same child would enjoy reading about a character his age who, perhaps with some adult guidance, discovers the light or the errors of his ways on his own. Not only is this more enjoyable to read, but it's also more meaningful for the child.

You shouldn't focus too much on animals either. Watch the tendency to bring animals to life. While some best-selling authors have successfully anthropomorphized bears, bunnies and turtles, writers have come to rely upon this device, to everyone's detriment. If any editor spots such a story, she's more likely to toss it aside, thinking "oh, just another dancing dinosaur."

As your story comes to its conclusion, beware of contrived endings that skew reality for children. In today's world, everything is not wonderful. Deal with issues and reality, but in a way that doesn't call too much attention to danger and fear. Children don't like to be lied to, and they truly are more sophisticated than we often give them credit for.

Selling Your Fiction

Whatever you choose to write, the work you submit to an agent or editor must be the best you can possibly create. Revision is your first selling tool. Don't be afraid to delete entire scenes, eliminate characters who serve no purpose and cut dialogue that doesn't move the story forward. Know the market you're submitting to, and make sure your work is similar to what the magazine or publishing house purchases.

For novels, it's vital that you take the time to develop a synopsis. Agents and editors cannot read your entire manuscript from start to finish. Therefore, a synopsis does the selling for you. This narrative summary of your main action can range from two to ten pages. It should be double-spaced, professionally typed and painstakingly precise.

Begin your synopsis where the excitement of the story starts. Don't spend valuable time giving too much background that elicits a yawn before the editor even gets going. You want your opening to be bold, full of conflict. You want it to hook the editor into requesting your completed manuscript.

Write your synopsis in the present tense and in the third person. Its form should be that of a running story, rather than chapter-by-chapter details. If you write "this happened, and then that happened . . . ," you will bore your agent or editor, and your synopsis will become a poor reflection of your writing abilities.

Keep action at the center of the synopsis, showing what the problems are for your protagonist and how they escalate throughout the remainder of your book. You must include the climatic scene and tell how the story is resolved. No editor will request your manuscript unless he has a feel for the entire work ahead of time. So don't hesitate or hint around. Write your conclusion concisely. If you've never read a synopsis before, it would be wise to read books that focus on fiction writing. Some of these may share a successful synopsis that sold a manuscript.

Because fiction is a much harder sell than nonfiction, many writers send their synopsis to an agent who specializes in fiction. Publishers rely heavily upon agents to screen work before it's brought to them. If you write both nonfiction and fiction, consider having two agents if you cannot find one to satisfy all your needs.

"I advise my authors who are dual personalities (fiction and nonfiction) to have two agents," says Pattie Steele-Perkins of the Elaine Davie Literary Agency. "My expertise is fiction. The editors I work closely with deal with fiction. I simply would be trying to spread myself too thin to deal in nonfiction."

But there is another way of looking at the agent search. "I feel it's very important to be with one agent so just keep going until you find the one who is willing to represent, and more importantly, is interested in both kinds of projects," says Alice Fried Martell of the Martell Agency. Martell cites many reasons for writers to use only one agent, namely that authors need overall career guidance that could get lost in the shuffle between two business partners reviewing work and making deals.

If you've selected an agent to represent your fiction or the entire breadth of your work, don't be surprised if he or she will suggest changes. An agent will only submit the best material to editors. Be willing to work cooperatively and take constructive criticism.

PUBLISHING OPTIONS

In the back of many writers' and women's magazines, you'll often spot ads calling for book-length manuscripts. "Pay us to publish your book," they seem to cry out to the aspiring author. If writers don't know much about the industry, such an offer sparks a ray of hope and excitement. But after reading this, I hope you'll have more information in order to make important decisions regarding your career as an author.

Most publishers make their money selling books. Some publishers—called vanity or subsidy presses—make their money by charging authors to publish their manuscripts. Publishers have a vested interest in your success as an author and in your book's sales record. If you and your books succeed, publishers can see a sizeable return on their investments. Therein lies the difference, as vanity presses have no vested interest in the success of either.

Vanity publishing is completely legal, but you should know that very few, if any, vanity published books are bought by bookstores or libraries. In fact, vanity publishing usually has a negative impact upon a writer's career. Frequently, writers pay large sums of money to have their books printed, and the results are often less than desirable. If any promotion takes place, it's at the author's expense. The entire process is filled with uncertainty and financial risk.

Don't confuse vanity publishing with self-publishing, however. Self-publishing means that you, as author, provide the capital to print your book. Desktop publishing has made this publishing option extremely viable, especially for those books appealing to highly targeted markets. Some self-publishers deal strictly through mail-order. Others use small book distributors to gain access into retail bookstores. Still others market their books through a combination of the two techniques.

Before you decide to self-publish, spend some time researching this business. If you thought writing a book was a challenge, just wait until you prepare, produce, print and promote every single word you write. Several books will help you discover the secrets to self-publishing success. Among these are *The Complete Guide to Self-Publishing* (Writer's Digest Books) by Tom & Marilyn Ross and *For All the Write Reasons*, self-published by Patricia C. Gallagher (Young Sparrow Press).

These books will help you from start to finish and make it clear that self-published books are nothing less than professionally written, designed and produced products. If you skimp on quality, your readers will not be fooled. Your book must rival the looks of those it will sit beside in any bookstore. So unless you're multitalented in every aspect of publishing, you'll most likely need to hire some services, including editing, design, layout, illustration, photography, printing, binding and distribution. Talk to other self-publishers to find out their mistakes and what they've learned along the way. If you do self-publish, establish a company name to add legitimacy to your efforts.

PROMOTING YOUR BOOK

You've spent months, maybe even years, writing a book, working with your editor and reviewing galleys before they went to press. Now your work is over, right? Wrong. You suddenly have a product to sell!

"But I have a publisher and an agent," I hear someone say. Well, unless your name is a literary franchise, demanding full-page ads in magazines, plan on spending a significant portion of your time (and advance) promoting your book.

Agents generally do not get actively involved in a book's promotion, but they will like to keep posted on your book's progress. "Clients should let an agent know about their successes," says Laura Cifelli of Richard Curtis Associates, Inc. "Send clippings, articles, reviews, publicity material, local news coverage, whatever you can . . . . We like to hear when good things happen with our authors' careers."

Publishers will help with promotion, to a certain degree. Smaller publishers, with limited resources, may not be able to offer too much assistance, but mid-sized to large publishers frequently have publicity directors who prepare releases, send review copies and compile catalogs with their recent and backlist titles. Work with your publicity director, returning author questionnaires promptly, arranging for and sending photos, if requested, and communicating on a regular basis.

If there's a specific audience or market you're aware of, let your publicity director know about it. If your book is suited for the educational market, promote it to teachers, college bookstore managers and students.

If you know of noted authorities who could endorse your book, especially for future printings, solicit their permission to quote them for promotional purposes and turn these over to the publicity department. Let everyone you encounter know that you've written a book. Write to your alumni publication, former professors, professional associations you belong to, and certainly, to the editors of newspapers and magazines that deal with your subject matter. Write articles based on the book or offer excerpts in advance of publication. Send reporters and talk show hosts a list of questions in advance. This just might ensure that you're booked as a guest. (See section on talk shows in chapter fifteen.)

While you may have to seek out these opportunities, some of them may come directly to you. "Many of the extra ways I've made money are ones that have found me," says Vicki Lansky, author of over twenty-six parenting titles. "I was approached about doing (and did) newspaper columns, magazine articles, speaking engagements, being a product spokesperson, writing magazine columns and participating in a 900 parenting advice line . . . All of these have come as spin-offs of my books and perceived expertise by others."

Offer to speak before conferences, community groups or gatherings of concerned citizens. Inform your publisher at least six weeks in advance of a speaking engagement so that sufficient copies of your book can be on hand for attendees to purchase. Bring a friend along or arrange for help in collecting money and selling your books.

Bookstore managers often welcome authors who want to sign their books because these events draw customers to the store. However, bookstores aren't always the best place to sell books. If your subject matter lends itself to maternity boutiques, sports departments, toy stores or gourmet shops, get in touch with these retailers.

Consider producing gadgets that deal directly with your book's subject matter. Some authors pay for bookmarks, mugs, T-shirts, magnets, pens or pencils — whatever they believe will remind their audience to buy their book.

SEVEN WAYS TO SELL EVEN MORE BOOKS

Be sure to include an index in your book as studies have shown they help sales, especially to libraries. Also, when the book is completed, prepare your own author bio sheet — a different version of what you used to sell the proposal in the first place. It's quite conceivable at large publishing houses that an employee in publicity may never have read your book, yet he or she may be writing the book jacket copy that sells your year-long effort. Leave nothing to chance, and offer one yourself.

Arrange for as many special events as you can dream up. Be innovative. Cookbook authors, for instance, might try preparing samples of their recipes to serve on trays at a book signing or speaking engagement. At autograph sessions, sign additional copies for the bookstore to sell in a special location after your event. Books that are signed cannot be returned to your publisher. And if you self-publish your books, slip an order form into your book, or devote a page in the back matter for future orders. Readers will often recommend books they've liked to friends and colleagues.

Get to know your publisher's sales force. Write a memo to the sales staff introducing yourself, your topic and offering assistance. Any extra information you can provide helps them sell your book to retailers. Ask your editor if you could speak before the sales force at the annual sales conference or book convention, where sales representatives learn of the new releases.

Finally, purchase the plates when your book goes out of print. Particularly if your book was successful, but just a little dated, you might be able to parlay that success into your own start-up self-publishing business.

HOW TO GET STARTED

Writing books isn't the mysterious undertaking it's often thought to be. Yet, it is difficult, and the odds don't favor the want-to-be author. But with the right idea, and a lot of persistence, a career in publishing could be meant for you.

• Learn as much as possible regarding the publishing industry. Work in a bookstore or library to get to know the reading public. Understand what sells and what gets sent back.

• Suggest a nonfiction project to a corporate client. If your client will purchase massive quantities for promotional use, you'll have an easier time finding a publisher since there's far less risk involved.

• While famous writers stretch the boundaries of genre fiction, beginners should stick to the accepted formulas.

• Write children's books with illustration in mind. Pictures make up at least half, if not more of, the content. Include lots of sensory detail that relates to the photos or illustrations.

• Create a sense of excitement about your book. Remember, most first books are remaindered quickly if they fail to sell. Keeping your name in the spotlight will ensure healthy sales and a bigger bank account.

• Two videos worth viewing are *Get Published!* (Peter Miller Agency, Inc., New York) and *The Publishing Game* (WSFP-TV, Bonita Springs, FL).

• To gain an edge on what editors are thinking, read *Editors on Editing: What Writers Need to Know About What Editors Do* edited by Gerald Gross (Grove Press).

I hope you've found a wealth of ideas in this book, and opportunities that lead to exactly that—wealth! While some may seem easy and effortless, others may strike you as impossible, perhaps even inappropriate during the initial stages of your career. But please believe me when I say there is no writing arena you cannot enter. If someone had told me at the start of my freelance career that I'd be writing a book, let alone a reference book for other writers, I would have laughed at the notion.

Know that the skills you have today will expand with each and every assignment you accept, and that the goals you have at this reading will certainly change during your writing life. Prepare for the days when the bills outnumber the checks, and savor the days when your confidence soars.

Why, maybe the next time you thumb through these pages, you'll be at an important juncture, undertaking new and exciting challenges and interesting assignments that will shape your career in ways you'd never imagined. Writing tends to do that. It can lead to incredible pleasure and lots of profit, if you give your work every ounce of energy you can muster as well as the passion you reserve for those subjects that genuinely move you.

Take time to discover which writing projects you enjoy. The process may take many months, or even years, tempered by disappointing rejections, and sometimes, your own unrealistic expectations. It's tempting to look at published authors—those whose names have sold millions of books—and try to duplicate their rise to success. But resist the urge. Instead, reap the inspiration these authors offer by reading their works, only channel that encouragement into your own projects.

In my writing, I've seen this happen. That's why my husband can usually tell whenever I've just finished another popular novel or category romance. All he needs to see is the fiction manuscript I've dusted off and curled up with, red pen in hand.

Reading good writing serves as inspiration of the best kind. So spend a little time with your favorite authors, and keep those good habits alive.

Talk to other accomplished writers and consultants in commercial writing endeavors. Carve out the time and space (in your life and in your home) to write every day, if you can manage it. And when you begin to publish, and publish often, don't hide from your readers. Teach a course. Speak before a writer's group. Get to know your readers and learn from them. They have just as much to give back to you as you have to offer them.

Whether you freelance full-time, part-time or on an occasional basis, I hope you'll keep this book as a handy guide. I believe everyone is given different gifts in this world. Writers, too, have different talents. I hope these pages have helped you discover your talents and that this book has inspired you to make your contribution as you begin or continue writing. May you use your gifts to their fullest potential!

I invite you to share with me your success stories, your suggestions and your innovative ways to make money through writing. Your contributions may be included in future editions of this book. Please write to me in care of this publisher or contact me directly. If you need a reply, please enclose an SASE. My address is:

Loriann Hoff Oberlin
P.O. Box 515
Monroeville, PA 15146-0515

Thanks for reading and recommending this book to others. And best of luck in your writing days ahead!

INDEX